THE GOD OF PEACE

Also by John Dear:

Disarming the Heart
Our God Is Nonviolent
Seeds of Nonviolence
Christ Is with the Poor
Jean Donovan: The Call to Discipleship
Oscar Romero and the Nonviolent Struggle for Justice

THE GOD OF PEACE

Toward a Theology of Nonviolence

John Dear

ORBIS BOOKS

Maryknoll, New York 10545

The Catholic Foreign Mission Society of America (Maryknoll) recruits and trains people for overseas missionary service. Through Orbis Books, Maryknoll aims to foster the international dialogue that is essential to mission. The books published, however, reflect the opinions of their authors and are not meant to represent the official position of the society.

Library of Congress Cataloging-in-Publication Data

Dear, John, 1959-
    The God of peace : toward a theology of nonviolence / John Dear.
      p.   cm.
    Includes bibliographical references and index.
    ISBN 0-88344-980-3 (pbk.)
    1. Nonviolence—Religious aspects—Catholic Church.   2. Peace—
Religious aspects—Catholic Church.   3. Catholic Church—Doctrines.
I. Title.
BX1795.N66D43   1994
24'.697—dc20   94-13049
                                         CIP

For the Pax Christi-Spirit of Life Plowshares
Philip Berrigan,
Lynn Fredriksson, and
Bruce Friedrich,
for beating swords into plowshares
and being faithful to the God of Peace.

The God of Peace is never glorified by human violence.

—Thomas Merton

Our community today is a gathering together of peacemakers. We pray that the God of peace may cleanse us in our will to war, that God may bestow on us some measure of wisdom and steadfastness in the tasks of peace. We gather, we pray together, and we disperse again, knowing that the work of peace cannot be accomplished by the churches; it can only begin there.

—Daniel Berrigan

Contents

Foreword

JAMES W. DOUGLASS

John Dear's life is the real foreword to this book. The truth written in John's life stands behind the prophetic truth of *The God of Peace*. The author writes what the Word has written in him. He says that "the blood of the martyrs makes peace." The transforming truth in those words is that the author is living them.

As I write this (June 1994), the author of *The God of Peace* is a prisoner in a North Carolina jail. As one of the Pax Christi Spirit of Life Plowshares, John Dear has been convicted of an act of nonviolent disarmament—swords into plowshares, the words of Isaiah made flesh.

At 2:30 A.M. on December 7, 1993, John entered Seymour Johnson Air Force Base in Goldsboro, North Carolina, together with Philip Berrigan, Lynn Fredriksson, and Bruce Friedrich. In the midst of hundreds of soldiers carrying out war games, the four waded through a stream. They then poured blood and hammered on an F15-E fighter jet for about thirty seconds before being arrested. Thus far they have served seven months in jail. They approach their sentencing expecting many more.

Seymour Johnson's F15-Es were used extensively in bombing runs during the Persian Gulf War. They are capable of dropping nuclear bombs.

The statement of John, Phil, Lynn, and Bruce reads in part:

> We seek the peace of Christ who requires that we put down the nuclear sword and love our enemies. We humble ourselves before the Spirit of Life to disarm F15-Es at the Seymour Johnson Air Force Base, expose these nuclear-capable weapons, and begin the process of disassembly and conversion. We use the symbol of blood to illustrate the murderous purposes of these weapons ... We beat the F15-E with household hammers—symbols of the creative force in our everyday lives, and of the transformation dictated by Isaiah.

These words explaining John's imprisonment can serve as a gentle warning to the reader of his book. If you read *The God of Peace* in the spirit in which it was written, you, like the author, may see the inside of a jail cell, walk the streets and share the suffering of our cities' homeless, struggle for the lives of Death Row prisoners, and go on missions of peace and justice to such places as Haiti, El Salvador, and the Pentagon.

John has written at the conclusion of *The God of Peace*:

> As Gandhi said, nonviolent social change does not come from governments, courts, or schoolrooms, but from within prisons and sometimes on the gallows. The praxis of nonviolence requires civil disobedience to preparations for war and nuclear destruction and divine obedience to the God of peace. Though we may be jailed or killed for proclaiming the truth of nonviolence, we will be found faithful. We will be blessed.

We are blessed now by the Word made flesh in community. The Word has brought John Dear into a community of truth and love in the fiery furnace of nonviolence. John's own prophetic words, in the context of the Word being written in his life, are in the end a simple, transforming invitation: Join us.

Acknowledgments

This work could not have been written without the help of many peacemaking friends. I would like to thank Don Gelpi, S.J., and Anne Brotherton, S.F.C.C., for their generous help and encouragement. I also thank Claire Ronzani and David Batstone for their help and comments.

Over the years that I worked on this project, I joined friends throughout the San Francisco Bay Area in witnessing to Jesus, the way of nonviolence, and I thank them for their witness and friendship: Ken Butigan, Louis Vitale, Cindy Pile, Sherry Larsen-Beville, Steve Kelly, David Hartsough, Peggy and Ed Gleason, Phyllis Kovacich, Faye Butler, Mary Burson, Molly Fumia, Francisco Herrera, Michael Harank, Ellen Jordan, Mev Puleo, Mark Chmiel, Ed DeBerri, and Anne Symens-Bucher. I also want to express my gratitude to my parents and my brothers; to my friends at Pax Christi and the Fellowship of Reconciliation; to Jim and Shelley Douglass; to Elizabeth McAlister; to Robert Ellsberg of Orbis Books for all his assistance; to the K Street Jesuit Community in Washington, D.C.; to Bill O'Donnell and Martin Sheen; and to the Casa San Jose Jesuit Community in Oakland—Tom Hoffman, S.J., Jim Gartland, S.J., Jim Flaherty, S.J., and Bill McKinney, S.J.

I am deeply grateful to Daniel Berrigan, S.J., for his friendship and lifelong nonviolence.

Finally, this book is dedicated to the Pax Christi-Spirit of Life Plowshares, Philip Berrigan, Lynn Fredriksson, and Bruce Friedrich, who helped me to "beat swords into plowshares" and climb the mountain to the God of Peace. Thank you, friends, for your gift of peace and disarmament.

Introduction

When six Jesuit priests, all of them theologians, scholars and peacemakers, were assassinated in El Salvador, along with Elba and Celina Ramos, on November 16, 1989, the world cried out in shock and horror. Though some seventy-five thousand people had already been killed in El Salvador, including Archbishop Oscar Romero and four North American churchwomen, many saw anew the suffering of the Salvadoran poor and the urgent need for justice and peace in that war-torn land. Perhaps because these men were priests, Jesuits, theologians and public figures, their deaths brought new attention to that old war. With the shift of global politics, including the fall of communism and the Berlin Wall, their martyrdom shocked people into imagining a new El Salvador—an El Salvador without war or violence, an El Salvador with justice and peace. It pointed to the dawn of nonviolence in a land that had come to define violence.

The Jesuit martyrs had long articulated the vision of God's reign of peace coming to El Salvador and the world. They worshipped the God of peace and proclaimed God's message of peace to a land of war and unimaginable violence. In particular, Ignacio Ellacuría, a noted liberation theologian, had outraged the military forces and the US military advisors by seeking peace with justice for the poor, specifically by pursuing a public dialogue between the revolutionary forces and the military. Because his prophetic voice for peace was so forceful, his days were numbered. Like the other Jesuit martyrs, like Romero and the martyred churchwomen, Ellacuría practiced gospel nonviolence to the point of laying down his life for the coming of God's reign of justice and peace.

I well remember sitting with Ignacio Ellacuría one afternoon in the summer of 1985 at the Jesuit University, listening to him explain the urgent need for God's reign of peace to come to El Salvador and the world. Later that night, at dinner in the Jesuit community house, Ellacuría pointed out all the bullet holes that marked their house, the dining room table, even the chair I sat on. They had been bombed and fired upon many times over the years and received scores of death threats, but they kept on preaching the gospel of peace and trusting in the God of peace. They were faithful disciples of the nonviolent Jesus, and I was deeply impressed by their costly discipleship, which they knew might mean their crucifixion.

1

When the Jesuits and the women were killed that terrible November night, I had just begun theology studies at the Jesuit School of Theology, at the Graduate Theological Union, in Berkeley, California. An hour after hearing the news, a group of us theology students prayed and held a vigil for peace outside the Salvadoran consulate in San Francisco. A few days later we held a prayer service that drew over one thousand people to San Francisco's Federal Building. Our worship of the God of peace culminated in prayerful, nonviolent civil disobedience in protest of ongoing US military aid to the Salvadoran government. Over one hundred and fifty people, including eighteen Jesuits and scores of priests, sisters and theology students, approached the main entrance of the Federal Building, knelt down in prayer, and were arrested for disturbing the peace. In jail, we sang hymns and gospel spirituals to the God of peace; it was an afternoon I will never forget. Those days of prayer and nonviolent action foreshadowed for many of us a new dawn in the North American faith community. Perhaps we too, in the United States, were beginning to worship the God of peace in our own context of superpower violence. Perhaps God's reign is indeed upon us, we began to think. Perhaps we too could give our lives over in Christ's nonviolent struggle for justice and peace.

These Jesuit martyrs lived and taught a new theology, rooted in the life of the poor, in the struggle for justice and in the witness for peace. With their very lives they denounced the injustices and systemic violence that kill so many poor people throughout El Salvador, Latin America and the whole world. At the same time they announced the real alternative of God's justice and peace, the nonviolent reign of God they knew was at hand, within reach, even tangible.

The Jesuit martyrs of El Salvador, like all the saints and martyrs of human history, shed new light on the gospel invitation to nonviolence. They revealed once again the image of Jesus as peacemaker, resister of evil and seeker of justice. Though they rarely used the word, they understood that Jesus was a practitioner of nonviolence, that he fulfilled God's own nonviolence and revealed God as a God of nonviolence. They invited us all to rethink our understanding of God, to renew our hearts in the gospel of peace, and to rededicate our lives to God's nonviolent struggle for the transformation of the world.

The theology we are learning from the Jesuit martyrs and other noble peacemakers, especially Mohandas Gandhi, Dorothy Day and Martin Luther King, Jr., leads us to understand Jesus anew in light of active nonviolence. Christian nonviolence, as a way of life, insists on justice and peace and sparks the nonviolent coming of God, the creation of God's beloved community on earth. Revealed in the light of nonviolence, God is now understood as a God of nonviolence, a God of unconditional love, who actively pursues justice and peace for all humanity, even to the point of taking on the world's suffering. This God, we are beginning to realize, transforms the world's evil through love in order to bring us all together into God's reign of peace.

The church has long taught the way of love and peace, but it has more often than not given in to the world's ways of violence and domination. Because the violence of our times has forced us to choose transformation or global annihilation, a deeper understanding of our vocation of nonviolence is opening up. The pressure of systemic violence in these kairos days offers us a new clarity. We stand now on the verge of a new theology, a theology of nonviolence; it can spell a new millennium of peace for humanity, a new age where faith in God means the practice of justice through lives of active nonviolence.

During four years of theological reflection at the Jesuit School of Theology, I grappled with the question of gospel nonviolence in a world of brutal violence. Those years were filled not only with classes, studies and heated discussion, but public experimentation in gospel nonviolence. They were years of discipleship to Jesus, the way of nonviolence.

The combination of public action for peace and justice, coupled with deep refection on God, scripture and the various areas of theology, combined to form this book. *The God of Peace* seeks to introduce and outline a theology of nonviolence, following the systematic approach used by theologians through the centuries. While not claiming to be the complete or definitive work, it offers another step in the ever-growing Christian movement of active nonviolence. Just as liberation theology has sparked a new movement of justice in Latin America and throughout the Third World, and a theology of feminism has opened new avenues for gender equality, so too a theology of nonviolence could spark the coming of God's reign of nonviolent love. God's reign includes justice and liberation, not only in the Third World, but in the First World, where the transformation is most needed. Such a theological transformation could help us imagine and realize a societal transformation, a movement away from destructive policies that bring us to the brink of nuclear annihilation and toward economic conversion, disarmament and a deeper love and service toward suffering humanity. These reflections are not intended for experts, although I hope the book will help promote a theology of nonviolence, but for the average North American Christian whose faith seeks understanding in an age of rampant poverty and incomprehensible violence.

With this book I am suggesting, as many have already done, that nonviolence is not simply a subtopic in the field of ethics or a significant tactic in the politics of revolution, but that nonviolence may be regarded as a hermeneutical lens which brings all the traditional topics of theology into a new focus for our age of global violence. Nonviolence is not some new value imposed on the gospel. Quite the contrary, nonviolence is a new way of talking about the essential mystery of God as revealed and embodied in Jesus Christ and about God's active transformation of humanity into God's nonviolent reign of peace and justice. Nonviolence is a key into the gospel itself and a new transforming theology for our times. Nonviolence is much more than a political strategy; it is a spiritual principle from which we can understand life in all its dimensions. Nonviolence does not mean passivity, nor does it mean simply a cessation of killing (though that is a clear starting point). It defines active peacemaking, persistent reconciliation and steadfast resistance to evil through a suffering love that speaks the truth in a global struggle for justice.

Just as liberation theology correlates the project of liberation from oppression with the theological mystery of human salvation, so too a theology of nonviolence correlates the transformation of human violence through active nonviolence with the theological mystery.

We begin here by exploring the framework for a theology of nonviolence. We reflect within a context of global violence, from El Salvador to the Persian Gulf, from Haiti to Somalia, from inner-city Washington, D.C. to the Pentagon. After defining violence, nonviolence and theology, we examine the perspective we bring to interpreting the scriptures, which we will employ in our systematic theology of nonviolence. Our perspective applies the viewpoint of Gandhi, King and Dorothy Day, the alternative of nonviolence, to both violence and traditional theologies. From this vantage point we look with suspicion on any theology or ideology that supports the status quo of institutionalized violence or violence in any of its forms and propose a theology of nonviolence which relates the nonviolent transformation of the world with the mystery of human salvation.

From this perspective we examine the traditional images of God and pose the image of the God of nonviolence. We begin with the gospel presentation of Jesus as the incarnation, teacher, model, prophet and sign of nonviolence. Then we examine God's nonviolence and, in particular, the Trinity as a peacemaking community, where God the creator is understood as creating a world of peace; where the Christ redeems the world of violence through nonviolence; and where the Holy Spirit of love is transforming the violence of the world into the nonviolent reign of God. Our Christology of nonviolence reflects on Jesus' identity as the redeemer, who offers us a way out of our addiction to violence. Next, we examine original sin from the perspective of violence and rethink God's covenant and grace in terms of God's nonviolence. Then we study theodicy, soteriology, eschatology, anthropology, ecclesiology, Catholic social teaching, the "just war" theory, feminism, liberation theology and the consistent ethic of life all from the perspective of Christian nonviolence. In the concluding chapters we investigate a spirituality of nonviolence, where peacemaking is rooted in the prayerful, contemplative truth that we all are united as God's children, already reconciled. We review the sacraments of the church as channels of God's nonviolent love, which reveal the God of nonviolence and manifest the in-breaking reign of God's peace. Finally, we explore the role of liturgy in the peacemaking community, the place where the God of nonviolence is worshipped and where we draw strength for the life of peacemaking.

Our reflections conclude with the primary role of the praxis of nonviolence. This new theology reflects our active lives of risky discipleship to the nonviolent Jesus. A theology of nonviolence is realized in the lived experience of bearing the nonviolent cross in the world and witnessing to the new life of the resurrection. In this new life of active nonviolence we meet the risen Jesus as he walks in the world today, resisting evil, reconciling us and uniting us with the God of peace.

CHAPTER 1

From Violence to Nonviolence

In 1988 I traveled with a delegation of North American Christians to a remote village in El Salvador in response to an invitation to stand in solidarity with the suffering people. We journeyed on rocky roads, over hills, through rivers and into the barren countryside. As we turned the corner into the small, country village, we gasped at the sight of hundreds of Salvadoran soldiers and US military advisers milling about everywhere. A fleet of ten helicopters rested in a nearby field. The villagers greeted us and asked us to stay only for a short while; they feared for their lives from the occupying military forces. But they appreciated our solidarity. They told us that our visit demonstrated to the Salvadoran military that North Americans were watching its every move.

During our visit one of the mothers handed me her child to hold. At that moment all the violence of the world suddenly became very clear to me. The child's dirty eyes were glazed over and covered with flies and his stomach was extended beyond belief. As I held that dying, malnourished child, I looked over a few feet away to see Salvadoran soldiers loading all the villagers' sacks of grain onto their trucks and helicopters. These villagers were literally starving, yet the soldiers, who threatened to kill them, were taking the little food they had. This scene summed up in a flash all the violence of our world.

In Washington, D.C., we see the same story. In some parts of town, at the Pentagon, the White House, the Congress, the Department of State and the Department of Energy, the most powerful forces of violence in the history of the world go about their day-to-day business, maintaining the structures of violence and planning the wars of the future. Elsewhere, indeed only a few blocks from the White House, single mothers with hardly any income struggle to raise their children, while drug wars tear up their neighborhoods leaving a record number of dead bodies strewn about the city's streets. In Washington, D.C., as in many other places, life for many people means the day-to-day business of death.

Levels of Violence

We are accustomed to recognizing violence when it is inflicted by weapons. But the violence of our world occurs on many levels, from the violence within us, to interpersonal and societal violence, to the global, structural violence of war, nuclear weapons, environmental destruction, hunger, sexism, racism, homelessness, abortion, torture, the death penalty and the rampant poverty that leaves over one billion people in misery. Though cancer, AIDS, heart disease, natural disasters and accidents of every variety kill people by the millions each year, the deliberate violence of war and systemic injustice kill human beings at an enormous rate—a plague that humanity has inflicted on itself.

The first level of violence includes the over-arching global, structured injustice which institutionalizes the worldwide oppression of poverty, systemically accumulates the world's resources in the hands of a small minority of rich people, and forces the vast majority of humanity to suffer starvation, misery and degradation. In recent decades the church has called this systemic injustice "institutionalized, legalized violence, whether in the form of economic exploitation, political domination, or abuse of military might."[1] These global systems of economic exploitation and political and military domination, which cause and maintain poverty, override all other forms of violence. Although the United States has only 5 percent of the world's population, it consumes nearly 60 percent of the world's resources. Twenty percent of the world's population controls 80 percent of the world's goods, another twenty percent lives in desperate poverty, and 60 percent just get by. As Gandhi said, "poverty is the worst form of violence."

Institutionalized economic injustice is only possible because of the worldwide weapons systems and military forces which wage war and threaten the nuclear destruction of the planet in order to protect this unjust arrangement. Francis of Assisi long ago summed up the link between war and greed. "If we want to own possessions," he observed, "we must also have weapons. From this comes all the quarrels and battles that make love impossible. And this," he concluded, "is why we refuse to own anything." The poverty of the Third World results from the greed and lifestyle of the first world and the maintenance of the first world's nuclear arsenal. Because the first-world elite hoards the world's goods, it needs an elaborate and lethal weapons system to protect through violence the goods that it has stolen from the rest of the world. The nuclear arsenal epitomizes the ultimate intent to kill the masses of poor people around the world who might one day demand that their resources and goods be returned to them. The catastrophic violence of the nuclear weapon and the entire nuclear and military arsenal, which can destroy cities in seconds and blow the world up a dozen times over, then forms a close second level of violence.

But as Catholic social teaching has long taught, economic systems and structures which maintain the lifestyle of the first world's wealthy already kill the poor of the world. As the Second Vatican Council declared, "The arms race is an utterly treacherous trap for humanity, and one which injures the poor to an intolerable degree."[2] "The arms race is to be condemned unreservedly," Paul VI wrote. "It is *in itself an act of aggression* against those who are the victims of it. It is an act of aggression, which amounts to a crime, for *even when they are not used,* by their cost alone, *armaments kill the poor by causing them to starve*"[italics in original].[3] In other words, the bomb has already gone off in the world of the poor. Poverty and militarism are inextricably linked.

The world spends nearly a trillion dollars each year on weapons of death. Though we produce enough food to feed adequately more than the current global population, 950,000,000 people are chronically malnourished.[4] Sixty thousand people, primarily children, die each day from starvation, while the best and brightest minds of the world's governments spend their energies and the world's resources on the business of war. Forty million people worldwide die each year from starvation and preventable diseases.[5] A child dies of hunger and hunger-related causes approximately every two seconds. Some fourteen million children die yearly of preventable disease. An additional 1.5 million children were killed in wars worldwide in the 1980s.[6]

Despite this forced, institutionalized suffering that affects so many human beings, global expenditures on arms and armies approach one trillion dollars a year—about two million dollars a minute—an amount that easily could reduce worldwide starvation, disease and poverty if it were spent on services for the world's poor.[7] World military expenditures from 1960 to 1990 add up to twenty-one trillion dollars ($21,000,000,000,000) in 1987 US dollars, equivalent in size to the value of all goods and services produced by and for the 5.3 billion people on the earth in the year 1990.[8]

Since 1500, when the history of war began to be recorded, there have been 589 "official" wars, and 141,901,000 people have been killed in these wars. In the twentieth century, there have been over four times as many war deaths as in the four hundred years preceding.[9] During the 1980s the number of wars reached an all-time peak and three-fourths of the people killed in them were civilians.[10] The world now has twenty-six million people in the regular armed forces, another forty million in military reserves, and sixty-four national governments under some form of explicit military control.[11] In the early 1990s over forty wars were being fought simultaneously around the world.

With the atomic bombings of Hiroshima on August 6, 1945, and Nagasaki on August 9, 1945, the destruction of the entire human race and the planet itself has become possible. Though changes have occurred since the late 1980s, most notably the collapse of communism and the Soviet Union, the world still maintains, as of 1993, nearly fifty thousand nuclear weapons, an explosive force sixteen hundred times the firepower released in three wars (World War II, the Korean war and the Vietnam war).[12] Six nations possess nuclear capabilities (the United States, Russia, Great Britain, France, China and Israel), and at least three other nations are developing them (South Africa, India and Pakistan). Loaded down with nuclear weapons, 745 ships and submarines continually circle the globe. Since 1945, 1,814 nuclear weapons have been detonated to "test" and thus "improve" their deadly power. The proliferation of nuclear weapons still threatens the world's destruction. Though the Cold War is over, the Clinton administration has declared that "the post cold-war world is decidedly not post-nuclear," and has thus re-

Making martyrs of those who are merciful. is part of the system of violence –

committed itself to maintaining the US nuclear arsenal.[13] The Pentagon will spend thirty-eight billion dollars in 1993 and $350 billion over the next ten years to prepare for nuclear war.[14]

Under these two levels of violence—global, systemic injustice and the nuclear weapons arsenal—lies a third level of violence, namely repression. In order to keep the masses of poor people around the world from attaining the resources they need to live, governments often rely on repressive military force to harass, intimidate and subdue people. Such government violence (often supported by superpower weapons, money and assistance) targets poor and marginalized peoples whenever they begin to demand their basic human rights to housing, food, clothing, education and medicine. The military forces of the unjust status quo lash out at the weaker, marginalized peoples who constitute the vast majority. Often in such repressive violence, key organizers and prophetic voices are publicly assassinated, while thousands disappear, are tortured and killed. Examples of repressive violence include the government brutality recently aimed at the suffering masses in El Salvador, South Africa, Palestine, Guatemala and Haiti.

As the violence of repression escalates, it often leads to a fourth level of violence, namely revolutionary violence. History records many cases of revolutionary violence, from the violent revolution of the Palestinian zealots against the Roman imperialism of Jesus' time, to the North American colonial struggle against the British troops in the 1770s, to the Salvadoran FMLN rebel attacks against the US-backed Salvadoran government. While they do not use nuclear weapons or support the systemic violence of imperialism which kills the poor, violent revolutionaries do kill people, and thus they sow seeds for further hostility and violence in the future. This fourth level of violence, although not equal to the massive institutionalized violence of systemic injustice or the nuclear weapons system, is still lethal.

Interpersonal violence, which is destroying the inner cities of the First World and is so characteristic of the entire world, comprises a fifth level of violence. This level encompasses the violence of murder and street violence; the violence of armed robbery and rape; and the psychological and physical violence used against children, women, gays and lesbians, and all marginalized peoples. Included in this category of interpersonal violence is the violence of personal assault and violent self-defense. These forms of interpersonal violence often find their roots in the poverty and despair of the first and second levels of violence.

Underneath this interpersonal violence is the personal violence within each human heart. When we examine the roots of human violence, we discover that we all have violence in our hearts and that we all need to be disarmed of the violence within. Because we live in a world of violence from our street corner to the nuclear arsenal, we have all been trained in violence, and we tend to give in to the darkness of violence. While violence is deadly in whatever form it takes, the global violence of systemic injustice backed up by the nuclear arsenal which threatens to destroy the planet (the first two levels) overshadow all other levels of violence.

personal violence

We are more social as human beings than we admit to consciousness Example: 1 peer pressure (letting others determine our value, etc.) 2 who's got more toys?

Underlying these interacting levels of violence is a prevailing myth which maintains that violence alone can bring about positive change. The myth of redemptive violence insists that violence is sometimes necessary and justified, that violence "redeems" a bad situation, that there is such a thing as "good violence." In this myth, violent retaliation is upheld as the only viable response to violence, whether on the interpersonal level or the global level. It insists that "violence is the only thing that works," that violence is necessary to teach our children—or another nation—a lesson. Theologian Walter Wink writes:

> Violence is the ethos of our times. It is the spirituality of the modern world. It has been accorded the status of religion, demanding from its devotees an absolute obedience to death. Its followers are not aware, however, that the devotion they pay to violence is a form of religious piety. Violence is so successful as a myth precisely because it does not seem to be mythic in the least. Violence simply appears to be the nature of things. It is what works. It is inevitable, the last, and often, the first resort to conflicts. It is embraced with equal alacrity by people on the left and on the right, by religious liberals as well as religious conservatives. The threat of violence, it is believed, is alone able to deter aggressors. It secured us forty-five years of a balance of terror. We learned to trust the Bomb to grant us peace.[15]

"An eye for an eye" sums up this worldwide philosophy of retaliation. The nonviolence of Jesus and Gandhi, on the other hand, teaches that "an eye for an eye only makes the whole world blind." Nonviolence maintains that violence only leads to further violence, that violence never ever solves anything. Nonviolence insists that violence does *not* work.

The Alternative of Nonviolence

The world's violence has brought humanity to the brink of self-destruction. We cannot continue this madness for long. Either we will kill ourselves in a global holocaust of violence, or we will renounce violence in every form on every level and learn to live at peace with one another. "The choice is no longer between violence and nonviolence," Martin Luther King, Jr., declared the night before he was assassinated. "It is nonviolence or nonexistence."[16] Gospel nonviolence offers us the only way out of the global catastrophe of violence.

Gandhi popularized the term *nonviolence*, taking it from the Sanskrit word *ahimsa* ("non-harm") to express the peaceful, loving means of proclaiming the truth. Nonviolence is a way of active peacemaking that both resists evil without doing evil and insists on truth and justice through love. From Gandhi to King and the movements of peaceful transformation around the world, nonviolence refers to active peacemaking and persistent reconciliation.[17] Nonviolence is the exact opposite of passivity (which the term *pacifism* often connotes). It is the active pursuit of peace and justice using peaceful and just means. It is active love and truth working together to transform every level of violence into God's realm of justice and peace. It is the unconditional love of God working within humanity to transform humanity into God's reign of justice and peace, to fulfill the reconciliation already created by God.

Nonviolence is a revolutionary tactic and a political strategy for the transformation of the world, but it is much more than that. It is a way of life, a principle underlying all human life. As a way of life, active nonviolence struggles through peaceful, loving means to promote the truth of God's reign of justice and peace for all. At every step along the way this struggle refrains from violence, so that every person is reconciled again to one another, to God and to the earth. The way of nonviolence therefore refuses to hurt others or kill others or wage war or support the institutionalized violence of poverty and systemic injustice.

Nonviolence recognizes that violence takes us down a never-ending spiral into ever-deepening violence. It breaks the cycle of violence simply by refusing to respond in kind. It turns the myth of redemptive violence upside down and opens up the way to reconciliation and justice through forgiveness, love and resistance to evil; violence only breeds further violence. Nonviolence reverses the cycle of violence by accepting suffering without retaliation in the loving insistence on truth, justice and peace. It injects the God of peace and unconditional love into the spiral of violence, and it opens a space for God to reverse the process of violence.

Nonviolence therefore offers a way to fight against injustice and war without using violence. It breaks through the world's violence, turns us to the God who created us to live in peace, and leads us along the steps of reconciliation and justice toward peace. As the force of love and truth that seeks positive social change for the benefit of all life, it resists injustice, refuses cooperation with violence, and looks beyond the systems of death to God's reign of life. Nonviolence requires active cooperation with good and active noncooperation with evil. Nonviolent resistance to evil willingly takes on suffering in order to right wrongs and transform the systems of death into life for all. It discovers the ends already present in the means and insists that only peace leads to peace, that only truth produces truth, and that only the practice of love itself toward every human being transforms and fulfills the human vocation to be a family of love, children of a loving God.

Violence makes us forget or ignore who we are, that we are all equal, all sisters and brothers of one another, all children of a loving God. Once we forget or ignore this fact of reality, we begin to hurt one another, to kill, to wage war, and to take from others. Eventually, we legitimize and systematize our violence. Nonviolence insists, on the other hand, that we are called to recognize the divine in every human being—even those who hurt or kill others or are labelled as enemies or nonhuman. From this inner journey of the heart we can create nonviolent structures and cultures that help us to affirm every human being as sister and brother so that we turn from the ways of violence toward justice and peace. Nonviolence, then, is a way of actively remembering, every day of our lives, who we are and what we are about, and returning to that core truth whenever we forget. It recalls us to our real identities as daughters and sons of the God of peace, peacemaking sisters and brothers of one another. It means noncooperation with violence, a refusing to forget. It enables us to regain the truth of human reality, that we are all God's children.[18] Activist Wally Nelson defines nonviolence as:

> the constant awareness of the dignity and humanity of oneself and others. It seeks truth and justice; it renounces violence both in method and in attitude. It is a courageous acceptance of active love and goodwill as the instrument with which to overcome evil and transform both oneself and others. It is the willingness to undergo suffering rather than inflict it. It excludes retaliation and flight.[19]

The Nonviolence of Gandhi, Day and King

Three contemporary apostles of nonviolence, Mohandas Gandhi, Dorothy Day and Martin Luther King, Jr., brought the world's attention to the possibility of nonviolence. Although a Hindu, Gandhi drew inspiration from the nonviolence of Jesus, in particular from the Sermon on the Mount. By teaching and practicing nonviolence, Gandhi revealed to the world that the teachings and practice of Jesus could be employed, not just by individuals, but by nations as well. Gandhi applied nonviolence to the political realities of poverty and injustice in South Africa and India to lead a nonviolent revolution from British oppression. In this struggle Gandhi experienced God as Truth, as the Spirit of nonviolence itself, pushing humanity to speak with love the truth of justice.

"Humanity has to get out of violence only through nonviolence," Gandhi declared. "Hatred can only be overcome only by love. Counter-hatred only increases the surface as well as the depth of hatred."[20] "Nonviolence is the greatest and most active force in the world. One person who can express nonviolence in life exercises a force superior to all the forces of brutality."[21] "The force generated by nonviolence is infinitely greater than the force of all the arms invented by humanity's ingenuity."[22] "Nonviolence and truth are so intertwined that it is practically impossible to disentangle and separate them. They are like the two sides of a coin or rather a smooth unstamped metallic disc," Gandhi observed. "Who can say which is the obverse and which the reverse? Nevertheless, nonviolence is the means and truth is the end."[23] "When the practice of nonviolence becomes universal, God will reign on earth as God does in heaven."[24]

Gandhi's teaching challenges Christian theology to return to Jesus' own nonviolence and to articulate what that nonviolence means for us today. Gandhi invites us to root our theology in Jesus' nonviolent struggle for justice, in the God of nonviolence, and in our own active nonviolence.

While Gandhi was practicing nonviolence in India, Dorothy Day was founding the Catholic Worker movement in New York City. She practiced nonviolence among the homeless poor of New York's Lower East Side and consistently voiced a strong rejection of war and the nuclear arms race in favor of justice and peace. While opening houses of hospitality that fed and sheltered the homeless, Day insisted that the United States stop waging war and developing nuclear weapons of mass destruction. She urged the nation to use its resources to serve the needs of suffering humanity, beginning at home. Her reflections, reported monthly in the *Catholic Worker* newspaper, grew from her day-to-day experiences of life among the poor, on the picket lines and in jail for nonviolent resistance to evil. Her theological reflections sprang from a lifelong immersion in the systemic injustice suffered by the poor, a serious analysis of global violence and regular application of gospel nonviolence.

"As you come to know the seriousness of our situation—the war, the racism, the poverty in the world—you come to realize it is not going to be changed by words or demonstrations," Day wrote. "It's a question of risking your life. It's a question of living your life in drastically different ways."[25] From this starting point, she applied the nonviolence of Jesus and went forth to serve the poor, walk with the poor, defend the poor, and proclaim the gospel vision of justice and peace. In this theology of nonviolence Day wrote that she met Christ in the poor and the enemy. We are called to love Christ present in every human being, especially in the poor and in the enemy, she declared. Such active love, she suggested, is transforming the world. "All my prayer, my own suffering, my reading, my study, would lead me to this conclusion. This is a great and holy force and must be used as the spiritual weapon. Love against hate. Suffering against violence. What is two thousand years in the history of the world? We have scarcely begun to love. We have scarcely begun to know Christ, to see him in others around us."[26]

In the late 1950s and early 1960s Dorothy Day and her friends refused to go indoors during air raid drills that sought to prepare the public for nuclear war. Instead, she sat in a New York City park and went to jail in opposition to the government's preparations for nuclear war. After her release from jail in 1957, she wrote, "It is a gesture, perhaps, but a necessary one. Silence means consent and we cannot consent to the militarization of our country without protest. Since we believe that air raid drills are part of a calculated plan to inspire fear of the enemy, instead of the love which Jesus Christ told us we should feel, we must protest these drills. It is an opportunity to show we mean what we write when we repeat over and over that we are put here on this earth to love God and our neighbor."[27] After two thousand people joined in the nonviolent protest in 1961, the air raid drills were cancelled. Until her death in 1980, Day continued to say no to war and yes to Christ's way of nonviolence.

During the 1950s and 1960s, Martin Luther King, Jr., captured the world's attention with his commitment to civil rights and peace through active nonviolence. King taught nonviolence not just as a method for promoting civil rights, but as the spirit that redeems and saves humanity. Thousands of people across the nation and the world learned the lessons of nonviolence from Dr. King. Even more than Gandhi and Day, King articulated a new theology of nonviolence. Through his sermons and published works King reflected on the wisdom of nonviolence, which he learned firsthand in the struggle for civil rights and peace. Early in his public life, Dr. King wrote:

MLK

> As I delved deeper into the philosophy of Gandhi my skepticism concerning the power of love gradually diminished, and I came to see for the first time its potency in the area of social reform. Prior to reading Gandhi, I had about concluded that the ethics of Jesus were only effective in individual relationship. The "turn the other cheek" philosophy and the "love your enemies" philosophy were only valid, I felt, when individuals were in conflict with other individuals; when racial groups and nations were in conflict a more realistic approach seemed necessary. But after reading Gandhi, I saw how utterly mistaken I was. Gandhi was probably the first person in history to lift the love ethic of Jesus above mere interaction between individuals to a powerful and effective social force on a large scale. For Gandhi, love was a potent instrument for social and collective transformation. It was in this Gandhian emphasis on love and nonviolence that I discovered the method for social reform that I had been seeking for so many months. The intellectual and moral satisfaction that I failed to gain from the utilitarianism of Bentham and Mill, the revolutionary methods of Marx and Lenin, the social-contracts theory of Hobbes, the "back to nature" optimism of Rousseau, and the superman philosophy of Nietzsche, I found in the nonviolent resistance philosophy of Gandhi. I came to feel that this was the only morally and practically sound method open to oppressed people in their struggle for freedom.[28]

MLK's eureka

"When the protest began," King wrote later on, "my mind was driven back to the Sermon on the Mount, with its sublime teachings on love, and the Gandhian method of nonviolent resistance. As the days unfolded, I came to see the power of nonviolence more and more. Living through the actual experience of the protest, nonviolence became more than a method to which I gave intellectual assent; it became a commitment to a way of life. Many of the things that I had not cleared up intellectually concerning nonviolence," King concluded, "were now solved in the sphere of practical action."[29]

When he received the 1963 Nobel Peace Prize in Oslo, King once again upheld the way of nonviolence:

comet

* He couldn't have been. The Zen mystics were long ahead of him. I wonder though if they married theology + politics together

This relates to the slave-owner mentality's vicious generational cycles

Nonviolence is the answer to the crucial political and moral question of our time—the need for people to overcome oppression and violence without resorting to violence and oppression . . . Nonviolence is not sterile passivity but a powerful moral force which makes for social transformation. Sooner or later, all the people of the world will have to discover a way to live together in peace . . . If this is to be achieved, people must evolve for all human conflict a method which rejects revenge, aggression, and retaliation. The foundation for such a method is love.[30] *Even Hillman admits this*

MLK

For Dr. King, nonviolence held the only way out of the downward spiral of violence and death. It offered a divine way into a new world of justice and peace.

In his book *Stride Toward Freedom*, King outlined six principles of Christian nonviolence which shaped his life and message.[31] First, nonviolence offers a way of life for courageous people. It means active resistance to evil through peaceful, loving methods, which always seek to persuade one's opponent of the righteousness and justice of one's cause. Dr. King described "the method" as "passive physically, but strongly active spiritually. It is no passive nonresistance to evil; it is active nonviolent resistance to evil."[32]

Second, nonviolence seeks to win friendship and understanding. It endeavors to make apparent the underlying unity and reconciliation that already exist in humanity, a unity forever sealed in the blood of Jesus, as St. Paul writes. Nonviolence uncovers and builds up the beloved community of humanity. As the way of God, it redeems, reconciles, and leads us to the nonviolent reign of God on earth.

Third, nonviolence seeks to defeat injustice, not people. Nonviolence looks on evildoers as themselves victims, rather than as evil people. The nonviolent resister seeks to defeat evil, not the people who do the evil. Nonviolence recognizes that every human being sins, that every human being does evil, that every human being commits violence. Active nonviolence seeks to halt evil and to heal the human family. It transforms injustice into justice, war into peace and death into life.

Fourth, nonviolence holds that suffering can educate and transform. Nonviolence struggles actively for justice and peace, but instead of inflicting violence and death on others, it accepts suffering without retaliation. In the nonviolent way of life, we refrain from violence, no matter how just the cause, King insisted. We never inflict violence on others or ever advocate it, but if necessary, we suffer it with a redemptive love that seeks to open the eyes of our opponent to the truth of justice and peace. Thus, nonviolence accepts the consequences of its actions. "Unearned suffering," King repeated everywhere he went, "is redemptive." It has the power to convert our opponent when reason fails. Redemptive suffering love, which insists on justice and peace, is the doorway to conversion and transformation.

Fifth, nonviolence chooses love instead of hate. It resists violence of the spirit as well as the body. This love flows spontaneously, unselfishly, creatively, sacrificially and unconditionally. Given the world's violence, active nonviolent love risks a return of hostility. Such active love never ceases to forgive but continues to insist on the beloved community of humanity. Nonviolence recognizes that all life is interrelated, that all is one. Love for the enemy, King explained, stands then at the center of the way of nonviolence. "Along the way of life," King wrote, "someone must have sense enough and morality enough to cut off the chain of hate. This can only be done by projecting the ethic of love to the center of our lives."[33] "Love, *agape*, is the only cement that can hold the broken community together. When I am commanded to love, I am commanded to restore community, to resist injustice, and to meet the needs of my brothers and sisters."[34]

Sixth, the nonviolent way of life flows from a deep belief that the universe stands on the side of justice, King wrote. The practitioner of nonviolence knows that God reigns, that God is nonviolent, that God's reign is a reign of nonviolence, and that God's way of nonviolence will eventually transform everyone into God's reign of justice and peace. The universe itself bends toward justice, he proclaimed. The deepest meaning in life, then, is to side with God in God's nonviolent transformation of the world into a reign of justice and peace.

Like Gandhi and Day, King's theology emerges from the nonviolent struggle for justice and peace. It springs from the poor and oppressed in their peaceful search for liberation and truth. Like Gandhi and Day, King learned that nonviolence is not just a tactic but a way of life, a way of living in God's reign here and now in a world of violence. Most important, King realized, the practice of nonviolence is teaching us that Jesus practiced nonviolence, that God is a God of nonviolence, and that we are called to be nonviolent, not just because it works, but because it reflects the very nature of God.[35] By articulating a theology of nonviolence, we may learn then what it means to be human in these days of violence and what it means to live in God's reign of nonviolent love.

Toward a Theology of Nonviolence

Theology simply refers to discourse about God. If our theology is to be credible, intelligible and real, it must address and grapple with systemic violence. From the perspective of the world's violence, theology refers to and reflects upon God's relationship and transformation of that violence, and our participation in God's transforming nonviolence. Our theology seeks to pinpoint God's way out of violence and enter into that struggle.

In light of the world's violence, a theology of nonviolence speaks of the God of peace. As Gandhi, Day and King have demonstrated, theological reflection on active nonviolence flows from the life and practice of active nonviolence as one struggles for justice and peace in the world. Their theology of nonviolence not only proclaims nonviolence but practices nonviolence for the transformation of the world. They show that we need to participate in the nonviolent struggle for justice and peace. Indeed, this new theology of nonviolence will be itself a form of our active nonviolence. Our theological reflections will emerge from our Christian peacemaking activity in the world. Since this theology is rooted in the living witness and daily practice of gospel nonviolence, it becomes a theology that literally can make peace in a world of war. It articulates our experience of making peace and seeking justice and so contributes to the spread of peace and justice among humanity. Our theology of nonviolence, rooted in our active peacemaking, will help us discover God as the source of our peace. It examines our discipleship to the nonviolent Jesus and our relationship to a nonviolent God who is transforming us all.

In our theology, we apply the insights of Gandhi, Day and King to Christianity, its scripture, tradition, faith life and praxis. We relate the perspective of nonviolence to traditional theology and the violence of the world. This theology evolves from the traditional theologies of Christian history but flows most explicitly from the liberation theology that has developed in recent decades in Latin America, Africa and Asia. It also includes feminist and other liberation theologies in order to address all the systems of violence, oppression and death that plague humanity. It builds on the foundations of theology, scripture, tradition and the insights of active nonviolence to help us understand who God is, what it means to be human, what it means to be a Christian, and how we can more faithfully serve humanity in its struggle for justice and peace. Just as liberation theology relates the liberating struggle from oppression to the traditional Christian theology of human salvation, so too a theology of nonviolence relates the nonviolent transformation of the world's violence into justice and peace with the traditional Christian theology of human salvation. A theology of nonviolence concludes that the human practice of nonviolence is a crucial factor in God's transformation of the world's violence. Nonviolence is the way God is saving us from our global, self-destruction violence. Active nonviolence is seen as a critical element in human salvation because God is now recognized as a God of nonviolence, a God who calls humanity to become a people of nonviolence. This theology of nonviolence looks critically at the world's deadly violence with the new insight of Christ's peacemaking alternative to help us transform ourselves, our church, and our world through the grace of God into God's nonviolent reign of justice and peace. Using the perspective of nonviolence articulated by Gandhi, Day and King, we approach theology systematically, over and over again, and learn to see new insights into God, ourselves, our world and what it means to be human.

Along the way, a theology of nonviolence will question any and every theology or ideology that supports violence in any form at any level. In our theology of nonviolence, we reflect on every level of violence in light of the nonviolent Jesus and then apply these insights to the area of theology under review. This interaction among the world's violence, Jesus' gospel of nonviolence, and our theological questions develops the theology of nonviolence. Throughout, we use a hermeneutic of nonviolence toward the scriptures. We question everything we have been taught about God, theology and the world in light of our self-destructive violence and the new possibility that God is a God of nonviolence. This interplay leads us to an entirely new theology, a new way of understanding God, Christ, the church, human life, the world, and what the future of humanity might be. By applying the standard of nonviolence to the traditional areas of theology, we reassess our understanding of God and human salvation. In the end, this new theology of nonviolence, then, can contribute to God's transformation of the world.

This theology of nonviolence holds that nonviolence is at the core of the gospel, the heart of Christianity, and the essence of the God revealed in Jesus Christ. Most people, however, especially most Christians, do not understand gospel nonviolence. Therefore, given the urgency of the day and the power of theology to support peace and justice, a theology of nonviolence needs to be articulated so that people of faith may come to a deeper understanding of who God is, how God responds to the world's violence, how God is transforming the world, and how humanity is called to become a people of nonviolence.

at the ♡ of Christianity

CHAPTER 2

The Nonviolence of Jesus

Good News of Peace

With the bad news of the world's violence coming at us from all sides, the Christian turns to the Christian scriptures and discovers God's good news of nonviolence. The gospels tell the story of nonviolence in the life of the peacemaking Jesus and his nonviolent alternative to the ways of the world. The Jesus of the Christian scriptures practices nonviolence and invites people to follow his way to the God of peace.

A theology of nonviolence begins with the historical Jesus (as opposed to the Trinity or the human person) because, for the Christian, Jesus reveals to us both who God is and what it means to be a human being. Jesus embodies nonviolence and is the reference point for a theology of nonviolence. Jesus is the basis from which all our Christian nonviolence and reflection on Christian nonviolence takes place. In a world of widespread violence and confusion, Christians find clarity in the life and message of Jesus. Jesus reveals the nature of the divine. Jesus shows us God, and the God he reveals to us is a God of nonviolence. As the incarnation of God, Jesus incarnates a nonviolent God; he spends his life teaching and practicing nonviolence. Christians seeking to learn and practice nonviolence need to begin, then, with the nonviolent Jesus.

The gospels present Jesus as the image of God's active nonviolence and the Way out of the world's cycle of violence. Five gospel perspectives sum up the nonviolence of Jesus: 1) Jesus, the incarnation of nonviolence; 2) Jesus, the prophet of nonviolence; 3) Jesus, the teacher of nonviolence; 4) Jesus, the model of nonviolence; and 5) Jesus, the sign of nonviolence. From these perspectives we can paint a simple portrait of Jesus Christ as God's revelation calling us to the life of active nonviolence, to share in the nonviolent reign of God. This image of Jesus grounds our understanding of theology, our understanding of God, and our understanding of the Christian life.

[handwritten margin note: Portrait of Jesus (God in Person)]

18

Jesus, the Incarnation of Nonviolence

The gospel proclaims that the God of peace became human and walked the earth making peace, speaking for peace, acting for peace, and suffering so that all humanity might live in peace with one another and with God. The gospel portrays Jesus as the incarnation of nonviolence, the fullest expression in human history of our nonviolent God.

The word *gospel* offers our first clue about this dramatic news. When a son of the Roman emperor was born, the news was proclaimed throughout the regions of the Roman empire as "the gospel," the good news of the birth of the emperor, indeed, the birth of a god since the Roman emperor claimed divinity. This "gospel" or "good news" grew over time to refer to any declaration or victory concerning the emperor, especially the latest conquest of the emperor's legions in the Mediterranean world.

When the evangelists—beginning with Mark—announce the "gospel" of Jesus, they speak directly of a new political victory, a new event of good news. The gospels announce a victory won not by any false god or emperor, but by the one true God. By choosing birth as a fragile human being, God has entered the struggle for justice and peace and has emerged victorious in order to transform the world into the reign of God's nonviolence.

Matthew and Luke's gospels describe Jesus' birth in poverty. Luke tells us that it happened in a stable on the outskirts of a brutal empire. The angels proclaim the nonviolent messiah's birth in Luke's gospel in a song of praise to God: "Glory to God in the highest and on earth peace to those on whom God's favor rests" (Lk 2:14). Matthew writes that God has intervened in human history as the child of impoverished, marginalized refugees (Mt 2:13-23). God has deliberately sided with the poor and oppressed of the world by embracing their vulnerability in the midst of a deadly empire. The birth of Jesus is marked not only by poverty, but by imperial violence. Herod the Great, the client of the imperial Rome, responds to the incarnation by trying to kill the child, the child of nonviolence, the son of the God of nonviolence. Thousands of male babies are killed at the news of Jesus' birth (Mt 2:16-18).

Perhaps the gospel of John best speaks of the good news of God's incarnation. John's prologue (1:1-18) declares that the Word of God came into humanity bringing life "and this life was the light of the human race" (1:4). "To those that accepted him, he gave power to become children of God" (1:12). "And the Word became flesh and made his dwelling among us, and we saw his glory, and the glory as of the Father's only Son, full of grace and truth" (1:14). Jesus incarnates divine love and radiates God's grace and truth, in other words, God's nonviolent response to human sinfulness.

Because God has become human, we are called to become human. The incarnation challenges us to resist every inhuman behavior, every level of violence. With the incarnation we are bound morally and spiritually not to hurt or kill one another, or else we hold the God of peace in contempt. The incarnation by its very happening rules out all killing and all injustice. God chooses to side with human beings and honors human life by becoming human, like us in all things but the violence of sin.

The incarnation of nonviolence challenges us to become a people of nonviolence, to incarnate the Spirit of nonviolence that God incarnated in Jesus. We too are invited to be transformed into God's Spirit of nonviolence present on earth in love and service towards others and nonviolent resistance towards all evil. We are called to receive "the grace and truth" offered by the incarnate Word of God. With this event we are called to be God's very sons and daughters, those whom the gospel of Matthew will later define as peacemakers (5:9).

Jesus, the Prophet of Nonviolence

From day one of his public ministry Jesus denounces violence and injustice and announces the good news of nonviolence. He calls us to enter God's reign, which leads him to walk the narrow path of nonviolence. He challenges the lies and false gods of the empire and witnesses to the truth of nonviolence. In this vocation of truth-telling and proclamation, Jesus, the prophet of nonviolence, voices God's message of peace and calls us to become God's people of peace.

Prophets speak the truth on behalf of God. The Greek word *prophetes* designates a person who serves as a channel of communication between the human and divine. Jesus' contemporaries saw him as a prophet. The disciples on the way to Emmaus, for example, describe Jesus as "a prophet mighty in deed and word before God and all the people" (Lk 24:19).

From the beginning of Mark's gospel, probably the earliest written of the four gospels, Jesus calls people to repent of their violence and to embrace God's nonviolent reign of peace. "The time is fulfilled and the reign of God is at hand," Jesus declares at the opening of Mark's gospel. "Repent and believe in the gospel" (Mk 1:14-15). Jesus' first words invite his hearers (and the readers of the gospel) to repent—to turn away from their sins. Heard in the political context of imperial oppression in first-century Palestine, Jesus' call invites his hearers to turn away from complicity in the systemic sin of imperial violence and all the ways of death. Moreover, Jesus' proclamation of God's reign sets him on a collision course with the temple priesthood and the Jewish nobility who collaborated with Roman oppression.

In describing Jesus' early ministry of proclamation, Matthew's gospel quotes Isaiah: "For those who sat in the region and shadow of death, light has dawned" (Mt 4:16). Jesus and his message bring the good news of life in the midst of a reign of death.

The gospel of Luke most clearly portrays Jesus as the joyful prophet of God's reign of nonviolence. According to Luke, Jesus announces the good news of the reign of God, which is explained in terms of mercy and compassion. "I must preach the good news of the reign of God," Jesus tells the disciples one morning, "for I was sent for this purpose" (Lk 4:43; see also Mk 1:38). In the course of his preaching, Jesus called people to repent from their violence so that they would not perish in violence (Lk 13:1-5). Luke's story of Jesus' inaugural sermon in Nazareth strikes the most dramatic portrait of Jesus as prophet. In the synagogue of Nazareth Jesus reads from the scroll of the prophet Isaiah:

> The Spirit of the Lord is upon me, because God has anointed me to bring good news to the poor. God has sent me to proclaim liberty to captives and recovery of sight to the blind, to let the oppressed go free and to proclaim a year acceptable to the Lord (Lk 4:18-19).

Lk 4:18-19

"Today this scripture passage is fulfilled in your hearing," Jesus boldly declares. God sends Jesus as a prophet to proclaim good news to the poor and a season of jubilee, like the Jewish year of jubilee, where all oppressive debts are cancelled and human rights upheld. Jesus works as a missionary of non-violence and justice, a prophet of God's peace.

In his call for repentance and his announcement of the reign of God, Jesus publicly tells the truth to all those who are willing to hear him. The proclamations made by Jesus in all four gospels reveal God's truth, the truth of nonviolence as the way to the fullness of life. "For this I was born and for this I have come into the world," Jesus explains to Pilate, "to bear witness to the truth. Everyone who is of the truth hears my voice" (Jn 18:37).

The truth of Jesus is announced as a law of nonviolence, God's law. Violence leads to further violence, Jesus says over and over again, but nonviolence leads to further nonviolence. Nonviolence, a law of nature, leads to life, love, justice and peace. Those who are nonviolent, Jesus declares, will find life. To live in God's reign of nonviolence, we need to be transformed into persons of nonviolence. "If you continue in my word, you are truly my disciples, and you will know the truth and the truth will make you free" (Jn 8:32). "Do not be anxious about your life, what you shall eat, nor about your body, what you shall put on," Jesus declares in Luke's gospel. "Which of you by being anxious can add a cubit to his span of life? If then you are not able to do as small a thing as that, why are you anxious about the rest? . . . Do not seek what you are to eat and what you are to drink, nor be of anxious mind. For all the nations of the world seek these things; and your God knows that you need them. Instead, seek God's reign and these things shall be yours as well" (Lk 12:22-32). As a PROPHET

As Jesus approaches Jerusalem to confront the ruling powers with the witness of nonviolence, including civil disobedience at the Temple, he denounces the injustices of the scribes, the Pharisees, Herod, Pilate, and all those who tell lies, lead people astray, hurt others, or partake of systemic injustice. As a prophet, Jesus denounces systemic violence and announces God's reign of nonviolence, the good news of peace, the truth of nonviolence. But besides his prophetic ministry, Jesus was a teacher of nonviolence as well.

Jesus, the Teacher of Nonviolence

Fundamentally, Jesus was a teacher who taught the way of nonviolence. Even Jesus' opponents, the Pharisees and the Herodians, recognized that Jesus taught with authority as no one else did. "Teacher," they said, "we know that you speak and teach rightly and show no partiality, and but truly teach the way of God" (Lk 20:21).

Jesus was often called "rabbi" or "teacher," and like other itinerant preachers or teachers of his time, he traveled about with a coterie of students, whom the gospels call "disciples." Throughout, Jesus the teacher guides his followers, encourages them, challenges them, questions their preconceptions, and urges them on to the wisdom of nonviolence.

As a teacher, Jesus explained the basic lessons of God's nonviolence; he taught an entirely new way of life, the way of divine justice and nonviolence. "Jesus lived and died in vain if he did not teach us to regulate the whole of life by the eternal law of love," wrote Gandhi.[1] Matthew's gospel in particular presents Jesus as a teacher of wisdom, the new lawgiver who teaches God's way of life. The centerpiece of Jesus' teaching is the Sermon on the Mount, his formal manifesto of nonviolence.

Matthew's Sermon on the Mount (like Luke's Sermon on the Plain) begins with the beatitudes, a list of blessings that outline the life of discipleship:

> Blessed are the poor in spirit, for theirs is the reign of heaven. Blessed are those who mourn, for they shall be comforted. Blessed are the meek, for they shall inherit the earth. Blessed are those who hunger and thirst for justice, for they shall be satisfied. Blessed are the merciful, for they shall obtain mercy. Blessed are the pure in heart, for they shall see God. Blessed are the peacemakers, for they shall be called the sons and daughters of God. Blessed are those who are persecuted for justice's sake, for theirs is the reign of heaven. Blessed are you when people revile you and persecute you and utter all kinds of evil against you falsely on my account. Rejoice and be glad, for your reward is great in heaven, for so people persecuted the prophets who were before you (Mt 5:3-12).

This upside-down vision of life calls us to be poor, mournful, meek; to hunger and thirst for justice; to be merciful and pure in heart; to be peacemakers, willing to be persecuted for justice's sake. Such qualities form the core of the way of nonviolence. Actual and spiritual poverty ground the authentic life of nonviolence. Mourners grieve the loss of those killed by war, injustice and imperial oppression. The life which is meek and gentle, hungers for justice, practices mercy, lives pure in heart, and makes peace leads to persecution by the empire of death. This life of nonviolence transforms the world's imperial violence, but not without brutal persecution. But if everyone adopts the way of nonviolence, as Jesus wants, then all wars, all injustices and all violence will cease; all nations and empires will abjure oppression, and God will reign on earth as God reigns in heaven—nonviolently.

Several of the antitheses that follow the beatitudes outline the way of violence the world teaches; they are contrasted with the nonviolent alternative Jesus commands. "You have heard that it was said to those of old, 'You shall not kill and whoever kills shall be liable to judgment.'" Jesus goes beyond the command not to kill: "But I say to you that everyone who is angry with his brother [or sister] shall be liable to judgment . . . So if you are offering your gift at the altar, and there remember that your brother [or sister] has something against you, leave your gift there before the altar and go; first be reconciled to your brother [or sister], and then come and offer your gift" (Mt 5:21-24).

Next, Jesus proclaims that not only are we not to commit actual adultery, we are not to commit adultery in our hearts, to look lustfully at another (Mt 5:27-28). Not only are we not to swear falsely, Jesus declares, we are not to swear at all. "Let what you say be simply 'Yes' or 'No,'" Jesus urges (Mt 5:33-37). Our hearts are to be pure in all things, so that the nonviolence we practice in the world reflects the nonviolent spirit in our hearts. "You have heard that it was said, 'An eye for an eye and a tooth for a tooth,'" Jesus recalls. "But I say to you, Do not [violently] resist one who does evil. If any one strikes you on the right cheek, turn to him the other as well. If a person takes you to law and would have your tunic, let him have your cloak as well. And if anyone orders you to go one mile, go two miles with him. Give to anyone who asks, and if anyone wants to borrow, do not turn away" (Mt 5:38-42). Here, Jesus clearly advocates nonviolent resistance to evil, a new, third alternative to the methods of passive acceptance or active complicity in violence.[2] Instead of passively accepting the oppressive and humiliating violence which lands on us like the back of a right hand slap across the face, we are to turn the cheek, look our oppressors in the eye, accept violence without retaliating. All the while we are to show our oppressors that we too are human, so that their hearts and eyes may be opened, the violence stopped and together we become reconciled.

The culmination of these antitheses is the command to practice unconditional love beyond the boundaries of empire.

> "You have heard that it was said, 'You shall love your neighbor and hate your enemy.' But I say to you, Love your enemies and pray for those who persecute you so that you may be sons and daughters of your God who is in heaven; for God makes God's sun rise on the evil and on the good, and sends rain on the just and on the unjust. For if you love those who love you, what reward have you? Do not even the tax collectors do the same? And if you salute only your brothers, what more are you doing than others? Do not even the Gentiles do the same? You therefore must be perfect as your heavenly God is perfect" (Mt 5:43-48).

Mt 5:43-48

Luke's version of the command to love enemies is even stronger. He repeats the command, adding the proscription to share one's possessions with one's enemies. "Love your enemies, and do good and lend, expecting nothing in

return; and your reward will be great and you will be sons and daughters of
the Most High; for God is kind to the ungrateful and the selfish. Be merciful
even as your God is merciful" (Lk 6:35-36). Love of enemies not only uni-
versalizes Christian love, it makes it nonviolent.

To the religious authorities who gather around him, Jesus declares, "Go
and learn what this means, 'I desire mercy, and not sacrifice.' For I came
not to call the righteous, but sinners [to repentance]" (Mt 9:13). As he is
about to heal a man with a withered hand in Capernaum's synagogue, he
asks pointedly: "Is it lawful on the sabbath to do good or to do harm, to
save life or to kill?" (Mk 3:4; Lk 6:9). He constantly challenges those
around him to choose life, to do good, to practice active, unconditional
love.

When he invites others to follow him, he has no illusions about the cost
they must pay. Following Jesus means entering upon the way of active resistance to evil, a narrow path that leads to nonviolent confrontation with the
forces of violence and eventually to the suffering and death that come with
persecution and execution.

> If any one would come after me, let [her] deny [herself] and take
> up [her] cross daily and follow me. For whoever would save his
> life will lose it; and whoever loses [her] life for my sake, [she]
> will save it. What does it profit a person if he gains the whole
> world and loses or forfeits himself? (Lk 9:23-25).

Likewise, the gospels take pains to point out that Jesus' way of nonviolence
runs counter to the ways of the world: "If anyone would be first, he must be
last of all and servant of all" (Mk 9:35). "Unless you turn and become like
children you will never enter the reign of heaven. Whoever humbles himself
like [a] child, he is the greatest in the reign of heaven" (Mt 18:3-4). "You
know that those who are supposed to rule over the Gentiles lord it over
them, and their great men exercise authority over them. But it shall not
be so among you; whoever would be great among you must be your servant, and whoever would be first among you must be the slave of all"
(Mk 10:42-44).

When Peter asks if he must forgive a brother who wrongs him "as many as
seven times," Jesus responds, "Not seven times, but seventy times seven"
(Mt 18:21-22). For Peter, "seven times" already meant an indefinite number
of times, but Jesus ups the ante. Jesus equivalently replies, "Forgive an infinite amount of times. Practice unconditional forgiveness."

In this way of nonviolence, with its discipline of love and forgiveness,
Jesus commands his disciples to practice voluntary poverty:

> Sell your possessions and give alms; provide yourselves with purses
> that do not grow old, with a treasure in the heavens that does not
> fail, where no thief approaches and no moth destroys. For where
> your treasure is, there will your heart be also (Lk 12:33-34).

When confronted with the question of capital punishment, Jesus responds with disarming compassion. The wisdom of his nonviolence invites people to put down their stones and to walk away from violence:

> The scribes and Pharisees brought a woman who had been caught in adultery and placing her in the midst they said to him, "Teacher, this woman has been caught in the act of adultery. Now in the law Moses commanded us to stone such [a person]. What do you say about her?" . . . Jesus said, "Let the one among you who is without sin be the first to throw a stone at her" (Jn 8:4-7).

On another occasion the authorities approached him and asked, "Is it lawful to pay taxes to Caesar or not? Should we pay them or should we not?" (Mk 12:14). His answer left them "amazed." "Render to Caesar the things that are Caesar's and to God the things that are God's" (Mk 12:17). As Dorothy Day explains, Jesus knows that once we give to God the things that are God's, there is nothing left to give Caesar.

When asked the greatest commandment, Jesus affirms the age-old teaching of the tradition:

> "The first is, 'Hear, O Israel: The Lord our God, the Lord is one; and you shall love the Lord your God with all your heart, and with all your soul, and with all your mind, and with all your strength.' The second is this, 'You shall love your neighbor as yourself'" (Mk 12:29-31).

John's gospel pinpoints the culmination of Jesus' way of nonviolent love, the love of neighbor and the love of God, as the laying down one's life for one's sisters and brothers, for those in need (Jn 15:13). In Matthew's closing parable of the last judgment Jesus identifies with all those in need and points to the consequence for those who practice such nonviolent, compassionate love:

> "Come, O blessed of my Father, inherit the reign prepared for you from the foundation of the world; for I was hungry and you gave me food, I was thirsty and you gave me drink, I was a stranger and you welcomed me, I was naked and you clothed me, I was sick and you visited me, I was in prison and you came to me . . . Truly, I say to you, as you did it to one of the least of these my sisters and brothers, you did it to me" (Mt 25:34-40).

"Peace I leave with you; my peace I give to you," Jesus told his disciples the night before he was executed by the empire (Jn 14:27). "Put away your sword," Jesus tells Peter, "for all who take the sword will perish by the sword" (Mt 26:53). Jesus in the gospels confronts us as the ultimate teacher of peace and justice, the great master of nonviolence.

Say what, means this:
* Jesus' peace is not the same as the peace the world gives

Jesus, the Model of Nonviolence

Besides incarnating, announcing and teaching the way of nonviolence, Jesus practiced it. As Gandhi wrote, "Jesus was the most active resister known perhaps to history. This was nonviolence par excellence."[3] In Gandhi's words, Jesus was "completely innocent, offered himself as a sacrifice for the good of others, including his enemies, and became the ransom of the world. It was the perfect act."[4]

After a life of active nonviolence, which included confronting those who practiced violence, accompanying the victims of violence, teaching nonviolence and offering prayerful, nonviolent love to everyone, Jesus walked towards Jerusalem from his Capernaum home in the outskirts of the empire to challenge the systemic violence of the world, symbolized in the Temple, the religious institution which oppressed the poor and blessed the empire's reign of death. He entered the Temple, turned over the tables, refused to let people pass by (staging a peaceful sit-in), and proclaimed the Temple "God's house of prayer." Significantly, every gospel tells the story of Jesus' nonviolent direct action in the Temple, but the gospel of Mark most clearly focuses on the incident as the culmination of a campaign of nonviolent resistance which Jesus waged from the rural countryside into downtown Jerusalem and finally to the Temple as the seat of power in Palestine.[5] Mark writes:

> Jesus entered the temple and began to drive out those who sold and those who bought in the temple, and he overturned the tables of the money-changers and the seats of those who sold pigeons; and he would not allow any one to carry anything through the temple (Mk 11:11; also Mt 21:10-17; Lk 19:45-46; Jn 2:13-17).

Jesus does not commit violence; he performs a symbolic act of nonviolent civil disobedience aimed at disrupting the business of the Temple and calling for true worship. Nonviolent civil disobedience enacted in the capital of a remote region of a brutal empire will almost inevitably result in arrest, torture and execution, not in the conversion of the masses that Jesus surely hoped and prayed.

The powers and principalities of death quickly decide to do away with Jesus because of his nonviolent activity for justice. His message of nonviolence calls for the transformation of all empires, nations and institutions that oppress people through systemic and institutionalized violence. The authorities in Jerusalem realize the threat which Jesus' civil disobedience posed and so they plotted quickly to do away with him.

Jesus' action in the Temple brings to a culmination an entire life of active nonviolence. Through civil disobedience he risks his life in order to invite us all to God's way of nonviolence. Through the arrest, jailing, trial, torture and public execution that follows, Jesus retains his nonviolent spirit—loving, forgiving and inviting everyone he encountered. In these final days, he shows how he is indeed the incarnation, prophet, teacher, model and exemplar of nonviolence. When struck by one of the temple guards, for example, he continues to insist on the truth. "If I have spoken wrongly," he asks, "testify to the wrong; but if I have spoken rightly, why do you strike me?" (Jn 18:23).

Each gospel portrays the steadfast spirit of Jesus' nonviolence, even and especially through his brutal passion. John's gospel, for example, culminates Jesus' life of nonviolence with a parable of service. As the community gathers at table on the night before he is executed, Jesus bends down and washes the feet of each of the disciples. The story continues:

> When he had washed their feet . . . he said to them, "Do you know what I have done to you? You call me Teacher and Lord; and you are right, for so I am. If I then, your Lord and Teacher, have washed your feet, you also ought to wash one another's feet. For I have given you an example, that you also should do as I have done to you . . . If you know these things, blessed are you if you do them" (Jn 13:12-17).

[handwritten margin note: Eucharist (Ln 5)]

According to the synoptic gospels, after that final eucharistic gathering, while praying in Gethsemane, Jesus asks that he might not suffer the violence of the world because of his active nonviolence. But he remains faithful to God by praying that God's will be done, not his own. "Father, all things are possible to you," he prays. "Remove this cup from me; yet not what I will, but what you will be done" (Mk 14:36; see also, Mt 26:26-46 and Lk 22:40-45).

At his trial before the Sanhedrin, "the high priest, all the chief priests, the elders, and the scribes," accused him, yet, we are told, "he was silent and made no answer" to their charges (Mk 14:61). They struck him, slapped him on the cheek and spat at his face (Mt 26:67; Mk 14:65; Lk 22:63). Matthew, Mark and John all present the same depictions of Jesus' suffering before the soldiers:

> Having scourged Jesus, [Pilate] delivered him to be crucified. Then the soldiers of the governor took Jesus into the praetorium, and they gathered the whole battalion before him. And they stripped him and put a scarlet robe on him and making a crown of thorns they put it on his head and put a reed in his right hand. And kneeling before him they mocked him, saying, "Hail, King of the Jews!" And they spat upon him, and took the reed and struck him on the head (Mt 27:28-30).

After he was crucified and as he died, according to Luke's gospel, he offered a prayer of forgiveness for those who crucified him, for all humanity. "Father, forgive them; for they know not what they do" (Lk 23:34). In this prayer of forgiveness, he lived out his nonviolence to the very end and he revealed his divinity, the nonviolence of God. Luke even portrays Jesus offering mercy and consolation to one of the men crucified with him (Lk 23:39-43). Jesus was obedient to the end. "Father, into your hands I commit my spirit!" he cried out with a loud voice. And having said this, he breathed his last (Lk 23:46).

Jesus not only revealed how to live and die humanly, but also how to love and forgive under the most violent experience imaginable. In this way Jesus overcame the violence of the world. As the book of Revelation later testifies, the victory was won through his blood. He could not be conquered by violence; he never swerved from the way of nonviolence. He proved to humanity the possibility of living nonviolently and thus opened the door to the transformation of humanity and to the redemption of the entire human race.

Jesus, the Sign of Nonviolence

All of the gospels agree that on the first day of the week the women who went to the tomb to anoint Jesus' body found an empty tomb. According to Mark's gospel, "They saw a young man sitting on the right side, dressed in a white robe and they were amazed." He said to them:

> Do not be amazed. You seek Jesus of Nazareth, who was cruci-
> fied. He has risen, he is not here; see the place where they laid
> him. But go, tell his disciples and Peter that he is going before you
> to Galilee; there you will see him, as he told you (Mk 16:5-7).

In the sign of the resurrection God vindicated and sanctioned Jesus' way of nonviolence. The resurrection revealed Jesus' way of life, the way of active nonviolence, as the path to eternal life, a path that offers redeeming life to others. In the resurrection Jesus' insistence on nonviolence stands vindicated in a way never before dreamed or realized. God definitively intervenes and raises Jesus to new life.

The risen Jesus' first words reveal that not even his own death altered his commitment to nonviolence. "Peace be with you!" (Lk 24:36; Jn 20:19), Jesus tells the disciples. He offers them God's gift of peace. After his ascension, the disciples recall this sign of peace every time they gather at the table of the risen Lord, in the breaking of the bread, where Jesus becomes present once again to the community of peacemakers in their lives of nonviolence (Lk 24:35). The disciples finally understand Jesus' way of nonviolence and commit themselves to following him. At the table they recall what he did the night before he was executed:

> He took bread, and when he had given thanks, he broke it and
> gave it to them, saying, "This is my body, which is given for
> you. Do this in remembrance of me." And likewise, [he took] the
> cup after supper, saying, "This cup which is poured out for you
> is the new covenant in my blood" (Lk 22:19-20).

In recalling Jesus they recommit themselves to walk the same nonviolent path.

In his resurrection Jesus revealed to humanity God's nonviolence. He simultaneously revealed that being fully human means living the life of active nonviolence. In light of the paschal mystery, we come to recognize the reign of God, the reign of Jesus, as a reign of nonviolence. "My kingdom is not of this world," Jesus said at his trial. "If my kingship were of this world, my servants would fight, that I might not be handed over to the Jews; but my kingship is not from the world" (Jn 18:36). Jesus' servants do not fight because, like him, they stand committed to nonviolence. With the resurrection Jesus' servants, his disciples and friends, finally understand his message of nonviolence, his drastically new way of life, and they go forth in his spirit to spread his way of nonviolent love, challenge the forces of darkness and share in his cross and resurrection.

The gospels proclaim an entirely new way of life, the way of nonviolence incarnated, announced, taught, modelled and signified in Jesus. Though each gospel takes a different perspective on the life of Jesus, his nonviolence shines through each testimony. This nonviolent Jesus forms the basis for our theology, our understanding of God and our understanding of the Christian life. Everything we do and say from now on will refer back to Jesus and to his way of active nonviolence.

CHAPTER 3

God Is Nonviolent

Images of the God of Peace

The God of Jesus is a God of nonviolence. The cross demonstrates to us that God suffers human violence without retaliating and transforms us with forgiving love. The God of the Christian scriptures emerges as a God of love, a God of compassion, a God of forgiveness, a God of justice, and a God of peace. God insists on justice and peace and still struggles to create a world of justice and peace, but does so through a suffering, unconditional love that refuses to retaliate in the face of violence.

Yet how far we have come from this image of the nonviolent God! Most Christians today imagine God as wrathful, vengeful, angry, bitter, mean, unjust, terrifying and violent, even though their personal experience of God may be as a living presence of love. The life of Jesus proposes a different picture of God. Jesus envisions God as the Spirit and the Truth of nonviolence. Jesus proclaims God as a loving parent to us all and calls us to dwell in that love and to share that love with one another, especially the poor and the oppressed. For Jesus, God is God because God is nonviolent.

Jesus' God does not use violence. Jesus' God always responds with nonviolent love. Jesus asserts that this presence of divinity, this spark of God's nonviolence, dwells within every human being; we all bear the presence of God in us. We all have the potential of delving deep into the nonviolence of God. Thus Jesus invites us to become like God, a people of nonviolence.

What does it mean that God is nonviolent? How does the image of a nonviolent God change our understanding of God? How does the nonviolence of God challenge our own lives? Such questions get to the heart of faith and human life today. We need to probe them as we begin a theology of nonviolence.

The God Who Knows, Sees, Takes Sides and Invites

As theologian Robert McAfee Brown has written, we can point to several basic insights, revealed in scripture, tradition and experience, into the God that we worship.[1]

30

First, God manifests the fullness of nonviolence. In the first letter of John, the writer declares decidedly: "God is love." Reflection on this God of love caused Augustine to advise, "Love and do what you will." Given the systemic violence of the world, we can translate this image of God to mean God is nonviolent love. In the Middle Ages, Aquinas insisted on the identity of essence and existence in God, writing that God's essence is "to be." In the light of nonviolence, we could say that nonviolence is being and that God then fulfills the essence of peaceful love. Violence, on the other hand, disintegrates us, takes us away from our full, true selves, and leads us into non-being (what might be called hell, the world of total violence).[2] God is the fullness of love. In a world of violence, God is the Spirit of nonviolence.

In our own time Thomas Merton offered a similar image of God. Writing at the end of his journal, *The Sign of Jonas*, Merton hears God ask: "Have you had sight of me, Jonas, my child? Mercy within mercy within mercy."[3] Merton imagines God as an endless sea of mercy, an ocean of nonviolence and love.

Second, God knows everything. God knows about every human being in every part of the world in every time in human history. God knows what happens everywhere—and what is not happening. God knows the futility and evil of violence and the creativity and beauty of nonviolence. As the God of peace, God knows the wisdom of nonviolence and shares that wisdom with humanity, most completely, in the person of Jesus.

Third, God sees all the violence of the world. God sees every injustice, every act of violence, every war, every murder, every act of complicity in the institutions that force sixty thousand children to die every day of starvation. More than that, God sees within every human heart. God knows the violence within each and every one of us. God also sees the potential for nonviolent love within every human heart. God sees the possibility of a disarmed world without war or injustice. God sees our destructive violence and sees every effort of nonviolence.

Fourth, God sides with the victims of violence, with the victims of oppression, with the victims of war. In God's preferential option for nonviolence, God takes a preferential option for the poor, for the oppressed, for all those who suffer the violence of war, poverty and injustice. From the side of the poorest people on earth, God offers a way of nonviolence. In the pain and agony of crucifixion God radiates nonviolent love and forgiveness for the healing of humanity and the world.

Fifth, God calls all of us to resist the forces of death, but only to do so with God's own active love. God invites us, primarily through the life of Jesus, to participate in God's own nonviolence. God does not sit idly by and allow the violence of the world to continue. God resists violence but does not use violence to resist. God's love is transforming the world's violence.

God does not and cannot use violence to change the world. Though ancient scriptures and texts portray God as violent, the life of Jesus reveals that God is nonviolent. Jesus teaches us that God does not use violence; rather, God uses active love and truth to resolve conflict and save humanity. For many, then, God is not all-powerful, as Aquinas wrote long ago, that is, if power is understood as violent force. Instead, God is powerless. Like the poor of the

earth, God is the power of nonviolence, the "powerless power" that refrains
from violence but insists on truth and justice through love. God does not use
the "power" of violence to change our hearts, to end war, to end systemic
injustice and world poverty. Instead, God sides with the poor, touches our
hearts, and invites us to become God's instruments of active nonviolence to
transform the world into God's reign of justice and peace. Such an image of
God invites our ongoing conversion toward a deeper, more active nonviolence.

Revelation and the God of Nonviolence

The word *revelation* (in Latin, *revelatio*; in Greek, *apocalypsis*) means "the
removal of a veil" or "disclosure."[4] According to the Second Vatican Council,
revelation refers to the action by which God freely makes known the hidden
purpose of the divine will and lovingly speaks to human beings as friends,
inviting them "into fellowship with God's self."[5] Through the scriptures and
the traditions that come from Christ and the peacemaking apostles, God is
revealed. God does not hold back. In this act of selfless love we learn that
God confronts us as open, vulnerable, selfless—truly nonviolent.

The church has long taught that the fullest revelation of God unfolds in
Jesus Christ, who incarnated, taught, proclaimed and practiced active nonviolence. In answer to the question "Who is God?," theologian David Tracy
answers: "For the Christian, God is the one who revealed Godself in the ministry and message, the cross and resurrection of Jesus Christ. A Christian
theological understanding of God cannot be divorced from the revelation of
God in Jesus Christ."[6] He continues:

> Christian theology understands the person and salvific event of
> Jesus Christ as the very self-revelation of who God is and who
> we are commanded and empowered to become . . . For the Chris-
> tian, God is the one who raised Jesus of Israel from the dead.
> God, for the Christian, is the one who revealed decisively who
> God is in and through the message and ministry, the incarnation,
> cross, and resurrection of none other than Jesus the Christ. The
> most profound New Testament metaphor for who God is remains
> the metaphor of 1 John: "God *is* love" (4:16). To understand that
> metaphor (which occurs, let us note, in the first theological com-
> mentary on the most theological and meditative of the four
> Gospels) is to understand, on inner-Christian terms, what has
> been revealed by God of God's very identity as agent and as love
> in the incarnation, cross, and resurrection of Jesus Christ. There-
> fore, for the Christian faithful the answer to the question "Who
> is God?," asked in relation to the self-disclosure of God in Jesus
> Christ, is: "God is love," and Christians are those agents com-
> manded and empowered by God to love.[7]

Tracy continues, "To affirm that 'God is love' is also to affirm that God, the origin, sustainer, and end of all reality, is characterized by the radical relationality of that most relational of categories, love."[8] This loving God then refrains from violence but loves every human being and all creation non-violently, unconditionally, peacefully.

The love of God, Roger Haight writes, "reaches out and engages human existence for its salvation."[9] Karl Rahner's explanation of the universality of God's grace, for example, is rooted in the experience of God as unconditionally loving. Haight explains:

> This experience indicates that the love of God is so universal that it intends the salvation of all human beings. God is experienced in the Christian community as the God of all; God is simply God. And this personal Creator-God loves not only God's creation as a whole but each thing in it as God's own. In respect to human beings, who are all subjects and personal, this love comes as a personal love fitting its human object: personal love, from freedom to freedom. This love reaches out in an egalitarian way to all of God's people: God's loving intent is the salvation of all.[10]

A theology of nonviolence roots its understanding of God in this image of God as Love. As Tracy explains, the combination of the mystical and the prophetic traditions in such a theology will enrich and transform not only our image of God but our very world.

> The recovery of the prophetic-apocalyptic traditions in new theologies of the cross, as well as in political, liberation, and feminist theologies, promises new ways to understand the hidden-revealed God: revealed under God's opposite—the cross, suffering, and oppression—and revealed best to those "preferred" by God— the marginal, the suffering, the oppressed . . . The prophetic and apocalyptic trajectories of the tradition will always develop the central Christian insight that "God is love" into more explicitly cross-centered understandings of that very God as revealed *in* hiddenness. The mystical trajectories of the tradition will always develop that same central Christian insight into deeper and often radically apophatic understandings of God's very incomprehensibility in and through comprehensibility . . . The theology of God of the future will be a full-fledged mystical-prophetic theology. That systematic theology of God will be both grounded in the revelation of God in Jesus Christ and credible to the quest for God that *is* the ultimate meaning of all the classic limit-experiences and limit-questions of human beings, who become human by facing both the personal questions of finitude, anxiety, transience, guilt, and death and the historical questions of oppression

and massive global suffering. A future mystical-prophetic theology of God will prove daring in its very fidelity to the central Christian meaning of the holy mystery: God *is* love. That classic Christian metaphor will inform every new naming of the hidden-revealed, the comprehensible-incomprehensible God of Jesus Christ.[11]

A theology of God that proclaims the nonviolence of God combines the mystical (and apophatic) theology which finds God in the absence of violence and injustice, and the prophetic theology that names the unconditional love of God as the basis for peace and justice in our world. This new theology discovers God as the absence of violence and the active presence of nonviolence. In a world of war and violence, God is Peace.

From the God of War to the God of Peace

The Hebrew scriptures are replete with portrayals of a warmaking God: the God who destroys creation and most of humanity in a flood; the God who kills; the God of battle; the God of military victory; the God of armies; the God who wipes out the enemies of Israel and who is tempted to destroy Israel as well. God rescues the suffering, oppressed people of the house of Israel in a definite act of solidarity with the poor, but uses violence to crush the brutally oppressive Pharaoh and his armies. In response to this image of the God of violence, the Christian scriptures portray Jesus as the God of nonviolence and selectively choose images of a peacemaking God from the Hebrew scriptures, most notably from Isaiah and Daniel. In the crucifixion of the nonviolent Jesus, God's image is transfigured into a God who suffers violence rather than inflicts it. As Walter Wink explains:

> The violence of the Old Testament has always been a scandal to Christianity . . . There are six hundred passages of explicit violence in the Hebrew Bible, one thousand verses where God's own violent actions of punishment are described, a hundred passages where Yahweh expressly commands others to kill people, and several stories where God kills or tries to kill for no apparent reason (e.g., Ex 4:24-26). Violence [Raymund] Schwager concludes, is easily the most often mentioned activity and central theme of the Hebrew Bible. This violence is in part the residue of false ideas about God carried over from the general human past. It is also, however, the beginning of a process of raising the scapegoating mechanism to consciousness, so that these projections on God can be withdrawn . . . The violence of scripture, so embarrassing to us today, became the means by which sacred violence was revealed for what it is: a lie perpetrated against victims in the name of a God who, through violence, was work-

ing to expose violence for what it is and to reveal the divine nature as nonviolent . . . The God whom Jesus reveals refrains from all forms of reprisal and demands no victims. God does not endorse holy wars or just wars or religions of violence. Only by being driven out by violence could God signal to humanity that the divine is nonviolent and is antithetical to the Kingdom of Violence . . . Jesus' message reveals that those who believe in divine violence are still mired in Satan's universe. To be this God's offspring requires the unconditional and unilateral renunciation of violence. The reign of God means the complete and definitive elimination of every form of violence between individuals and nations.[12]

From the very start of the Bible, God is portrayed as a creator who looks on creation and sees that it is very good (Gn 1:31). The scriptures tell of a covenant God makes with Israel, a covenant of faithful love that insures, if Israel remains faithful, that God will be their God and grant the gift of peace (Lv 26:3-16). As the prophets begin to condemn not only the idolatry and injustice of the ages but the infidelity of the chosen community, they condemn violence and begin to speak of God's everlasting covenant of peace. Ezekiel in particular speaks of a new covenant in which God would establish an everlasting covenant of peace with the people (Ez 37:26).

As *The Challenge of Peace*, the US Catholic Bishops' pastoral letter, notes, the prophet Isaiah explicitly connects fidelity to God with the consequent gift of peace.[13] "Oh, that you had hearkened to my commandments!" God cries out. "Then your peace would have been like a river, and your righteousness like the waves of the sea" (Is 48:18). The God of Amos, Isaiah, Jeremiah, Micah, Zechariah and Daniel, likewise, desires justice and peace with great passion. In this new messianic age of God's covenant, the prophets proclaim, God's own peace and justice will be present everywhere because the God of peace and justice will reign on earth. In this justice, there will be peace, and people will "abide in a peaceful habitation and in secure dwellings and in quiet resting places" (Is 32:15-20).

One of the most provocative images in the Hebrew scriptures envisions the God of the mountain where God's people go to live, where they renounce war, transform their weapons of war into instruments of human service, and then live in peace:

In days to come, the mountain of the Lord's house shall be established as the highest mountain and raised above the hills. All nations shall stream toward it; many peoples shall come and say: "Come, let us climb God's mountain, to the house of the God of Jacob, that God may instruct us in God's ways, and we may walk in God's paths." For from Zion shall go forth instruction and the word of the Lord from Jerusalem. God shall judge between the nations, and impose terms on many peoples. They shall beat their

swords into plowshares and their spears into pruning hooks; one
nation shall not raise the sword against another, nor shall they
train for war again. O house of Jacob, come, let us walk in the
light of the Lord! (Is 2:1-5).

Though several authors wrote the book of Isaiah over different time periods, it
culminates as it began with this vision of God's nonviolent reign (a vision which
will return in the Christian textbook of nonviolence, the book of Revelation):

Lo, I am about to create new heavens and a new earth; the things
of the past shall not be remembered or come to mind. Instead,
there shall always be rejoicing and happiness in what I create;
for I create Jerusalem to be a joy and its people to be a delight; I
will rejoice in Jerusalem and exult in my people. No longer shall
the sound of weeping be heard there, or the sound of crying. No
longer shall there be in it an infant who lives but a few days, or
an old man who does not round out his full lifetime; a person
dies a mere youth who reaches but a hundred years . . . They
shall live in the houses they build, and eat the fruit of the vine-
yards they plant; they shall not build houses for others to live in,
or plant for others to eat. As the years of a tree, so the years of
my people; and my chosen ones shall long enjoy the produce of
their hands. They shall not toil in vain, nor beget children for
sudden destruction; for a race blessed by the Lord are they and
their offspring. Before they call, I will answer; while they are
yet speaking, I will hearken to them. The wolf and the lamb shall
graze alike and the lion shall eat hay like the ox. None shall hurt
or destroy on all my holy mountain, says the Lord (Is 66:17-25).

Isaiah's portrayal of a suffering servant messiah hints at the nonviolence of
the Anointed One. Even more pointedly, the apocalyptic tales of Daniel, which
chronicle stories of nonviolent resistance and uphold the coming of "the Human One" (an incarnation of nonviolence), conclude with the bold assertion
that those nonviolent resisters, the *maskilim* of God, will rise and "live forever," while "those who lead the many to justice shall be like the stars forever"
(Dn 12:2-3).

Given this emerging vision of God as a God of peace and justice, it seems
natural that the developing scriptures of the Christian community should proclaim a God of peace, a nonviolent God who has become incarnate to reveal
to humanity, once and for all, the true image of God. God makes the clearest
self-revelation in Jesus Christ, who undergoes suffering and execution for his
love of justice and redemptive passion for humanity, but does so with a forgiving love, a nonviolent spirit. The image of the crucified Jesus epitomizes
the image of the God of nonviolence. God would rather suffer and die in the
nonviolent struggle for justice and peace than hurt or kill others.

Jesus is deliberately portrayed in the Gospels as using the words and examples of the prophets of peace and justice, most notably, Daniel and Isaiah.

Jesus speaks of fulfilling the Jewish scriptures; he fulfills the scriptures by repudiating the God of violence and war, instead imaging, portraying and incarnating the God of peace and love. Jesus deliberately presents a correction of past understandings which portray God as violent. The US Catholic bishops speak directly to the new image of God portrayed in the Christian scriptures:

> There is no notion of a warrior God who will lead the people in an historical victory over its enemies in the New Testament. The only war spoken of is found in apocalyptic images of the final moments, especially as they are depicted in the Book of Revelation. Here war stands as image of the eschatological struggle between God and Satan. It is a war in which the Lamb [a symbol of nonviolence] is victorious (Rev.17:14). Military images appear in terms of the preparedness which one must have for the coming trials (Lk.14:31;22:35-38). Swords appear in the New Testament as an image of division (Mt.12:34; Heb.4:12); they are present at the arrest of Jesus, and he rejects their use (Lk.22:51 and parallel texts); weapons are transformed in Ephesians, when the Christians are urged to put on the whole armor of God which includes the breastplate of righteousness, the helmet of salvation, the sword of the Spirit, "having shod your feet in the equipment of the gospel of peace" (Eph.6:10-17; cf. I Thes.5:8-9) . . . Jesus challenged everyone to recognize in him the presence of the reign of God and to give themselves over to that reign. Such a radical change of allegiance was difficult for many to accept and families found themselves divided, as if by a sword. Hence, the gospels tell us that Jesus said he came not to bring peace but rather the sword (Mt.10:34). The peace which Jesus did not bring was the false peace which the prophets had warned against . . . All are invited into the reign of God. Faith in Jesus and trust in God's mercy are the criteria.[14]

Nonviolent love, the bishops point out, stands at the heart of Jesus' life and message and thus reveals our God:

> Jesus described God's reign as one in which love is an active, life-giving, inclusive force. He called for a love which went beyond family ties and bonds of friendship to reach even those who were enemies (Mt.5:44-48; Lk.6:27-28). Such a love does not seek revenge but rather is merciful in the face of threat and opposition (Mt.5:39-42; Lk.6:29-31). Disciples are to love one another as Jesus has loved them (Jn.15:12). The words of Jesus would remain an impossible, abstract ideal were it not for two things: the actions of Jesus and his gift of the spirit. In his actions, Jesus showed the way of living in God's reign; he manifested the forgiveness which he called for when he accepted

all who came to him, forgave their sins, healed them, released them from the demons who possessed them. In doing these things, he made the tender mercy of God present in a world which knew violence, oppression, and injustice. Jesus pointed out the injustices of his time and opposed those who laid burdens upon the people or defiled true worship. He acted aggressively and dramatically at times, as when he cleansed the temple of those who had made God's house into a "den of robbers" (Mt.21:12-17; Jn.3:13-25). Most characteristic of Jesus' actions are those in which he showed his love. As he had commanded others, his love led him even to the giving of his own life to effect redemption. Jesus' message and his actions were dangerous ones in his time, and they led to his death—a cruel and viciously inflicted death, a criminal's death (Gal.3:13). In all of his suffering, as in all of his life and ministry, Jesus refused to defend himself with force or with violence. He endured violence and cruelty so that God's love might be fully manifest and the world might be reconciled to the One from whom it had become estranged. Even at his death, Jesus cried out for forgiveness for those who were his executioners: "Father, forgive them . . . "(Lk.23:24). The resurrection of Jesus is the sign to the world that God indeed does reign, does give life in death, and that the love of God is stronger even than death.[15]

"As his first gift to his followers, the risen Jesus gave his gift of peace," the bishops observed.

Jesus Christ is our peace, and in his death-resurrection he gives God's peace to our world. In him God has indeed reconciled the world, made it one, and has manifested definitively that God's will is this reconciliation, this unity between God and all peoples, and among the peoples themselves . . . Because we have been gifted with God's peace in the risen Christ, we are called to our own peace and to the making of peace in our world. As disciples and as children of God, it is our task to seek for ways in which to make the forgiveness, justice and mercy and love of God visible in a world where violence and enmity are too often the norm.[16]

In response to this Gospel of peace the early Christians understood God to be a God of peace and nonviolence; many of them renounced war and went to their deaths as martyrs of nonviolent resistance to evil and faithful disciples of the nonviolent Jesus. As the bishops note: "Moved by the example of Jesus' life and by his teaching, some Christians have from the earliest days of the church committed themselves to a nonviolent lifestyle. Some understood the gospel of Jesus to prohibit killing. Some affirmed the use of prayer and other spiritual methods as means of responding to enmity and hostility."[17]

Writing in the second century, St. Justin affirmed the Gospel vision of nonviolence and peace:

> We who delighted in war, in the slaughter of one another, and in every other kind of iniquity have in every part of the world converted our weapons into implements of peace—our swords into ploughshares, our spears into farmers' tools—and we cultivate piety, justice, charity, faith and hope, which we derive from God through the crucified Savior.[18]

St. Cyprian of Carthage wrote that Christians did not fight against enemies. "They do not even fight against those who are attacking since it is not granted to the innocent to kill even the aggressor, but promptly to deliver up their souls and blood that, since so much malice and cruelty are rampant in the world, they may more quickly withdraw from the malicious and the cruel."[19] St. Martin of Tours renounced his military life in the fourth century, saying, "Hitherto I have served you as a soldier. Allow me now to become a soldier of God . . . I am a soldier of Christ. It is not lawful for me to fight."[20] The bishops conclude:

> In the centuries between the fourth century and our own day, the theme of Christian nonviolence and Christian pacifism has echoed and re-echoed, sometimes more strongly, sometimes more faintly. One of the great nonviolent figures in those centuries was St. Francis of Assisi. Besides making personal efforts on behalf of reconciliation and peace, Francis stipulated that laypersons who became members of this Third Order were not "to take up lethal weapons or bear them about, against anybody." The vision of Christian nonviolence is not passive about injustice and the defense of the rights of others; it rather affirms and exemplifies what it means to resist injustice through nonviolent methods.[21]

The Experience of God in the Nuclear Age

In this age of total violence, where we have enough weapons to destroy the entire planet and the whole human race, we are also experiencing a new revelation of God within our own tradition, in our own human experience. During the unparalleled violence of World War II—from Auschwitz to Hiroshima—Mohandas Gandhi revealed the power of nonviolence on a massive scale as a spiritual way of life that can even overthrow empires. Behind Gandhi's revelation of active nonviolence lay a living faith in the God of nonviolence. "Nonviolence is a power which can be wielded equally by all— children, young men and women, or grown-up people—provided they have a living faith in the God of Love and have therefore equal love for all humanity. When nonviolence is accepted as the law of life it must pervade the whole being," Gandhi wrote.[22] "To me, God is Truth and Love. God is the source of Light and Life and yet God is above and beyond all these . . . God is love."[23]

Since the witness of Gandhi, Christians such as Martin Luther King, Jr., Dorothy Day and Archbishop Oscar Romero, as well as thousands of others around the world, have begun to experience God as the Spirit of active non-violence moving among the poor and the oppressed to liberate both the oppressors and the oppressed from violence, injustice and death. This new revelation of God deepens the witness of Jesus, a life of perfect nonviolence. It calls us to a renewed witness to the Gospel of peace, to the life of nonviolence. This God of peace, Thomas Merton noted, can never be glorified by human violence, and so Merton dedicated himself to exploring nonviolence, justice and peace.

As we struggle for justice and peace we experience God in new ways and a renewed image of God emerges. Gone is the warrior god of old, the god who kills people in anger, the god who supports suffering and systemic injustice, the god who threatens to destroy all humanity. Instead, through the witness of Gandhi, Day, King and countless practitioners of nonviolence throughout the world, the face of God is reemerging: the God who reconciles, the God who loves enemies, the God who heals, the God who disarms, the God of the Sermon on the Mount, the God of the cross, the God of resurrection, the God who unites all, the God who sides with all by siding with the poor and oppressed, the God who abhors war, who hates hatred and overcomes violence with a suffering, patient love, the God who never blesses violence. God's self-revelation to us in this age of total violence shows a God of peace.

The practice of nonviolence transformed Martin Luther King, Jr.'s, understanding of God. "I can't make myself believe that God wants me to hate," King declared. "I'm tired of violence and I'm not going to let my oppressor dictate to me what method I must use. We have a power, a power that can't be found in Molotov cocktails, but we do have a power; a power that cannot be found in bullets and guns, but we have a power. It is a power as old as the insights of Jesus of Nazareth and as modern as the techniques of Mahatma Gandhi."[24] Following the mandate of the nonviolent Christ to love our enemies, King concluded: "We are potential sons and daughters of God. Through love that potentiality becomes actuality. We must love our enemies, because only by loving them can we know God and experience the beauty of God's holiness. We shall never be true sons and daughters of our heavenly God until we love our enemies and pray for those who persecute us."[25] The nonviolent God of Martin King invites us all through the life and death of King to experience God's own nonviolence.

Dom Helder Camara, the prophetic bishop of Recife, Brazil, who inspired Latin America's base community movement and liberation theology, turns to the example of Jesus for further insight into who God is and what God wants us to do. Camara once told an interviewer:

Jesus encountered suffering. He wept. He took pity on the crowds. He tried to heal, to feed, to console. He even gave a child who had died back to her parents. When he was in agony himself, he asked for mercy. He never said that suffering was good or necessary or just. He never gave edifying sermons. Our God was willing to create a universe. In doing so, God had to be willing to take the blame for having given life to what is imperfect. But God has given men and women the power and responsibility not to resign themselves to the misfortune and suffering of the innocent, but to fight it. This is our task.[26]

For Camara, this task of fighting misery calls us to active nonviolence, a stead-fast witness with the poor and oppressed for peace. Camara invites us to follow the God of peace, the risen Jesus, who lives now among the poor of the world, organizing people into campaigns of nonviolence to transform injustice into God's own justice.

Theologian Walter Wink observes that Jesus' teachings in the Sermon on the Mount and his death on the cross reveal the very nature of God. "This strange God," proposed by Jesus, Wink writes, "loves enemies, the ungrateful and the selfish, the good and the evil, the just and the unjust, in an all-inclusive embrace" (Mt. 5:43-48/Lk. 6:27-28, 32-36).[27] Through the cross, "the ultimate paradigm of nonviolence," "God is revealing a new way, tried many times before, but now shown to be capable of consistent, programmatic embodiment."

Jesus' nonviolent response mirrored the very nature of God, who reaches out to a rebellious humanity through the cross in the only way that would not abridge our freedom. Had God not manifested divine love toward us in an act of abject weakness, one which we experience as totally noncoercive and nonmanipulative, the truth of our own being would have been forced on us rather than being something we freely choose. By this act of self-emptying, Jesus meets us, not at the apex of the pyramid of power, but at its base: "despised and rejected by others," a common criminal . . . In Jesus we see the suffering of God with and in suffering people.[28]

This new understanding of our faith, granted to us in a new insight into the nature of Jesus as actively nonviolent, has led the US Catholic Bishops to call for the renunciation of violence. They concluded their peace pastoral by declaring:

The whole world must summon the moral courage and technical means to say "no" to nuclear conflict; "no" to weapons of mass destruction; "no" to an arms race which robs the poor and the vulnerable; and "no" to the moral danger of a nuclear age which places before humankind indefensible choices of constant terror or surrender. Peacemaking is not an optional commitment. It is a

the move to integrate theory and praxis

requirement of our faith. We are called to be peacemakers, not by some movement of the moment, but by our Lord Jesus.[29]

Similarly, theologian William Shannon concludes his book on prayer, *Seeking the Face of God*, with this new insight into the reality of God as the God of nonviolence:

> God is supremely the contemplative One: God always IS in total awareness of all that is. God is supremely nonviolent. God lets God's sun "rise on the bad and the good, God rains on the just and the unjust" (Mt. 5:45). God gives to each creature that which constitutes its identity and its uniqueness; and God never violates what God has given. Jesus Christ is the Contemplation and the Nonviolence of God made visible among us. When Jesus calls us to be "perfect as our heavenly God is perfect" (Mt. 5:48), he is, I should like to suggest, speaking about the perfection of contemplation and nonviolence . . . The greatness of nonviolence consists in this: it releases the greatest healing, purifying, unifying power in all the world. This is what Jesus did in his life and especially in his death. He refused to fight violence with violence. He had only one weapon: love . . . Jesus resisted those who betrayed and oppressed the poor. He resisted those who profaned the Temple. He resisted those who struck him on the cheek. But he resisted in a nonviolent way. He refused to allow people to make him hate them. He refused to allow anything to make him forget that inviolable dignity that is God's gift to every human person. His most unforgettable words are the prayer he cried out from the cross to his Father on behalf of those who had so wrongfully oppressed him: "Father, forgive them, for they do not know what they are doing." Surely, it was the noblest moment of nonviolence in the pages of human history.[30]

Toward the God of Nonviolence

"In his nonviolent teaching, life and death, Jesus revealed a God of nonviolence," Walter Wink writes. "Christians are to be nonviolent, not simply because it 'works,' but because it reflects the very nature of God (Mt. 5:45/ Lk. 6:35). Nonviolence is not a fringe concern. It is the very essence of the gospel."[31] This new insight into the divine nature leads us to reflect on the trinitarian dimension of God and how the Trinity reveals the nonviolence of God.

CHAPTER 4

The Peacemaking Trinity

Model of the Nonviolent Community

In the tumultuous times of today's world, humanity cries out for community. Humanity longs for reconciliation between all human beings and God, for a real communion rooted in justice and peace. Nationalism, race, gender, religion, class and cultural differences divide the human family into warring factions. The truth of our common humanity, our worldwide human communion, suffers under daily assault. The continued development of nuclear weapons and the economic and environmental catastrophes they bring still hang our heads, threatening us all with a complete division, a "final solution."

Into such a world comes the God of peace, more and more revealed as a community of divine persons. From the tens of thousands of base Christian communities scattered throughout Latin America, Asia and Africa a new understanding of the age-old Christian doctrine of the Trinity has emerged. God encompasses more than just three persons in one nature; God exemplifies a community of love and sharing and models within the divine nature what the human community might be if we entered into a similar communion of love. The light of nonviolence focuses on the love and sharing in this divine community and calls us to reject violence and division and instead to incarnate the same communal love and sharing.

Even in the North American church a growing appreciation of humanity as social community has begun to break through. In her theology of personalism, Dorothy Day, for example, stressed the importance of building communities of justice and peace on behalf of the human community. Her autobiography, *The Long Loneliness,* culminated with this point: "We have all known the long loneliness, and we have learned that the only solution is love and that love comes with community."[1] For Dorothy Day, Christianity requires community. Community, we are slowly grasping, stands at the heart of God. Indeed, God is a community of love, sharing and equality. God is a community of nonviolence.

43

To explore the community of God we need to examine the roots, development and new understanding of the triune God as a community of nonviolence. Why do Christians speak of three persons in God and what does their unity mean? How do contemporary theologians understand the Trinity as social and communal? In particular, what does Leonardo Boff, among others, mean by the Trinity as a model for human community? Finally, and most important, how then does gospel nonviolence affect our understanding of the Trinity? The nonviolent community of God, we conclude, models the human community of nonviolence.

The community of God implies nonviolence as the very nature of the divine. It overflows as a community of peace calling us to be a people of peace. Jesus reveals that the Triune God is a community of nonviolence that interrelates in eternal communion as the nonviolent Creator, the nonviolent Redeemer, and the Spirit of nonviolence at work on earth and in heaven. Such a vision of communal nonviolence invites us to become a community consisting of communities of nonviolence.

The Christian Understanding of God as Three Persons in One

Christianity upholds a God of peace who lives as one interpersonal community of persons. This image of divine community as the model for human community has its roots in the scriptures and develops through the tradition into new, contemporary insights about God. The Hebrew scriptures maintain a steadfast monotheism, which the Christian faith, through its scriptures and tradition, name as the Trinity. Jesus incarnates the liberating God, the God of active, nonviolent love who takes sides with the poor and oppressed in a divine effort to bring life to all. In the experience of Pentecost the followers of Jesus, inspired by Jesus' Spirit, form a nonviolent, liberating community of disciples who name God as Father, Son and Spirit.

The narratives about Jesus' life begin the process of proclaiming this Trinity. The opening scene of Mark's gospel, for example, refers to Jesus' special relationship with God, describing how a voice comes from the heavens during Jesus' baptism and declares, "You are my beloved Son; with you I am well pleased" (Mk 1:11). The same words are later spoken as Jesus is transfigured on the mountaintop. A voice proclaims: "This is my beloved Son. Listen to him" (Mk 9:7). The divine relationship of God as Father and Jesus as obedient Son clearly develops.

In Matthew's gospel Jesus speaks of his deep relationship to the Father. "All things have been handed over to me by my Father. No one knows the Son except the Father, and no one knows the Father except the Son and anyone to whom the Son wishes to reveal him" (12:27; see also Lk 10:21-22).

Throughout the synoptics Jesus is portrayed as a liberator, healer and peacemaker who nonviolently resists untruth and systemic injustice, even unto death, in a spirit of unconditional love and compassion. This Jesus depends on God, sides with the poor, does justice, reconciles all and loves unconditionally.

The gospel of John, written as late as 120 C.E. according to some scholars, reflects more intentionally than the synoptics Jesus' relationship to God, the coming of the Spirit and the meaning of this Triune God for the persecuted Christian community. The prologue of John proclaims that the Word, which was God from the beginning, is the Christ who came in our midst and lives forever. "The Father loves the Son and has given everything over to him," we are told (Jn 3:35). The religious authorities soon plot to kill Jesus "because he called God his own father, making himself equal to God" (5:18). The image of God as Father and Son sharing with each other is repeated: "For the Father loves his Son and shows him everything that he himself does, and he will show him greater works than these, so that you may be amazed . . . the Father has given all judgment to his Son, so that all may honor the Son just as they honor the Father . . . For just as the Father has life in himself, so also he gave to his Son the possession of life in himself. And he gave him power to exercise judgment, because he is the Son of [Humanity]" (5:20-21,26-27). "The works that the Father gave me to accomplish," Jesus declares, "these works that I perform testify on my behalf that the Father has sent me" (5:36). "For on the Son [of Humanity], the Father, God, has set his seal" (6:27). "Everything that the Father gives to me will come to me . . . I come down from heaven not to do my own will but the will of the One who sent me" (6:37-38).

John's gospel offers the divine communion of the Father and Son (and then the Spirit) as a metaphor and a model for the communion of humanity with God: "Just as the living Father sent me and I have life because of the Father, so also the one who feeds on me will have life because of me" (Jn 6:57). When threatened and persecuted, according to John's gospel, Jesus continued to testify to his loving communion with God: "The one who sent me is with me. God has not left me alone, because I always do what is pleasing to God" (8:29). "I am the Good shepherd," Jesus continues. "I know mine and mine know me, just as the Father knows me and I know the Father; and I will lay down my life for the sheep" (10:1-15). From this union of love, Jesus clarifies their union: "The Father and I are one" (10:31). "The Father is in me and I am in the Father" (10:38). As Boff writes, they share one reality of communion.[2] "Whoever believes in me believes not only in me but also in the one who sent me, and whoever sees me sees the one who sent me" (12:44-45).

In the last supper discourse Jesus speaks directly to his relationship with God, and the implications of love and service that this communion entails for his followers:

> Whoever has seen me has seen the Father . . . That Father who dwells in me is doing his works. Believe me that I am in the Father and the Father is in me, or else, believe because of the works themselves (14:7-11) . . . If you love me, you will keep my word. And I will ask the Father, and he will give you another Advocate to be with you always, the Spirit of truth (14:15-17) . . . On that day, you will realize that I am in my Father and you

> are in me and I in you (14:20) . . . Whoever has my command-
> ments and observes them is the one who loves me. Whoever loves
> me will be loved by my Father, and I will love him and reveal
> myself to him (14:21) . . . Whoever loves me will keep my word
> and my Father will love him and we will come to him and make
> our dwelling with him (14:23) . . . As the Father loves me, so I
> also love you. Remain in my love. If you keep my command-
> ments, you will remain in my love, just as I have kept my Father's
> commandments and remain in his love (15:9-10) . . . When the
> Advocate comes whom I will send you from the Father, the Spirit
> of truth that proceeds from the Father, [she] will testify to me
> (15:26) . . . Holy Father, keep them in your name that you have
> given me, so that they may be one just as we are (17:12).

Later, when the risen Jesus appeared to Mary Magdalene, he told her, "Tell my brothers, 'I am going to my Father and your Father, to my God and your God'" (20:17). For Jesus, communion with God the Father in the Spirit stands in the center of all reality.

Although there is no doctrine of the Trinity per se in the Christian scriptures, an understanding of Jesus, the Father and the Spirit as God develops in the "formulas" of the early community (mentioned, for example, in Mt 28:19, 2 Cor 13:13, 2 Thes 22:13-14, and 1 Cor 12:-6). For the early community, faith in the Trinity of Father, Son and Holy Spirit originally named an experience rather than a well thought-out doctrine. The Christian communities of the first three centuries enacted a faith committed to the love of God, each other and all humanity, a faith in a loving God which demanded steadfast nonviolent resistance to imperial might and a divine obedience that risked martyrdom. They envisioned a God of unconditional love as the Father of Jesus, Jesus himself as the Christ, and the Holy Spirit of God's love. Their worship of an interrelating, communal God who is one and who is three led them to form communities of nonviolent resistance to evil and cooperation with that Spirit. Unfortunately, when Christianity was co-opted by the empire, a new image of the Trinity developed, one which stressed power and domination rather than nonviolent, communal love.

The doctrine of the Trinity had clear social implications for early Christian writers, but by the end of the Roman empire the emphasis had shifted. Instead of confronting imperial violence and injustice in light of Jesus' divine obedience to a God of love, they began to focus on the nature of the three, distinct, divine Persons in one God. Their questions had changed, and so had the image of a communitarian, nonviolent God. Instead of focusing on the praxis of Jesus and the demands of discipleship under the empire, they focused on the nature of Jesus. Orthodoxy became the primary concern. Gospel nonviolence took second place to this rising orthodoxy.[3]

Nonetheless, even with the focus on orthodoxy, a communitarian image of God was still possible. The Council of Nicea in 325 responded to the heresy of Arianism (which denied the divinity of Jesus) by declaring that Jesus Christ lives "from the being of the Father, God from God, Light from Light, true God from true God, begotten, not made, one in being with the Father." This creed sowed the seeds for social trinitarianism. As Boff suggests: "God could no longer be thought of as the solitude of the eternal One. The unity of God is something proper and specific, being made up of a unity of Persons ever interacting with each other." Though the image of God has overtones of domination, Boff notes that this image offers a glimpse of God as persons "in communion with one another, in mutual giving and freedom."[4]

Augustine insisted that "God is the Trinity," and he saw the Persons as eternally related subjects. He suggested that each divine Person is a Person in a different way, but he kept the term *person*. "You see the Trinity when you see love," Augustine wrote. Boff translates that to mean, "It is the practice of love that opens up true access to the mystery of the Trinity."[5]

Richard of St. Victor believed that the good is necessarily diffusive, and thus that God, who is love and the Good, naturally wants to share that love and goodness with others (within God). He maintained that "love and enjoyment require a society of three."[6] For Richard, God is love, and love is "the most distinctive characteristic of God's oneness of nature." God's unity of nature is dynamic, "grounded in a community of persons." Richard's social model of the Trinity submits that the infinite and transcendent divine love demands a second and a third in God. "God's perfect love of friendship demands another person in God so that friendship can be experienced between two. But truly perfect love demands even a third (to go beyond three is superfluous), and love becomes social. Perfect lovers want a third so that they can altruistically share with that third their love for one another."[7] In his analogy of "the lover, the beloved, and the love itself," Richard formally presents a social trinitarianism that also models a God of nonviolent love.

Thomas Aquinas began with the divine essence in his reflections on the One and Triune God and defined the divine Persons as subsistent relationships, permanently and eternally related, forming one God or one divine nature. The doctrine of the Trinity, formalized over the centuries in the creeds of the church, began to express the social characteristic of the Trinity. As Boff explains, the Persons exist because of their mutual love. "They are distinct in order to unite and unite not in order to fuse into each other, but so that one may contain the others."[8] Eventually, social Trinitarianism emphasizes the Trinity's perichoresis (or communion), where the three persons are one in the others, through the others, with the others and for the others.

The Trinity as the Model for Human Community

Leonardo Boff reflects on the Triune God from Brazil's barrios. He sees God as the God of the poor, the God who liberates the oppressed. "The preferential option for the poor is rooted in the very nature of God," he insists.

"Being drawn to the oppressed and unjustly impoverished comes from the depths of God's being. An offence against the poor is an offence against the nature and glory of God."[9] Boff suggests that Christianity demands a just society modelled on the communion of the Triune God, one that reaches out in communion with the poor and oppressed. Human society is called to practice the communal love, solidarity and sharing which marks the very nature of God. Boff writes, "A society structured on these lines would help us in understanding the communion of the Trinity. But as long as the present social inequalities remain, faith in the Trinity will mean criticism of all injustices and a source of inspiration for basic changes."[10]

"A disunited society affects our understanding of faith," Boff observes. "It cannot create favorable conditions for an integrated expression of the mystery of the Trinity." A patriarchal society models a religion of the Father alone—and is thus based on (vertical) domination. A society based on the figure of a ruler alone is "religion of the Son alone," a horizontal relationship. Finally, Boff argues, a religion of the Spirit alone is the fanatic, inward-looking religion that relates only with the inner self, not the masses of the poor and oppressed classes, who are denied participation in society. Each facet of life must be respected and, in the social Trinity, a model of this complete sharing can be found. "Communion," Boff concludes, "is the first and last word about the mystery of the Trinity . . . The Trinity is our true social program."[11] For Boff, social trinitarianism models "the ultimate structure of the universe and of human life: communion and participation."[12]

> The complete communion of three Persons, the full perichoresis of one in the others, for the others, by the others and with the others, destroys the figure of the one and only universal Monarch, the ideological underpinning of totalitarian power. Only a human community of brothers and sisters, built on relationships of communion and participation, can be a living symbol of the eternal Trinity.[13]

Thus, for Boff, "God is not a solitary power, but an infinite love opening out to create other companions in love."[14]

Boff describes the unity in the Trinity as communion between the three divine persons:

> Communion means union with. There can be unity only between persons, because only persons are intrinsically open to others, exist with others and are one for one another. Father, Son and Holy Spirit live in community because of the communion between them. Communion is the expression of love and life. Life and love, by their very nature, are dynamic and overflowing. So under the name of God we should always see Tri-unity.[15]

Boff's vision of God is a perfect communion of sharing, equality, inclusivity and participation. Such an image of the Trinity encourages a theology of liberation. "The oppressed struggle for participation at all levels of life, for a just and egalitarian sharing while respecting the differences between persons and groups," Boff writes. "They seek communion with other cultures and other values, and with God as the ultimate meaning of history and of their own hearts."

As these realities are withheld from them in history, they feel obliged to undertake a process of liberation that seeks to enlarge the space for participation and communion available to them. For those who have faith, the trinitarian communion between the divine Three, the union between them in love and vital interpenetration, can serve as a source of inspiration, as a utopian goal that generates models of successively diminishing differences . . . [Perichoresis] speaks to the oppressed in their quest and struggle for integral liberation. The community of Father, Son and Holy Spirit becomes a prototype of the human community dreamed of by those who wish to improve society and build it in such a way as to make it into the image and likeness of the Trinity.[16]

The revelation of the community of God urges us to practice perichoresis in our world. "Despite all ruptures," Boff suggests, "the Trinity seeks to see itself reflected in history, through people sharing their goods in common, building up egalitarian and just relationships among all, sharing what they are and what they have." This mystery of the communion among the three divine Persons needs to be modelled by the church, Boff insists. "Inspired by the communion of the Trinity," this church would be characterized

by a more equitable sharing of sacred power, by dialogue, by openness to all the charisms granted to the members of the community, by the disappearance of all types of discrimination, especially those originating in patriarchalism and *machismo,* by its permanent search for a consensus to be built up through the organized participation of all its members.[17]

The Trinity models a just interaction among economic, political and symbolic structures in society, Boff continues. "The more a society develops structures of interactions in which human beings, in private and in society, can find their lives and their hopes promoted and set free, the more it will reflect the Trinity, which is a living-together of diversity in the communion and unity of one life and mystery."[18] As the model integrated society with full participation and equality, the Trinity upholds justice and well-being. "The Trinity understood in human terms as a communion of Persons lays the foundations for a society of brothers and sisters, of equals, in which dialogue and consensus are the basic constituents of living together in both the world and the church."[19]

"The sort of society that would emerge from inspiration by the trinitarian model," Boff writes, "would be one of fellowship, equality of opportunity, generosity in the space available for personal and group expression. Only a society of sisters and brothers whose social fabric is woven out of participation and communion of all in everything can justifiably claim to be an image and likeness (albeit pale) of the Trinity, the foundation and final resting-place of the universe." Boff continues:

> As this communion, participation, and equality are at present denied to a majority of men and women, who remain oppressed and permanently marginalized, it has become urgent that a process of liberation should start from the oppressed themselves. Oppressed Christians find an incomparable inspiration for the liberation struggle in the God of their faith. This liberation aims to bring about participation and communion, the realities that most closely mirror the very mystery of trinitarian communion in human history.[20]

This understanding of the Trinity calls for "a vision of a church that is more communion than hierarchy, more service than power, more circular than pyramidal, more loving embrace than bending the knee before authority."[21]

"We are called to live together and to enter into the communion of the Trinity," Boff concludes. "Society is not ultimately set in its unjust and unequal relationships, but summoned to transform itself in the light of open and egalitarian relationships that obtain in the communion of the Trinity, the goal of social and historical progress."[22] The three Persons want "to introduce all of us and the world we live in to their overflowing life of community."[23]

The Trinity as Community of Nonviolence

Boff's Triune God models a society that espouses full equality and communal love. This image of the community of God models the human community of nonviolence which we are called to become. The God of peace lives in eternal community—nonviolently. The Trinity comprises a community of divine love that gets involved in human history, liberates humanity from systemic injustice and the original sin of violence, reconciles all and makes peace with all, just as the community of God is at peace, reconciled and in love. In the Sermon on the Mount, Jesus invites humanity to practice unconditional love toward every human being, a love that transcends borders and embraces enemies. In this nonviolent love, Jesus declares, we will be like God. By loving our enemies we become the sons and daughters of the God "who makes God's sun rise on the bad and the good, and causes rain to fall on the just and the unjust" (Mt 5:45). "Be perfect [that is, compassionate, unconditionally loving] just as your heavenly Creator is perfect," Jesus urges (Mt 5:48). This text declares God's very nature as unconditional love and reveals that God is the fullness of nonviolence, an eternal wellspring of communal love for all humanity and for God's own community. The peace that is God, then, is found for us relationally with every human being, including our enemies, in a worldwide human community.

If the Trinity models for us the supreme communion of persons in free, selfless love, then the totality of this selflessness rules out all violent disruptions of communion. The communion of the Trinity forbids violence. It perfects nonviolence. For Christians who worship the Trinity of peace, then, nonviolence becomes the norm. The Trinity of nonviolence invites us to put away our violence and to practice nonviolent love and seek reconciliation with every human being on earth.

Such a vision of the Trinity inspires us to become a species of people at once reconciled, at peace, sharing our food and resources, so that God's nonviolent justice becomes a reality on earth as it is in heaven. Martin Luther King, Jr., understood this vision of God and humanity:

> In a real sense all life is interrelated. All men and women are caught in an inescapable network of mutuality, tied in a single garment of destiny. Whatever affects one directly affects all indirectly. I can never be what I ought to be until you are what you ought to be, and you can never be what you ought to be until I am what I ought to be. This is the inter-related structure of reality.[24]

The Trinity as such an interrelated, social reality of nonviolent love calls us to become likewise, what King called, "the beloved community." As we become the beloved community and learn to transcend the boundaries of race, gender, class and every other division, we become more like the God of nonviolence who calls us to be a people of nonviolence. For Christians in the mainly white, middle-class peace movement, the challenge of the peacemaking Trinity calls us to side with African-American, Hispanic, Latino, Asian and Native American sisters and brothers, and with all those marginalized in the culture so that together, as one people, we can work for justice and peace.

This image of God as a community of nonviolent love encourages humanity to become a sharing community that is reconciled, liberated and at peace. The beloved community of God invites us to be who we are, the nonviolent community of humanity, like Jesus, God's very daughters and sons.

CHAPTER 5

The Christ of Peace

A Christology of Nonviolence

With the image of God as a peacemaking community, the image of Christ stands before us as a peacemaker. A Christology of nonviolence proposes that Jesus continues to practice nonviolence and make peace as the Christ of God. This new vision of the peacemaking Christ invites us to see Jesus as the incarnation of nonviolence, the revelation of God's nonviolence, and the redeemer who invites us to practice God's nonviolence. Indeed, this Christology holds that Jesus is the way, the truth and the life of nonviolence.

The Question of Christology

Christology examines Jesus' self-understanding and the titles and concepts used about Jesus. In faith we Christians proclaim Jesus of Nazareth Lord, true God from true God, the Christ, the Anointed One. In the light of scripture, tradition and our experience of God today, Christology pursues a variety of questions: Who is Jesus Christ? Is the Jesus of history the same as the Christ of faith? What are the implications for our understanding of and commitment to Jesus Christ?

The Christian community has understood Jesus Christ in a variety of ways: as messiah, teacher, ruler, judge, king, high priest, holy one, mediator, liberator, master, friend, brother, savior, Son of God, Lamb of God, Lord of history, prince of peace and the Human one. No one questions that Jesus of Nazareth really lived. We have plenty of evidence for this. The question of Christology arises over whether this same Jesus of history is also the Christ of faith proclaimed by the Christian scriptures.[1] The gospels embody the final edited version of the oral and written proclamation of the early church regarding Jesus Christ.[2] To dig deeper into the historical Jesus, biblical scholars have used form criticism, historical criticism, redaction criticism and socio-literary approaches to get to the meaning of the texts. Until the last two centuries the gospels were by and large taken literally, but now we have begun to search out the cultural, historical and theological perspectives of the evangelists as well as the early theologians who defined the terms of Christology. These new insights based in a critical reading of scripture have pushed us back to the basic question about the identity of Jesus. They have shed new light on our own cultural, political and spiritual struggle for justice and peace and how God may be trying to transform our world.

Liberation theologians Jon Sobrino and Leonardo Boff stress the historical Jesus who liberates the poor from oppression and calls us to the work of liberation and justice. Through Jesus, they write, God sides with the poor and oppressed of the world and calls humanity to convert to God's reign of justice and love. "The norm of truth is the historical Jesus," Sobrino writes.[3] He suggests that as we reflect on the gospels of Jesus and come to experience his living presence in the world of the poor, then we are moved to carry on his mission with the poor to struggle for justice and peace and to proclaim God's reign at hand. Sobrino's Christology is rooted in the praxis of a lifelong struggle with the poor of the world for justice and peace. "We do not get to know Jesus personally by reading the witnesses to his words and deeds, or hearing sermons, or taking solid courses," Sobrino suggests. "The only way to get to know Jesus is to follow after him in one's own real life; to try to identify oneself with his own historical concerns; and to try to fashion his reign in our midst. In other words, only through Christian praxis is it possible for us to draw close to Jesus. Following Jesus is the precondition of knowing Jesus."[4] Our image of God, Christ, and what it means to be human is transformed as we perceive a God who suffers with humanity in its struggle for justice.

In a similar way feminist Christology struggles with the sexism and patriarchy in the institutional church's traditional Christology. It challenges us to reject a Christology that dominates for a Christology that liberates. The good news, Rosemary Radford Ruether writes, breaks through the dominating Christology of empire to the Jesus of the gospels, the Christ of the martyrs. "Once the mythology about Jesus as [militaristic, dominating] Messiah or divine Logos, with its traditional masculine imagery, is stripped off, the Jesus of the synoptic gospels can be recognized as a figure remarkably compatible with feminism."[5] The Jesus Christ who emerges from the feminist critique stands for equality and justice. This Christ reflects a God of the poor, a God of love, a God of justice and a God of peace.

Jesus, the Peacemaking Christ of God

When we look at the actual life of Jesus, based on the Christian scriptures and other texts of the first century, we can draw some basic, indisputable facts. Jesus was a Jew who lived in the Palestine ruled by imperial Rome. Neither a Zealot nor an Essene, Jesus nevertheless opposed the structured injustice of his day and called people to new life in God. He preached the reign of God, a new nonviolent realm of justice and peace where everyone treated one another equally in love. He gathered disciples, associated with the poor and organized a campaign of nonviolent resistance that challenged the laws and structures which divided and oppressed people. His campaign culminated in an act of nonviolent civil disobedience in the Jewish Temple of Jerusalem. This act resulted in his immediate arrest, trial, torture and execution. Three days later, on the first day of the week, the women who followed him from Galilee to Jerusalem discovered an empty tomb and began to announce that he had risen from the dead.

At the center of this profile stands the empty tomb, an event which pushes us into the realm of faith: Do we believe that Jesus was raised from the dead, and if so, what does this mean for us today in a world of systemic violence? Christians are beginning to affirm anew that the God of life raised the nonviolent Jesus to new life after Jesus had suffered execution for his opposition to the world's ways of violence and death. If the God of peace raised the revolutionary, peacemaking Jesus from the dead, after Jesus had been executed by the state as a criminal, then the God of peace affirmed Jesus' way of active nonviolence and peaceful resistance to systemic injustice. We his followers, then, are called to embark on that same path of nonviolence. The gift the risen Jesus gives to his community is the gift of his peace. The risen Christ, the community testifies, continues to make peace, to offer the alternative of God's nonviolence. In an age where crucifixion was legal (just as nuclear war and the death penalty are legal today), the resurrection was "illegal." According to the "rules," Jesus was supposed to stay dead. But his active nonviolence breaks the laws of death and once again invites us to the way of life. Jesus commits the ultimate act of civil disobedience in his resurrection. His followers testify that the risen Christ is alive and continues to call us to take up the journey he began, a journey of peace and nonviolence in which we risk our own arrest, execution and resurrection.

Who is Jesus then? In a world of violence and death, people of peace are naming Jesus as the peacemaking Christ of God. By calling Jesus the peacemaking Christ, we declare that Jesus was and is a peacemaker; indeed, that Jesus is our peace (as Paul wrote). We conclude that Jesus is the way of nonviolence, that he practiced and taught nonviolence, and that his entire life revealed God's nonviolence to the world. As Christ, he reconciles all humanity to one another and to God through his own nonviolent love, a love that suffers our violence, transforms it and overcomes it forever.

A Christology of Nonviolence

This new insight into the nonviolence of Jesus calls for new study of the peacemaking Christ, indeed, for a Christology of nonviolence. Such a Christology explores the nonviolence of Jesus, its implications for our faith and the ramifications for all Christians living in a world of violence and death. This new understanding of the peacemaking Christ will push us to make peace in the world.

A Christology of nonviolence approaches traditional Christologies with a hermeneutic of suspicion. It notes how some Christologies have been used to defend the systemic violence and injustice that plague our world. It spotlights those Christologies of violence which portray an otherworldly Christ unconcerned with the wars and injustice of this world. It challenges those Christologies concerned only with obeying the government, fulfilling religious observances and getting to heaven on our own. These false Christologies defend the status quo and the violence of the world by invoking a god of violence, war and injustice. They are sometimes used to justify violent revolutions. They wrongly imagine a violent Christ, a warmaking Jesus, a dominating messiah who rules as all emperors do—through violence. A Christology of nonviolence shatters such militaristic imagery. It envisions a God of nonviolence and thus a Christ whose nonviolence turns over the tables of the world's systemic injustice. This Christology of nonviolence sees Jesus as a nonviolent, unarmed revolutionary, disarming and transforming the world of violence. This subversive theology breaks the complacency and apathy of the false Christologies which support systemic violence. It challenges us to reimagine the nonviolent Jesus and to join with this peacemaking Christ in the nonviolent transformation of the world.

A Christology of nonviolence has its starting point in the historical Jesus who practices, teaches, proclaims, incarnates and signifies the nonviolence of God. It centers itself in the Sermon on the Mount; in the active nonviolence of Jesus' life, especially in his nonviolent direct action in the Temple; in the crucifixion as the consequence of nonviolent action; and finally, in the resurrection as God's affirmation of nonviolence.

A Christology of nonviolence affirms the divinity and humanity of Jesus, suggesting that Jesus reveals his divinity by fulfilling the deepest expression of nonviolence, thus revealing that God is a God of nonviolence, a God of peace. Jesus *is* Christ, that is, the divinely Anointed One; he is the fullness of nonviolence. The incarnation of nonviolence in Jesus of Nazareth reveals to all the world the divine potential for every human life. Had Jesus employed, supported or encouraged violence in any form, he would have been neither fully human nor fully divine. Because he fulfilled nonviolence perfectly, he fulfilled both human and divine potentials. The image of Christ, then, envisions the union of the divine and the human, where the fullest possibilities of human life are joined with the fullness of God. Because of his extraordinary nonviolence, Jesus becomes the risen Christ of nonviolence, uniting both ordinary human life (especially for the poor and oppressed) with the highest dimensions of spiritual peace itself. His presence on earth, including the plunge into human suffering love on the cross, becomes a spiritual explosion of nonviolence that has transformed all humanity. His death and resurrection are the ultimate expression of the nonviolence of God. In particular, in the resurrection of Jesus into the Christ of peace, God reverses the values of the world, condemns the world's violence, and affirms the way of nonviolence in the most dramatic act of nonviolence in human and salvation history.

By pinpointing the nonviolence of Jesus, this Christology also pinpoints all that is *not* Christ, indeed, that which is against Christ. By highlighting the truth of Christ as the way of nonviolence, this Christology helps us to see that those institutions and systems which practice total violence are anti-Christ: the Pentagon, the C.I.A., the Trident submarine system, Livermore Laboratories, the Strategic Air Command Base, the Nevada Test Site, the Pantex Weapons Center, the Salvadoran death squad system, the South African police force (which defended apartheid) and the spirit of "ethnic cleansing" in the war-torn former Yugoslavia. Torture cells, execution chambers, gas chambers, concentration camps, bomber planes and nuclear missile silos stand in complete contrast to the way of nonviolence, and thus they are anti-Christ, anti-peace, pro-violence, pro-death.

A Christology of nonviolence suggests that Jesus was sinless; he did not commit violence to others, as the gospels point out. His nonviolence reveals his sinlessness. Rather than practice the world's original sin of violence, Jesus loves everyone in active nonviolence; he practices the active nonviolence of God. Nonviolence, Jesus teaches, rejects violence in any form and always responds to other human beings with unconditional love. Jesus repudiates the world's violence and lives out, as no one before or since has done, the covenant and grace of God's nonviolence.

The implications for such a Christology push us as followers of the nonviolent Jesus to practice and teach the way of nonviolence in our lives and in the midst of the world's violence, even if that means risking our very lives in dramatic acts of nonviolent resistance. A Christology of nonviolence highlights the active, risky peacemaking that Jesus practiced and challenges us to take Jesus' nonviolence seriously and put it into practice in our own lives if we are going to be recognized as faithful disciples. It demands commitment to nonviolence. It moves us to continue the nonviolence of Jesus, to walk the way of nonviolence and to participate in God's nonviolent transformation of humanity. It knows that practitioners of nonviolence will share in the new risen life of God's reign of nonviolence. It proclaims the nonviolent reign of God, which is at hand in the midst of the world's violence, calling us to become a people of nonviolence, followers of Jesus. Thus, a Christology of nonviolence has serious social and political implications for Christians.

In *A Christology of Peace* James Will calls for such a new peacemaking Christology. This Christology, he writes, needs to go beyond the "Jesusology" of peace, which is based only in the ethical teachings of the historical Jesus. "Though the churches' 'dangerous memory' of the historical Jesus is crucial to our faith, only a full-orbed Christology can provide an adequate basis for understanding our personal experience of peace or our social witness and activity for peace," Will asserts. He continues:

> The gospel interpreted by the church in the last decade of the twentieth century must provide a more comprehensive understanding of peace if it is to be genuinely good news for so complex and conflicted a world as ours has become. Nothing less than a full Christology of peace will suffice. That is, the issues that the church has sought to clarify through its faith in Jesus as the Christ must provide a paradigm for our interpretation of the Christian meaning of peace. Our understanding of peace must interpret, and our work for peace must express, how our humanity may ultimately be united with God's eternal wisdom and purpose . . . A

fully trinitarian Christology illumines our ethical struggle for peace in a peaceless world as the gracious gift of participation in the power and pathos of the trinitarian life of our Creator and Redeemer. Since many Christians become disillusioned because of a much simpler understanding of the possibility of peace, the articulation of such a Christology is essential to sustain the peace work and witness of the ecumenical churches.[6]

Such a Christology of nonviolence will take the peacemaking Jesus seriously, study the Christ of nonviolence and reflect on the implications of this new image of Jesus Christ for all Christians everywhere.

The Peacemaking Christ Invites Us To Make Peace

Christian discipleship and praxis are essential for a true Christology of nonviolence, because Christian nonviolence is not only reflection but action in the face of systemic violence. What Sobrino writes in *Christology at the Crossroads* applies to a Christology of nonviolence:

> What is necessary is a decision to follow Jesus Christ and a praxis based on that following, together with a passionate concern for the reign and a resultant yearning to experience the gratuitous historical mystery of Jesus and make our own life an inescapable part of it. It is that mystery that will break down our preconceptions, just as it did those of his contemporaries, and give impetus to a historical process of liberation for the oppressed peoples of the world.[7]

"If the end of Christology is to profess that Jesus is the Christ, its starting point is the affirmation that this Christ is the Jesus of history," Sobrino declares.[8] Sobrino urges us to return to the historical Jesus, "the person, teaching, attitudes, and deeds of Jesus of Nazareth insofar as they are accessible, in a more or less general way, to historical and exegetical investigation."[9] "Access to the Christ of faith comes through our following of the historical Jesus," he concludes.[10]

"When we insist that theology can be done only from within the context of praxis," Sobrino writes from war-torn El Salvador, "we are saying that people can understand and appreciate the Jesus who sends the Spirit only if they live a life in accordance with that Spirit."[11] Sobrino urges us to "see how Jesus lived his history" so that, in that spirit, we might "learn how to live, not his history, but our own."[12] In a world of institutionalized violence, our new lives based in the historical Jesus will be lives of persistent, active nonviolence that seeks nothing less than the transformation of the world.

In a world of oppression and systemic injustice, Sobrino's Christology is good news. It calls for the end of poverty and war and the implementation of God's justice and peace here and now. In this regard Sobrino defines Christian discipleship as "not giving up," an expression that easily can be grasped in the bloody context of El Salvador, Haiti, Peru, the Philippines, South Africa or South Central Los Angeles.[13] As Sobrino notes, Jesus showed us a way to become sons and daughters of God, and Christians must get on with the task of becoming those sons and daughters by following Jesus.[14]

A Christology of nonviolence remembers that to be sons and daughters of God, we need to become peacemakers, like Jesus (Mt 5:9). It invites us to practice nonviolence, oppose systemic violence and participate with God in the nonviolent transformation of humanity. This new Christology of nonviolence not only speaks for the liberation of the oppressed and points out a way to peace, but it liberates Christology itself from the dead theologies used to justify the world's violence. It brings new life to our reflection on God and gives us new vision to carry on with the life mission to make peace. While it challenges us to take seriously the active nonviolence of Jesus, it puts new hope into our lives for the journey of transforming the terrible violence that is tearing our world apart. It puts our focus back on the peacemaking Jesus so that we become the nonviolent Christ in action, transforming the world's violence into God's reign of peace.

CHAPTER 6

The Sin of Violence

The Covenant and Grace of Nonviolence

For the last fifteen hundred years Christian theologians have discussed the topic of sin more than any other subject, including Jesus. Gospel nonviolence does not tone down the emphasis on sin. It admits right from the beginning that we are drowning in our sinful violence. It points out that unless we repent of our sinful violence, we are all doomed to a nuclear hellfire and brimstone of unparalleled proportion.

But the good news of nonviolence does not yell at congregations with the bad news of violence. Instead, it has something much more powerful to offer: a way out of our madness through the grace of active nonviolence. Gospel nonviolence invites Christians to renounce sin and move on to the higher ground of peace. It points to God's covenant of love and peace with humanity and the grace that flows from this life in God.

A theology of nonviolence takes up the old concepts of sin, covenant and grace and transforms them through today's crises of war and violence. In a sinful world of systemic violence, what does it mean to be in a covenant with a nonviolent God? it asks. How does our understanding of grace change in light of our reflections on violence and nonviolence? Reflection on these questions from the perspective of Christian nonviolence may lead us to a renewed understanding of our Christian identities as sons and daughters of the God of peace. Indeed, in the light of our sinfulness and the transforming grace of God's nonviolence, the questions may help us become graced people of nonviolence.

The Sin of Violence

The tradition defines sin as a break in the relationship between human beings, individually and corporately, and God. This break is illustrated in the biblical paradigm of the fall and the contemporary insight regarding our "deviation" from God. Both speak of sin and name our break with God as a selfish turning away from God into our own nothingness, the chaos of violence.

59

Church tradition teaches the doctrine of original sin, which explains that we are all born into this systemic break with God, that we are socialized into sin and ultimately choose it. In the paradise of Eden, as the Genesis story explains, the first humans freely disobeyed God, gave in to their own selfish desires, began to kill one another (detailed in the story of Cain and Abel) and eventually created a tower in Babylon that rose into the heavens to "make a name for themselves." The Genesis narrative of sin culminates (in chapter 11) with the nations themselves turning against God, becoming idolatrous and sowing the seeds of oppression. The paradigm of the fall declares that humanity has created a fundamental rupture in our relationship with God, which remains to this day. William Stringfellow defines the fall as "a profound disorientation, affecting all relationships in the totality of creation, concerning identity, place, connection, purpose, vocation." He continues:

> The subject of the fall is not only the personal realm, in the sense of you or me, but the whole of creation and each and every item of created life. The fall means the reign of chaos throughout creation now, so that even that which is ordained by the ruling powers as "order" is, in truth, chaotic. The fall means a remarkable confusion which all beings—principalities as well as persons—suffer as to who they are and why they exist. The fall means the consignment of all created life, and of the realm of time, to the power of death.[1]

Jim Wallis of *Sojourners* reflects that this image of the fall has political consequences for us as a nation. "The fall is the principal political and spiritual fact of America and other nation-states," Wallis writes. "That is what the Bible teaches and what the churches refuse to believe. If we had believed the Bible at this point, we would not be so inclined to ignore the violence and oppression inflicted upon the poor, upon racial minorities, and upon those whom the nation designates as enemies." He continues:

> The Bible teaches that the whole of creation has become alienated from God and, thereby, from itself. The biblical description of the fall and its consequence in alienation is that it is pervasive, affecting not only people and their relationships but also institutions, nations, governments, corporations, ideologies, systems, bureaucracies, movements, idols—all those structural realities that are biblically referred to as principalities and powers. Meanwhile, the preaching and the practice of most of our churches serve to deny the reality of the fall, or, perhaps, to claim a special exemption from the fall for their nation, preferred institutions, or favorite idols.[2]

Contemporary theology defines sin as "any thought, word or deed that deliberately disobeys God's will and in some way rejects the divine goodness and love."[3] Sin includes any deviation from God and God's way of nonviolent love. Sin is not just passive; it is deliberate infidelity to the will of God.[4] In this light the Christian tradition distinguished between mortal and venial sins. Mortal sins "deliberately and radically turned away from God with clear knowledge and full consent in a truly serious matter" and bring the loss of grace and the risk of eternal damnation. Venial sins "harm one's relationship with God and others, but do not entail a fundamental option against God."[5]

Until the last few decades Christian tradition has relied on the teachings of Augustine and focused almost completely on sin as an individual, personal matter. Now we are beginning to examine the social dimensions of sin and to speak of systemic and institutionalized sin. The key to understanding the human community's deviation from its relationship with God is found in the way we relate to one another as peoples and nations, which, as we have discussed, is rooted in the global violence of war and systemic injustice. In this age of total violence we are beginning to understand sin itself as violence, as forgetting who we are—all sisters and brothers of one another, children of a loving God. The one great commandment that Jesus teaches commands us to love God, to love one another, to love ourselves, to practice *agape*, a nonviolent, unconditional love toward all (Mt 22:34-40). Sin violates the command to love; it does violence. It remains indifferent and apathetic in the face of relievable, human misery. When we cease to love God, our neighbors, suffering humanity and ourselves, we sow the seeds of violence and soon give in to our culture's despair and the world's violence. When we forget our identities as God's beloved children, we hurt ourselves, others, humanity and God. We turn away from God, our loving Parent. Our sin flows from this inner, heartfelt turning away, this inner division which causes us to hate ourselves, to hate others and to hurt others. For hundreds of generations we have continued to turn away from the love of God and neighbor. Now, with the nuclear age, this forgetting who we are, this turning away from God, has become high art and threatens the destruction of us all. Now we systematize and institutionalize this forgetting; we wage war, execute people, torture people and create such vast unjust structures that more than 800 million people suffer malnutrition, sixty thousand children die every day from starvation and related illness, and tens of thousands of nuclear weapons, enough to destroy the planet fifteen times, are stockpiled and maintained. This systemic violence is sin; this violence reveals the break in our relationship with one another and with the God of peace.

The Christian understanding of the fall teaches that human beings are responsible for the evil of violence in the world, not God. It is in Christ that we are redeemed from this sin of violence and shown a way out of our sinful condition into the new creation of God's justice and peace. Though we are born into the "original sin" of violence, God did not intend us to live violently; instead, God is seeking to lead us into a new, transforming life of nonviolence. In this light sin refers not to punishment from God but the punishment of violence we do to each other, our own rejection of the God of

nonviolence, our participation in the world's rejection of God and humanity
and the natural consequence of our inner hostility.

The massive deception of social sin has reached unimaginable levels, as in
South Africa's system of apartheid, the "ethnic cleansing" and systematic rape
and warfare in the former Yugoslavia, the extermination of Jews at Auschwitz
and the creation of the Trident submarine system. Society is addicted to sin,
to violence. We are so out of control that the abnormal is normal and the
world's violence is accepted as a fact of life. Retaliatory violence and oppressive structures, most of us presume, are meant to be. Given this despair, many
sit back in quiet acquiescence. Others actively work at maintaining this systemic sin of violence; indeed, many profit from the sin of violence. All of us
partake in the sin of violence; we are all sinners. Every human being commits
acts of violence. At some point we all consciously deviate from the God of
nonviolence. We consciously reject God and accept our socialization into a
world addicted to violence and death. By participating in the world's sin we
worship the idols and false gods of violence, the god of war and the god of
death. "For Paul, the essence of sin is the desire to be God," Walter Wink
writes. He continues:

> Desire thus transforms God into an idol on whom human beings not
> only project their own violence and hatred, but whom they also de-
> pict to themselves as the sanctifier of the violence at the heart of all
> religious systems. To desire to usurp the place of God inevitably
> leads a person to create God after the image of a jealous rival, and
> fosters an unconscious death wish against God. The human desire
> to be God is countered by the divine desire to become human.[6]

The good news of nonviolence tells us that the God of peace forgives us,
still loves us unconditionally and calls us to break from our sinful patterns. In
his active nonviolence Jesus shows us how to resist the world's violence, how
to be human, how to become a people of nonviolence. Jesus invites us to
worship the God of nonviolence, the God of peace. Indeed, as the scriptures
explain, God invites us to a new relationship of peace through a covenant of
nonviolence. Given our sinful violence, this covenant and grace of nonviolence offer us great hope for a future of peace.

The Covenant of Nonviolence

Just as the sad reality of original sin has been passed down from generation to generation, so too has an original covenant with God rooted in God's
way of nonviolence. This covenant of nonviolence still binds us today with
God and invites us into God's own life of nonviolence, the life of grace. The
life of covenantal, graced nonviolence unleashes God's healing nonviolence
in the world. By cooperating with the God of peace in this covenant, God
transforms our sinful, violent ways and turns us into a people of nonviolence.

A covenant signifies a formal agreement between two parties with each side assuming some obligation. The Jewish scriptures proclaim a covenant that God made with Israel at Sinai (Ex 19-24). As part of the covenant, God presented ten commandments which summarized Israel's duties (Ex 20:1-7; Dt 5:1-21; Jer 11:1-8). Like the political covenants of early biblical times, this covenant identifies God's side of the agreement (Ex 19:4-6; 20:2); holds various stipulations (20:3—23:33); and includes a treaty recital (24:7) and a ceremonial meal (24:9-11). God calls the people of the covenant (Israel), God's children, and the stipulations and the covenant itself, the Torah (Dt 31:25-26). If Israel does not keep this covenant, we are told, it will suffer the consequences. The covenant serves as a basic image for the human relationship with God. When Israel breaks the covenant, the relationship, though not destroyed, receives a serious setback.[7] Faithful as ever, even in light of human infidelity, God responds by promising a new covenant, which will ensure growth and prosperity for God's people (Jer 31:27-37). As the gospel explains, God initiates this new covenant in the peacemaking life, death and resurrection of Jesus.

This biblical concept of covenant occurs twenty-six times in the Christian scriptures. In Jesus we are told of a new and eternal covenant, what we call today a covenant of nonviolence, which God creates not just for Israel but with all of humanity. God seals this covenant of peace with the blood of the nonviolent Jesus, who refuses to retaliate with violence, dies on the cross in a spirit of loving forgiveness and rises into an eternal reign of nonviolence (see Lk 22:20; 1 Cor 11:25; Heb 7:22,8:8-13). Jesus refers to his blood as "the blood of the covenant" (Mt 26:28; Mk 14:24) and "the new covenant in my blood" (Lk 22:20; 1 Cor 11:25). The narrative of Jesus' life and specifically his death presents the beginning of this new covenant (Mk 14:24). As the blood of the old covenant united the partners in one relationship, similarly the blood of Jesus functions as the bond of union between the covenant parties, that is, God and the followers of Jesus, and ultimately, all humanity.

As the gospel stories explain, Jesus embodies the covenant of nonviolence. He incarnates it, teaches it, practices it, suffers through it and remains obedient to the God of nonviolence even unto death. Paul writes later that the apostles are sent as ministers of this new covenant (2 Cor 3:6) to proclaim the good news realized in Jesus and now available to all humanity. We are reconciled to God through Christ, who gave us the work of handing on this reconciliation, Paul writes (2 Cor 5:18). In the letter of the Hebrews we read that God has taken the initiative in this new covenant to redeem God's people (7:22; 8:8-13; 9:15; 12:24).

The new covenant, we are slowly learning, demands an active life of nonviolence. This covenant with the God of peace calls us to become a people of peace. To fulfill our end of the bargain we need to be transformed (by God) into a people of nonviolence. As Jesus reveals a God of nonviolence, we realize that God does not enforce this covenant by threatening us or punishing us with violence or death. Rather, God suffers death on the cross and continues to suffer today in those who resist the world's systemic violence with nonviolent, suffering love. The violence which afflicts the world today is not a punishment from God but the natural consequence of our violent actions. Violence only breeds further violence. Every act of violence, including silent complicity in systemic violence, leads to further violence. Only covenantal nonviolence breaks the spiral of violence and leads to the new life of peace. God is helping us fulfill our part of the covenant. In reality, as Paul notes, God does all the work.

To fulfill our side of God's covenant of nonviolence, according to the gospel, we have to renounce all our violence, make peace, seek justice for poor, love our enemies, forgive one another and reconcile ourselves with every human being. Then we will be living out the reconciliation with God already granted to us in Jesus. To fulfill God's side of the covenant God simply has to be God—protecting us, loving us nonviolently with God's gift of peace and justice and raising us up as we hand over our lives in nonviolent struggle for peace and justice. The scriptures, tradition and current experience of humanity assert that God has kept and continues to keep the covenant of nonviolence, even through this very moment. Human beings, however, have broken their side of the covenant and continue to break it daily. We set up structures maintaining this brokenness and institutionalize our rejection of the covenant of nonviolence when we create the Pentagon, Trident submarines, death squads, thousands of nuclear weapons and racial and class divisions. Yet we have the audacity to declare that God has abandoned us, that our chaotic violence is all God's fault, or that God has been unfaithful. But God always has been faithful to the way of nonviolence, since nonviolence is the very nature of God. Humanity has rarely been faithful. We have barely begun to try nonviolence, though we are experts at violence.

Jesus calls us to be faithful to God's way of nonviolence. The covenant of nonviolence begun in Jesus calls us now to turn over the idols and false gods of violence and to place all our trust in the God of peace, even to the point of our own civil disobedience, arrest, trial and execution. This covenant invites us to practice nonviolence; it requires that we do what God asks of us—to renounce violence and to embrace the way of nonviolence. Instead of relying on nuclear weapons or instruments of death, we are summoned by the God of the covenant to rely solely on God's creative alternative of nonviolence—for the rest of our lives.

In the life, death and resurrection of the nonviolent Jesus we are given a primary example of how to be faithful to God and God's covenant of nonviolence. As we learn to practice the nonviolence of God, we learn to share in the life, death and resurrection of Jesus Christ, to live in God's reign of justice and peace. When we all finally become faithful to the covenant of nonviolence, God will reign on earth as in heaven.

The Grace of Nonviolence

Grace names the presence of God and God's active love for humanity at work in our hearts and in the world. Though in sin we consciously move away from God, God still moves closer to us and invites us to embrace non-violence. God continues to work in us, to be present to us, to love us, and to invite us into God's own nonviolent life. Grace bespeaks an experience of God; it encompasses any gift from God, especially the gift of God's own life. Grace describes favors from God—those generous, loving, free, unexpected, undeserved gifts given us in abundance. These include the gift of creation and, above all, the utterly basic gift of being saved in Christ through faith (see Rom 3:21-26; 4:13-16,25; Eph 2:5-8), a grace that God is giving to all human beings (1 Tim 2:4-6).[8]

In the light of the gospel of peace and our world's violence, grace can be understood as nonviolence itself. A graced life does not turn away or deviate from God; it does not reject the God of nonviolence. Rather, the life of grace embraces the God of nonviolence and endeavors, like the nonviolent Jesus, to be faithful to the way of nonviolence, to fulfill God's covenant of peace. The grace of nonviolence is freely bestowed by God on all who renounce violence and choose to live the nonviolent life. God's grace pours out on all those who risk their lives along the path of nonviolence in discipleship to the peacemak-ing Christ. As they deepen their practice of nonviolence and publicly resist the systems of violence with loving, disarmed hearts, the Spirit of nonvio-lence transforms their hearts and lives more and more into images of the nonviolent Christ and leads them into God's reign of peace.

Though we are caught up in the sin of violence, God's grace of nonvio-lence continues to be showered upon us, offering us the possibility of justice and peace here and now, an eternal life of nonviolence that begins anew this very moment. With God's grace we can become faithful and fulfill the cov-enant of nonviolence.

The world's systemic violence can only be transformed by the grace of God's nonviolence. God invites us to renounce our sinful ways and to accept the grace of a new life of nonviolence. Since our world hangs on the brink of violent destruction and God works through us, we need to accept that grace, allow God to disarm us and live out God's covenant of nonviolence. As lib-eration theologians explain, God's grace of nonviolence liberates us from the personal, social and systemic sin of violence. In the light of nonviolence God's grace heals us personally from our violence, roots us in the peace of Christ, transforms us into peacemakers and transforms our violent world into God's nonviolent reign of justice and peace. The social grace of nonviolence can be seen in the transforming movements of Gandhi, Day, King and all those who confront systemic violence with Christ's transforming nonviolence.

The way of nonviolence teaches us ultimately that we are a graced people, God's own beloved children, called to be a people of nonviolence. Though we sin and turn from God's way of nonviolence to our own violence, God still invites us back to God's covenant of new life through the grace of nonvio-lence. Such an invitation offers new hope for the transformation of the world.

CHAPTER 7

Human Suffering and the God of Peace

Theodicy and Nonviolence

In late 1981 hundreds of US-trained and armed Salvadoran soldiers massacred over one thousand people in the remote northeastern village of El Mozote in El Salvador. Only one villager, Rufina Amaya, survived to tell what happened. She recalls how the villagers, including many children, were rounded up and shot or macheted to death. Twelve years later, as the war in El Salvador drew to a close, investigators exhumed the bodily remains of the El Mozote massacre and shocked the world with the reality of life and death in El Salvador.[1]

Newspapers daily report the violence that human beings do to one another. We can categorize massive human suffering in two ways: 1) the intentional violence inflicted deliberately on other people, such as the massacre of twenty-four people in a California McDonald's restaurant, the slaughter of nearly half a million Iraqis by the US military or the brutal warfare that has systematically killed so many people in the former Yugoslavia; and 2) the unintentional, catastrophic violence which kills millions of people annually, such as the deadly Hurricane Andrew, the Oakland Firestorm of October 20, 1991, the 1990 earthquake in Armenia which killed tens of thousands and the AIDS epidemic. From Dresden, Auschwitz and Hiroshima to Vietnam, Panama and Haiti, people deliberately do terrible things to other people. The details of human suffering inflicted on others extend from centuries of slavery and the execution of millions of people to the millions who are now starving to death in Africa (particularly in Somalia and the Sudan) to children who have been killed by their parents. On top of this awful suffering deliberately inflicted by some people on others, there stands the terrible reality of unintentional, catastrophic suffering: the death of a child to cancer; the earthquakes, fires, hurricanes and floods that kill people; and the senseless accidents that daily claim human lives. While there is a deep mystery in the unrelievable suffering and tragedy that comes from such catastrophic violence, the deadly violence deliberately and systematically carried out by some people on others cries out to be stopped.

A theology of nonviolence looks honestly at the suffering of the world and the violence human beings do to one another and reflects on the nonviolence of God in order to find a clue to stopping relievable suffering. Let us explore this question first by asking the basic question: If God is indeed nonviolent, then why did God create a world filled with violence and suffering? Next, let us examine the powerlessness of God and God's call to humanity in the face of our total violence. Finally, let us look to the example of Jesus' way of nonviolence and his own horrible death on the cross for a deeper understanding of the reality we face and our response.

If God Is Nonviolent, Why Did God Create a World Filled with Violence and Suffering?

Many human beings imagine God as a violent, vengeful, wrathful being who wills, or perhaps even intends, to destroy us all. As theologian Richard McBrien concludes, the differing opinions of God and evil have led to drastic conclusions about the inevitability of suffering and the evil of God:

> At the extreme left, God is portrayed as not involved at all in evil because God is not much involved in good either. At the extreme right, God is directly and immediately implicated in evil. God deliberately, almost callously, inflicts suffering and pain upon us in order to teach us a lesson or gain some unknown greater good. And in the middle, we have the usual traditional explanations that God does not cause evil; God only permits it. Or that evil is nothing in itself; it is simply the absence of good. For many, of course, the very existence of evil (natural disasters, the terminal illness of a young child, the sudden death of a father or a mother, a brutal murder, an act of terrorism, Auschwitz) is the single most persuasive argument against the existence of God, or at least against the existence of the God of Christianity. They cannot readily explain, on the other hand, how there can also be so much goodness and heroic charity in a world without God.[2]

Indeed, the basic question, which forces our disbelief or belief in God (and then our image of God), rests in our understanding of the violence that tears apart the human family. If God is essentially nonviolent, as the Christian scriptures and a theology of nonviolence proclaim, then why did God create a world filled with violence and suffering?

Ancient myths posed images of good versus evil and images of a sinful, warmaking god. The scriptures and traditional theology teach that God is good, and that this good God created the world and saw that world as good. Human choice brought violence and radical evil into the picture. God did not create a world of violence; on the contrary, the God of the scriptures created a world of nonviolence. Everything has been set up within the framework of nonviolence; even nature is meant to fit in to the worldwide mold of nonviolence. Revelation suggests that God created the world in order to enter into loving union with creation. God created a world that could sustain the human race and all life in peace, justice and nonviolence.

This biblical understanding of God and creation suggests that God did not have foreknowledge about the future of humanity's evil. In this understanding of God we note that God does not know the future; for God, the future is possibility and probability. In granting freedom to human beings, and knowing that humans may well choose to do violence and evil, God decided it was worth the risk of violence and evil to have that free, loving union with humanity. God then concluded that if humans choose to do violence and inflict suffering, then God would likewise choose to enter the world's suffering through the incarnation. By this incarnation, by this life of active nonviolence, God would show us how to transform suffering and evil into nonviolent, loving union with God. In this light God chooses our freedom, takes the risk, encourages us to say no to violence and shows us how to become people of nonviolence.

As a God of nonviolence, God cannot coerce us or do violence to us. The constant free choice by humanity to act violently and turn away from this nonviolent God has built up so dramatically over time that we now have a world of war and systemic violence that threatens to destroy the entire planet and the entire human race. This "sedimentation of thousands of years of human choices for evil (not wrong choices merely, but actual choices for evil)," as Walter Wink explains it, has led us to this precipice of massive human suffering and global annihilation.[3] Still, the God of nonviolence calls us to transform ourselves and our world through suffering love, a way that takes on suffering for the sake of justice and peace.

The Powerful Powerlessness of God

From Job to the crucified Jesus to the suffering masses around the world, people of faith have wrestled with this image of a loving, nonviolent God in light of the world's total violence. Theodicy probes this question: What can we say about God, given the massive suffering and systemic violence that continues to kill people in our world? How can God be God and allow such suffering to happen? How can we believe in God when such terrible things occur? What does this world of violence say about God?

Traditionally, Christian theology has taught that God is at the same time all-knowing, all-loving and all-powerful. In recent times theodicy has begun to question, in light of human suffering, whether God can have all three of these characteristics. A theology of nonviolence suggests that God is all-knowing and all-loving—that is, perfectly, actively nonviolent—but *not* all-powerful in the traditional sense of power (as the violent force of domination and control). Through the ages the church has taught that God is omnipotent, but that such omnipotence cannot include contradiction or an incompatibility with the divine reality. A theology of nonviolence sees God as pure nonviolence, unconditional love, perfect truth, never-ending mercy and boundless compassion. Such an image of the God of nonviolence suggests that God is *powerless*, that God does not contain one drop of violence and that God cannot use violence to change human beings or to stop the violence that occurs in our world. Instead, God radiates the power of powerlessness, an active nonviolence which stands up to violence with love, insists on truth and transforms violence into nonviolent love and justice—all without the violence of domination.

Walter Wink points out that the Christian scriptures approach the reality of evil from an entirely different perspective. "I have long been struck by the virtual absence of any attempt to explain evil (theodicy) in the New Testament," he writes. He continues:

> The early Christians devoted a great deal of energy to discovering the meaning of Jesus' death, but nowhere do they offer a justification of God in the face of an evil world. They do not seem to be puzzled or even perturbed by evil as a theoretical problem. When they encountered persecution or illness, they never asked, "How could God have let this happen?" . . . To the question, Why was Jesus crucified, the early church had a ready answer: he was crucified by the Powers because what he said and did threatened their power. The burning question for them was not *why* but *how*: How has God used this evil for good? How has God turned sin into salvation? How has God triumphed over the Powers through the cross? Likewise, persecution did not evoke surprised reactions of "Why me?" The early Christians *expected* to be persecuted; they were surprised when they were not! For them the question was not *why* but *how long*? . . . The early Christians *expected* to be assaulted by the Powers. Never once do they seem puzzled by this fact. It would have been unthinkable for them to ask, "Why do bad things happen to good people?" The Powers that had crucified Jesus had an equal stake in crushing this new movement, though full recognition of this fact did not dawn on the empire until the second century, when systematic and widespread persecution began. In short, for the early church, the problem of justifying the existence of evil in a world created by God can scarcely be said to have existed. The first Christians never—astonishingly—blamed God for their unmerited sufferings . . . We should respect the New Testament's refusal to become preoccupied with evil as a theological problem. Its concern is instead practical. It wishes to overcome evil, not explain it. Christians should expect the Powers to do evil. The more pressing question is: What can God do about this or that concrete evil facing us today? Can these rebellious Powers be tamed? On a practical level, then, the problem of evil is dealt with through prayer and action, in the everyday attempt to bend evil back toward the purposes of God.[4]

As the Christian scriptures make clear in no uncertain terms, God knows about the violence of the world and, through Jesus, confronts that evil head on, taking on the violence of the world with a transforming spirit of love. With the revelation of the nonviolent Jesus as the fullest image of God, we discover that God grieves over human violence and is actively nonviolently trying to stop human beings from doing violence to one another and to the planet. God is laboring that we might learn to live at peace with one another and with God in God's own nonviolent reign of justice and peace here and now on earth. This vision of the God of nonviolence rejects the age-old image of a wrathful, violent god who inflicts suffering on humanity as a form of punishment. It breaks the image of a God who wants us to suffer and insists that the living God does *not* will violence or injustice. It refuses to let us justify evil, and pushes us to resist nonviolently every injustice and act of violence. It understands that God is calling us to be a people of nonviolence. It recognizes that we are responsible for our own violence, that human violence has consequences, and that we are called to break through the world's violence with an uncompromising nonviolence. This image of a nonviolent God, who resists the world's systemic and personal violence, offers us the freedom to join in that nonviolence and redeems us from our violence through nonviolent love. God is continually transforming humanity into a beloved community of nonviolence.

Even more than that, this image suggests that if God, who created the earth and humanity, is indeed nonviolent, then we have all the resources we need to live together in peace and justice on the planet earth. God has given us the grace to live in nonviolence in the basic relationship we are offered with God and each other. That means that once we stop killing one another and waging violence against each other and learn to live together in peace with justice, we may even find ways to respond to the world's unintentional, catastrophic violence. When we end war, the arms race, human conflict and the institutionalized violence of poverty and starvation, we finally may be able to apply our resources, talents and money to finding cures for such diseases as cancer and AIDS and to alleviate disaster in the face of natural events.

God Calls Humans to Resist Evil Nonviolently

Though the world has become structured and institutionalized to benefit a wealthy elite at the expense of the suffering masses who die from poverty and war, the faith and revelation of nonviolence teach that God in no way approves this unjust arrangement. A careful study of the evil of violence in our world in light of the God of nonviolence leads us to the conclusion that God does not approve of violence in any form; that God actively opposes violence; that God never intended people to kill one another or suffer and die in poverty and violence; that God suffers and dies with all those who suffer and die, especially with those who nonviolently resist evil; and that we are called to join God in actively resisting evil through the unconditional love and steadfast insistence on truth, which is the way of nonviolence.

As the fullness of nonviolence, God calls humanity to practice nonviolent resistance. In this image of God confronting the world's violence we are moved to follow the steadfast life of active nonviolence lived by such people as Gandhi (in his confrontation of imperial Britain); Day (in her solidarity with the poor and her witness for peace); Romero (in his outspoken criticism of the forces of violence and his willingness to risk his life so that the killing and injustices might stop); and Jägerstätter (the Austrian peasant who was executed by the Nazis because of his refusal to kill). Martin Luther King, Jr., spoke to this movement of nonviolence, which accepts suffering in the loving struggle for justice and peace:

> I've seen too much hate to want to hate, myself, and I've seen hate on the faces of too many sheriffs, too many White Citizens Councilors, and too many Klansmen of the South to want to hate; and every time I see it, I say to myself, hate is too great a burden to bear. Somehow we must be able to stand up before our most bitter opponents and say: "We shall match your capacity to inflict suffering by our capacity to endure suffering. We will meet your physical force with soul force. Do to us what you will and we will still love you. We cannot in all good conscience obey your unjust laws and abide by the unjust system, because noncooperation with evil is as much a moral obligation as is cooperation with good, and so throw us in jail and we will still love you. Bomb our homes and threaten our children, and, as difficult as it is, we will still love you. Send your hooded perpetrators of violence into our communities at the midnight hour and drag us out on some wayside road and leave us half-dead as you beat us, and we will still love you ... But be assured that we'll wear you down by our capacity to suffer, and one day we will win our freedom. We will not only win freedom for ourselves, we will so appeal to your heart and conscience that we will win you in the process and our victory will be a double victory."[5]

Jesus and the Suffering Love of God

Because Jesus confronted the structured injustice of his day, symbolized and actualized in the Temple, he was tortured and publicly executed on a cross by the ruling authorities. By continuing to maintain a spirit of nonviolence, forgiveness, unconditional love and faithfulness to the God of nonviolence, Jesus transformed the empire's brutal violence. His resurrection, life, message and nonviolent love have given hope and provided an example to billions of people throughout history. Such is the power of redemptive, suffering love enacted through steadfast nonviolence.

The cross of Jesus, the fullest expression of God's active nonviolence, reveals how nonviolent love insists on truth through a spirit of forgiveness, which can transform violence, even systemic, imperial violence. It stands as the ultimate witness of God's reaction to human suffering and radical evil. God takes on the suffering of the world by insisting on justice and peace and, through the world's suffering, offers us a way out of our total violence and a way into God's reign of nonviolence. Theologian Jim Douglass writes:

> I believe that through the cross of Jesus, the cross of suffering love, humanity is being saved and made free from our own violence. The cross was to Jesus' world as the electric chair, the firing squad and nuclear weapons are to our world. Crucifixion was a form of the death-penalty which the Romans inflicted on the lower classes, in particular slaves, violent criminals, and the rebellious. Crucifixion had a political and military purpose: to silence and deter rebels. Jesus was one of those thousands of Jews executed publicly on crosses, because what they represented had to be suppressed in order to safeguard law and order in the Roman state . . . Once we recognize the reality of the cross in its original context of total violence, its use as a symbol of nonviolence is astounding. It is as if the electric chair became our symbol for life. To take up the cross is, in Jesus' transforming vision, to assume the suffering of the oppressed. It was the oppressed and enslaved who suffered and died on Roman crosses. Jesus was one of them. Yet Jesus was also one with the God he revealed, that God who loves both justice and enemies. When the God of Justice and Love assumes the suffering of the oppressed at the point of deterrence, in Jesus' cross, then the systemic violence of the empire has been overthrown. Through our acceptance of his cross of suffering love for everyone, we are all liberated from violence. The inconceivable change that occurred at Jesus' cross was that an empire's terrifying deterrent was transformed through the nonviolent power of God's love, truth and forgiveness.[6]

"When Jesus suffered and died on the cross he had taken up," Douglass observes, "the cross was transformed. The divine possibility of its nonviolent side, life through suffering, was to become visible. The violence of a crucifixion, meant to keep total violence in power through a terrible kind of capital punishment, was revealed instead, to the eyes of the oppressed, as the transforming power of a suffering, nonviolent love. The cross is Jesus' and our own resurrection from violence. Through his cross Jesus entered into the crucifixion of the world. In this, he revealed the other side of violence, which is suffering as a way of divine love, forgiveness, and transformation—a way of transforming total violence into total life . . . Through our acceptance of Jesus' cross of suffering love for everyone," Douglass concludes, "we are liberated from violence."[7] Nonviolence as an active lifestyle of vulnerable, mutual love does not divinize suffering but risks suffering, persecution and death for ourselves as an accepted consequence, not a goal, for the transformation of the world's systemic violence into God's reign of justice.

Our Response to God's Way of Active Nonviolence

In *The Nonviolent Cross* Douglass speaks of God as Suffering Love, ultimately revealed in Christ on the cross, and further elaborated in history in people like Gandhi, who applied the way of the cross to nonviolent social movements in South Africa and India. According to God's way of dealing with suffering by entering and transforming it, human beings are invited to enter the world's violence, risk our lives in the struggle for justice and thus to participate in God's transformation of the world's violence through our own nonviolence. Understanding the nonviolence of Jesus as God's way of responding to systemic violence, Gandhi concluded that human beings are called to embrace systemic violence as fully as possible with heartfelt love and a steadfast insistence on truth:

> The greater the repression and lawlessness on the part of the authority, the greater should be the suffering courted by its victims. Success is the certain result of suffering of the extremist character, voluntarily undergone.[8]

If God is Suffering Love (that is, Love willing to suffer in the course of the act of loving), and if God responds to the world's violence by entering it and transforming it through the way of nonviolence, then humanity is called by God to join in the way of nonviolence as the best response to the world's systemic violence and radical evil. This proposal requires nothing less than our very lives and risks temporary failure, but nonetheless, it stands as a definitive response to injustice and war. We are called by the God of nonviolence to respond to the evil of violence by the active life of nonviolent resistance, a life that risks suffering and death in the struggle for justice. Douglass explains:

> The logic of nonviolence is the logic of crucifixion and leads the person of nonviolence into the heart of the suffering Christ. The purpose of nonviolence is to move the oppressors to perceive as human beings those whom they are oppressing. Men and women commit acts of violence and injustice against others only to the extent that they do not regard them as fully human. Nonviolent resistance seeks to persuade the aggressor to recognize in his victim the humanity they have in common, which when recognized fully makes violence impossible. This goal of human recognition is sought through the power of voluntary suffering, by which the victim becomes no longer a victim but instead an active opponent in loving resistance to the one who

has refused to recognize him/her as human. The person of non-violence acts through suffering love to move the unjust opponent to a perception of their common humanity, and thus to the cessation of violence in the commencement of brotherhood and sisterhood. The greater the repression, the greater must be the suffering courted by its victims; the greater the inhumanity, the greater the power of suffering love necessary to begin restoring the bonds of community. Suffering as such is powerless. Love transforms it into the kind of resistance capable of moving an opponent to the act of mutual recognition . . . The suffering of his victim must be acknowledged by the oppressor as being human before he will cease inflicting it, and it is the love manifested in that suffering undergone openly and voluntarily which will bring him finally to this acknowledgment.[9]

"At the cross suffering love received its fullest expression," Douglass concludes. In response to the suffering and total violence of the world we are not to seek suffering for its own sake or avoid it out of fear; rather, we are to confront suffering on behalf of life through a lifestyle of active nonviolence. We are called to live lives of active nonviolence, and thus to risk and undergo our own suffering, even death, in the active nonviolent struggle for justice and peace, a struggle that seeks to end, first and foremost, the suffering that the First World has inflicted upon the world's poor. Like Jesus, who risked and underwent execution on a cross for turning over the tables against the system in an act of dramatic, nonviolent, civil disobedience, we are called to turn over the tables of our culture which permit and defend systemic injustice, even at the risk of our own suffering and death. We are called to confront society's apathy in the face of relievable human suffering as nations and corporate powers continue to wage war and practice systemic violence. We are called to transform the suffering of the world by going to the cross in a spirit of suffering love that nonviolently resists the systemic violence of the world. We are called to enter the suffering and crucifixion of God and humanity and thus to enter into the resurrection and eternal life of God and humanity where peace, justice and nonviolent love reign forever.

How do we respond to radical evil, to human suffering, to the God who created our world and who redeems it through active nonviolence? For too long the poor and oppressed peoples of the world have been told that God blesses them because they suffer, as if God supports and maintains oppression. A theology of nonviolence holds, quite the contrary, that the God of active nonviolence resists evil and suffering, walks with the victims of violence and oppression, takes on the evil and violence of the world in order to transform it—but without using the methods of evil, without resorting to violence. God takes on the world's violence and undergoes all the suffering of the world so that we might have a world without violence and suffering, so that we might live here and now in God's nonviolent reign of peace. God invites us to join in that task of nonviolent transformation.

As we choose each day to follow Jesus in his response to the world's violence and injustice, we take on the violence of the world in the struggle for justice and peace and become God's nonviolent instruments for the redemption of humanity and transformation of the world. Then, in that struggle, in that dying and rising again, in that full entrance into suffering humanity, we no longer ask, "Where has God been and where is God in light of the world's violence?" Instead we ask, "How do I experience God as I nonviolently struggle for God's justice and peace in the midst of the world's violence?" Like the suffering masses of the world, like Jesus, we find ourselves standing in fidelity to God and being granted the new life of justice, peace and God's own love.

While living and working in 1985 in a church-run camp for displaced peoples in El Salvador, and witnessing the daily US bombings, the poverty and sufferings of the people, I discovered that most of the suffering people maintained a deep faith in God. They felt God was actually, if not tangibly present to them despite all the violence and injustice they suffered. To my astonishment I experienced in their faith that the God who suffers with humanity, a God of nonviolence, takes a preferential option for the poor and oppressed who suffer injustice. Because of our cultural blindness and idolatry, most comfortable First Worlders like myself do not see God in our midst. On the contrary, the poor of the Third (and Fourth) World, suffering under institutionalized violence and unjust domination, and struggling for liberation and justice, experience God's real presence in their midst. God joins them in their nonviolent struggle for justice and peace. God is present with the poor and enters their struggle, suffers with them and begins again the process of transforming humanity into the beloved community of God. Given this divine preference to suffer with the world's poor and oppressed in their struggle for justice, those who benefit from their suffering (such as the first-world elite and other oppressors) only know God in God's absence. As they remain apart from the suffering masses and their nonviolent struggle for justice, indeed, as they inflict violence, poverty and death on the world's poor, they also inflict violence, poverty and death on God.

The choice before us, then, is whether or not we want to be like God, to be with God and to enter into the suffering of humanity in order to relieve that human suffering and offer humanity a new way into God's nonviolent reign of justice and peace. This life response to human suffering entails risky, nonviolent action for justice, work for real disarmament, unconditional love for enemies, solidarity with the poor and constant prayer to the God of justice for an end to relievable human suffering. As Jesus demonstrated, though we may end up on the cross, we know that we can trust that we too shall share in the resurrection and the eternal life where God's reign of justice and peace are realized for all. This choice on behalf of suffering humanity can indeed become good news to the poor. If we have the faith to accompany the nonviolent Jesus in his struggle for justice and peace, we find ourselves on the road to eternal life.

CHAPTER 8

A Soteriology of Nonviolence

Salvation as Gospel Peacemaking

In a world of violence, war and starvation, what does it mean to speak of salvation? What does salvation in Christ mean to Mayan peoples who live in the mountains of Guatemala and are killed by government death squads comprised of born-again Christians; to Somalian parents who watch their children starve to death while first-world Christians overeat in comfort; to South African children who are not free to live in peace because of the color of their skin; or to homeless families on the streets of Washington, D.C.? What does it mean that those who live in comfort and defend the unjust status quo spend their lives imagining a salvific afterlife of eternal comfort and satisfaction— while those who live in absolute poverty and degradation do not know what comfort is and cannot imagine any kind of happiness, justice or peace?

From the perspective of nonviolence, what does it mean to say that we are saved? How does nonviolence transform our traditional understanding of salvation? Gospel nonviolence, we are beginning to realize, challenges us to break through the illusions of false piety that keep us complacent in the face of systemic violence and to struggle for a salvation that means food for the starving masses, homes for the homeless and real justice for all who suffer under global oppression. Gospel nonviolence pushes us to enact salvation here and now in God's reign of justice and peace for all humanity, beginning with the poor and oppressed, who suffer the brunt of the world's institutionalized violence. A brief exploration of these connections will deepen our theology of nonviolence and perhaps lead us to a fuller understanding of salvation.

Soteriology as God's Saving Action in Jesus

Christian scripture and tradition hold that we are saved into eternal life by Jesus Christ. The Jewish scriptures tell the great of story of salvation in the

76

Exodus narrative, how God acted in human history to liberate the suffering peoples from slavery to imperial oppression. The gospel takes up that story of liberation by announcing the definitive act of God in human history for the salvation of all humanity: Jesus the Christ and his proclamation of God's reign. As Paul writes to the Ephesians, God "has made known to us in all wisdom and insight the mystery of God's will, according to God's purpose which God set forth in Christ as a place for the fullness of time, to unite all things to Christ, things in heaven and things on earth" (Eph 1:9-10). The gospels portray Jesus as the liberator who teaches, practices and incarnates the way of salvation. After his execution and resurrection, Jesus sends forth his community of friends to enflesh this way of salvation in the world.

In general, salvation explains how God has delivered us from personal and collective suffering and evil and called us to a life-giving relationship with God in God's reign of peace. It describes how humanity has been liberated from evil, its suicidal addiction to violence and death. As a systematic interpretation of Christ's saving work for humanity, soteriology explores salvation in Jesus Christ and teaches that by the unmerited grace of God in Jesus Christ we have been redeemed and saved from the sin of violence and the reign of death. It explores the proclamation of the Christian scriptures that Christ lived, acted, died and rose to save humanity from its sin, its violence, its injustices and its addiction to death (Jn 11:49-51; Rom 4:25; 5:6-11; 1 Cor 15:3). Most notably, we read how Jesus offered bread and wine to his peacemaking community of disciples the night before his execution, and declared, "Take and eat; this is my body . . . Drink, for this is my blood of the covenant, which will be shed on behalf of many for the forgiveness of sins" (Mt 26:27). As Paul elaborates, through Christ's salvific action we are saved from sin and the reign of death itself and offered the eternal life of God's reign beginning here and now.

Today, however, in a world of nuclear violence, starvation and systemic injustice, the language of salvation poses a grave problem. For nearly two thousand years people claiming to have been saved by Jesus Christ have killed others, waged war, oppressed others, designed nuclear weapons and created a worldwide structure that forces most of humanity into desperate poverty. The crisis of violence that threatens the world has forced us to realize that, in light of Jesus' nonviolence, we can no longer live off the agony of the poor and oppressed or support systemic injustice if we want our salvation in the peacemaking Jesus to possess any real meaning. Such claims on top of complicity in systemic violence make a mockery of the gospel, the teachings and crucifixion of Jesus. The poor, the oppressed and the starving masses challenge the comfortable first-world church and the wealthy Christians who benefit from global systemic injustice. Those who live and die in the nonviolent struggles for justice and who claim salvation in Jesus dare the rest of us to take human salvation more seriously by joining with the risen Jesus as he struggles today for the liberation of the oppressed and the oppressors and the transformation of humanity. The gospel suggests that salvation means struggling for peace with justice, that it entails consequences. Though given to us freely, it requires entrance into Jesus' nonviolent struggle for justice. Though the world's addiction to violence plagues us all, signs of our salvation, of the possibility of sobriety through nonviolence, can be seen "if one has eyes to see." Jesus observed that these signs of salvation hailed the coming of God's reign.

If people have been saved by a person of nonviolence dedicated to the liberation of the poor and the oppressed for the coming of God's reign, why do many of them continue to do violence, kill others, oppress peoples and war against others, even in his name? The poor and oppressed of the world challenge our lack of faith and invite us to take the gospel promise of salvation seriously by renouncing our oppressive violence and joining them in God's reign of peace. For if humanity has been saved in Christ, as the Christian scriptures announce, then we can dismantle all our weapons, renounce all our violence and place all our security in God alone. Then, all humanity can feel free to adopt Jesus' nonviolent way of life. Because many Christians continue to kill, wage war, and support systemic injustice, non-Christians and poor people throughout the world question the claim of salvation and wonder why Christians do not practice what they preach. The challenge of the gospel, the summons of the poor, the opportunity of this historic moment urges us to prepare now for salvation by renouncing violence and embracing nonviolence.

A Soteriology of Nonviolence

A soteriology of nonviolence approaches the question of salvation from the perspective of gospel nonviolence. If we are truly saved in Christ, as the gospel asserts and as many people believe, then we can no longer kill people or participate in the structures of violence which oppress people. Our lives need to model Jesus' life, for the nonviolent Jesus has become our salvation. We need to become a people of nonviolence, a people who stand in solidarity with the poor, a people who struggle for justice and make peace, a people who resist the systems of injustice, a people who risk crucifixion in their fidelity to Jesus and the reign of God. The first sign of our salvation, then, will be the seriousness with which we live the gospel, that is, our love for one another and for our enemies, our practice of nonviolence toward everyone, our peaceful resistance to injustice, and our steadfast devotion to God and God's will. When Christians around the world begin to live the gospel, to practice the nonviolence of Jesus, to show compassion to the marginalized and to work for justice, then the world will see that we have been saved in Christ. Indeed, the violence which threatens to destroy humanity and the earth itself will be transformed, and we will be saved from our destructive, genocidal violence. Salvation, from the perspective of nonviolence means renouncing violence, practicing the nonviolence of Jesus and cooperating with the God of nonviolence who is rescuing us from ourselves and transforming the world into a haven of justice and peace.

We can sum up several basic insights into a soteriology of nonviolence. *First, we are saved from violence.* This soteriology emphasizes that there is a way out of the worldwide addiction to violence and systemic injustice that threatens to destroy all humanity and the planet. It proclaims that God has intervened and offered us a way to become sober, a way to live life to the full—if we choose it. The salvation that the scriptures announce declares that this systemic violence need not continue forever in an everlasting hell of violence, revenge, retaliation, war and death. We are saved from poverty, apartheid, racism, sexism, patriarchy, homelessness, disease, oppression, war, consumerism, greed and nuclear weapons. We have been invited into a new reality of peace with justice. As Paul writes in his letter to the Romans, Jesus saves us from sin, law and death—from the sin of violence, which is killing us all; from the laws which legalize injustice, torture, execution and nuclear weapons; and from the reign of death, which fills every human being with fear. As Paul explains, we are saved by Jesus for an eternal life of nonviolent love in God's reign of peace.

Second, we are saved by the nonviolent Christ. Jesus Christ is the way of salvation. To walk that way of salvation, as we have discussed, means to walk the way of nonviolence, to seek justice, make peace, resist injustice and love unconditionally. The nonviolent Christ speaks about the way of salvation in texts, such as the Sermon on the Mount, which command us not to resist evil with violence and instead to love our enemies. This way frees us from each and every act of violence. We no longer have to be violent to one another; we do not have to take revenge, retaliate, kill, oppress or sit idly by while millions of human beings suffer and die in poverty. The way of salvation demands that we place our faith in Christ, that we believe him and take up where he left off on the life journey of nonviolence. To have faith means to act like Jesus, to practice active nonviolence.

Third, the salvation offered to us in Christ requires a particular way of living. This salvation demands action. It charges us to take on the violence of the world; indeed, to uncover the latent violence of systemic injustice by denouncing and resisting it and then being willing to take on that violence when the system lashes out the only way it knows how. Christ's salvation transforms violence through nonviolent resistance to systemic violence even to the point of taking on the violence of world, as Christ did, so that the violence stops there, in our bodies. When we put this salvific way into practice, the eyes of many are opened and the world is brought a little closer to God's reign of justice and peace. This way of salvation willingly embraces violence and death, as Jesus did on the cross, and thus ushers in the reign of God.

Fourth, Jesus' salvation insists that our survival is already guaranteed. Because his suffering love and sacrificial life has transformed us, and because God raised Jesus from the dead, we can follow the risen Christ along the way of nonviolence by risking our lives in resistance to systemic violence. We can risk persecution, arrest, trial, imprisonment, suffering, and execution knowing that as followers of the nonviolent Jesus, we too will be raised. Jesus promises that we will enter eternal life. All he asks is that we continue his life of peacemaking. This new life in Christ begins now and lasts for an eternity of peace. Thus we need no longer fear death. We can resist the forces of death through nonviolent love knowing that the risen Christ lives and that we will follow him to the cross and into his risen life of eternal nonviolence. As more and more Christians live out Jesus' salvific way of nonviolence, God's reign of justice and peace will be further realized. More and more people will begin to enjoy life now in the nonviolent reign of God.

Salvation and Nonviolence, Here and Now

The gospel does not leave us with our heads lost in the clouds. It speaks of salvation here and now, that is, of good news to the poor, liberation to those held captive, sight to the blind, justice, mercy and peace for all. The salvific way of Jesus is meant to be lived in the present. We are called to make the salvation offered by Christ a reality for all humanity; thus, we are called to become peacemakers, practitioners of nonviolence, doers of justice.

A theology of nonviolence holds that the life of faith necessitates a life of nonviolent action for justice and peace, a life of selfless service for suffering humanity that strives for the reign of God here and now so all humanity can experience God's justice and peace. The tradition teaches that our faith needs to be informed by active love, by the deeds of justice and peace. As the letter of James declares, faith without works is dead (Jas 2:17). In his letter to the Galatians Paul proclaims that only "faith working through love" leads to salvation (Gal 5:6). In other words, to be faithful people of Christ we cannot merely accept the salvation won by Christ for us on the cross and in the resurrection and then go about our daily business in silent complicity in the world's systemic injustice. We are called to put that salvific nonviolence into action. We cannot claim salvation in Christ and still support systemic violence; we are charged to renounce violence and embrace the way of nonviolence with our very lives.

A soteriology of nonviolence, therefore, demands that we practice nonviolence. It maintains that Christ has indeed saved us from violence and death. It confirms that we are free now to follow Christ, make peace, seek justice, forgive everyone, love our enemies and worship the God of nonviolence. This good news of salvation will be proclaimed to the poor and oppressed peoples of the earth when they see us joining God's struggle for justice and peace. When they see us alleviating suffering, feeding the hungry, tearing down the structures of oppression, renouncing war and dismantling nuclear weapons, they will know that "the reign of God is at hand" and "salvation has come to God's people."

A soteriology of nonviolence realizes that we live in a kairos time, a time of special opportunity. Indeed, practitioners of nonviolence understand every age since the nonviolent Christ as a time of opportunity, as a time of salvation if we but choose to live in God's reign of justice and peace. In this light we understand the urgency of the Christian scriptures, which cry out to us to wake up, turn our hearts to God and accept the salvation offered to us in Christ. As Paul's letter to the Romans explains:

You know the time has come: it is the hour now for you to awake from sleep. Our salvation is even nearer now than when we first believed. The night is almost over, it will be daylight soon—let us give up all the things we prefer to do under cover of the dark and put on the armor of light. Let us live decently as people do in the daytime; no drunken orgies, no promiscuity or licentiousness, and no wrangling or jealousy. Put on the Lord Jesus Christ (Rom 13:11-14).

The scriptures announce a salvation rooted in real justice for the poor and a deep peace given to us from God. As the book of Isaiah describes, salvation names the time of justice and peace when God reigns supreme, when the poor and oppressed are liberated, when violence and war no longer occur. Isaiah's text envisions salvation as the time when all nations shall stream to the mountain of God, when God instructs humanity in God's ways, when people shall "beat their swords into plowshares and their spears into pruning hooks; [when] one nation shall not raise the sword against another, nor shall they train for war again" (Is 2:2-5). As Isaiah elaborates, this reign of justice and peace is at hand, if we but choose it and enact it. As we do, the God of peace will declare:

> I will make my justice come speedily;
>   my salvation shall go forth;
> in me shall the coastlands hope,
>   and my arms they shall await . . .
> My salvation shall remain forever
>   and my justice shall never be dismayed . . .
> How beautiful upon the mountains
>   are the feet of the one who brings glad tidings,
> announcing peace, bearing good news,
>   announcing salvation, and saying to Zion,
>   "Your God is God." . . .
> Observe what is right, do what is just;
>   for my salvation is about to come,
>   my justice, about to be revealed . . .
> I will appoint peace your governor, and justice
>   your ruler.
> No longer shall violence be heard of in your land,
>   or plunder and ruin within your boundaries.
> You shall call your walls "Salvation"
>   and your gates "Praise." . . .
> No longer shall the sound of weeping be heard
>   there,
>   or the sound of crying;
> no longer shall there be in it
>   an infant who lives but a few days,

or an old one who does not round out his full
    lifetime;
they shall live in the houses they build,
    and eat the fruit of the vineyards they plant;
they shall not build houses for others to live in,
    or plant for others to eat . . .
The wolf and the lamb shall graze alike,
    and the lion shall eat hay like the ox.
None shall hurt or destroy
    on all my holy mountain, says God (Is 51:5-6;
      52:7; 56:1; 60:18; 65:19-25).

These days of making peace and seeking justice are the days of salvation. The Christ of nonviolence, who is our salvation, announces the good news that our salvation approaches. Indeed, for those who believe in the God of peace, the days to come have arrived. We are called to live out the salvation granted to us. We are saved. We no longer need to be slaves to violence. Jesus has shown us a way out of our madness. The salvific way of nonviolence is good news indeed.

CHAPTER 9

An Eschatology of Nonviolence

God's Reign of Peace at Hand

To speak of heaven and hell in a world of total violence requires addressing the present condition of suffering humanity. From the perspective of the world's violence, God's way of nonviolence turns upside down traditional theological reflections on the end time, heaven, hell, judgment and death. It refocuses those theological terms in the violence actually inflicted upon the poor and oppressed and propels us into their nonviolent struggle for justice here and now. In other words, it challenges us to proclaim God's reign of peace and justice on earth now as it is in heaven. For many, such a proclamation cuts to the heart of our belief and lifestyle. Indeed, as the scriptures explain, this announcement declares the fall of the principalities and powers, the end of imperial violence and the nonviolent coming of God. While this insight means bad news for the rich and powerful, it proclaims good news of change to the poor and oppressed. *But: it liberates the rich too*

Many preachers and evangelists speak of the second coming of Christ as a final cataclysmic, apocalyptic, global holocaust. Through the ages this event, the parousia, has been portrayed as the ultimate catastrophe of violent destruction, when the world literally will blow up and a wrath-filled Christ will judge us and condemn many to an eternity of terror. In an age of nuclear weapons and imperial politics, where self-declared "born-again" presidents have prepared secretly for the annihilation of the earth in nuclear hellfire, such an outcome, the horrific destruction of the planet in a global nuclear war, has become quite imaginable. It is not only possible, but even probable.

The revelation of Christian nonviolence, however, reframes the entire question and poses a much more compelling, much more hopeful image. It shatters the false god of hellfire and brimstone as an aberration and proclaims the living God of nonviolence. Reflecting upon the end of time and the world as we know it, Christian nonviolence announces the transformation of the world's systemic violence and death into God's nonviolent reign of justice, peace and unconditional love. Since the world overflows with systemic violence and brutal injustice, the vision of a nonviolent reign of God's justice on earth indeed marks the end of the world as we know it, the transformation into an entirely different world, a new realm of justice and peace. An eschatology of nonviolence envisions the world's fulfillment in God's nonviolence, the complete transformation of humanity and the earth. Instead of blowing up in a global firestorm of nuclear destruction, the world matures into nonviolent love and justice so that God reigns on earth as in heaven, as Jesus prayed. As the Christian scriptures hope, the lives of the saints and martyrs of nonviolence will be vindicated, and God's reign of peace will be at hand. Indeed, as Karl Rahner wrote, in this parousia, the world will come to the God of peace in the fulfillment of God's teachings rather than Christ coming to the world.[1] The nonviolent, risen Christ, this new eschatology holds, dwells among us now, leading us to this moment of global and spiritual transformation in God.

How might this culmination of God's nonviolence on earth look? I believe we have seen and are seeing glimpses of its coming, even in this dark age of world wars, holocausts, Hiroshima, Nagasaki, Gulf wars, starvation and unparalleled misery. Even now we have moments of breathtaking light that have captured the world's imagination and point to a transforming time of nonviolence. While Hitler and the world's armies waged war throughout Europe and the Pacific Rim in the 1930s and 1940s, Gandhi and his followers were experimenting with nonviolence and truth on a massive level as never before. Gandhi's public nonviolence led to Britain's peaceful withdrawal from India; a remarkable fast ended violence in Calcutta. Similarly, at the height of the civil rights movement, we witnessed the vision of God's reign as white and black people came to celebrate Martin Luther King, Jr.'s dream of a new world of justice and peace, in Montgomery, Washington, D.C., and Selma. We have seen the nonviolent People Power movement turn away the Marcos dictatorship, and we have witnessed the determination of ordinary people using nonviolent direct action who brought down the Berlin Wall and frustrated a military coup that threatened to plunge the Russian people back into the darkness of oppression. In the Plowshares movement, first enacted by Daniel and Philip Berrigan and their colleagues on September 9, 1980, in King of Prussia, Pennsylvania, we see dedicated peacemakers enact Isaiah's vision by symbolically beating nuclear bombs into plowshares of peace as a first step toward nuclear disarmament. Such experiences herald a future of nonviolence and peace, where God one day reigns on earth as in heaven.

This new reign bears the marks of nonviolence—justice for the poor, liberation for the oppressed, reconciliation between all peoples, and Christ's own peace—as its hallmark. To imagine such a day requires that we pray for its coming and prepare for its arrival. A theology of nonviolence needs to reflect on this image of a nonviolent parousia, where the world is given over in a global transformation to the God of peace.

Eschatology

Eschatology, the study of the last things, reflects on the coming of God's reign on earth. It considers such biblical themes as the second coming of

Christ, death, judgment, heaven, hell and resurrection. It examines the end of human existence in God, and thus our basic hope as Christians. It points to Christian destiny, not as distinct from the destiny of the world and its history, but as the destiny of all humanity toward God and in God's reign.[2] According to Jesus, God's reign is at hand; it is already here and, at the same time, not here. As liberation theologians have written, the movements for liberation, justice and peace on earth struggle for God's reign. In this light Walter Wink writes that "the reign of God is not 'built,' but sampled. We have a foretaste, an appetizer, an aperitif, a down payment (Rom 8:23; 2 Cor 1:22; 5:5; Eph 1:14)."[3] We are on a journey toward God. As we make that journey, we discover more and more that the God of peace walks toward us to meet us and draw us into the divine mystery of peace. Even while we seek it, we begin to experience God's reign in our midst.

Eschatology, Jesus and Nonviolence

Christian nonviolence looks at these last things in the light of the life, teachings, death and resurrection of Jesus Christ, that is, from the way of nonviolence. As it looks at the world's violence, it hears the invitation to nonviolence which comes from God in the life of Jesus. It prophetically announces, as Martin Luther King, Jr., declared on the night before he was killed, that "the choice before us is no longer violence or nonviolence; it is nonviolence or nonexistence."[4] It invites us to turn from the violence of the world, a violence which has the capacity to destroy all humanity and the entire planet, and instead to choose the spiritually explosive nonviolence of God, which can transform every human heart and the face of the earth into a new realm of justice, peace and love. Jesus "proclaimed to his people, and to all people, a double prophecy, contingent in the choices it offered: the nonviolent kingdom of God or the destruction of Jerusalem, and ultimately of the world," Jim Douglass writes. "The deepest implications of that contingent prophecy have been brought home finally by our nuclear age."[5] This choice, Douglass observes, "was the same for Jesus and his people as it is for us today. Choose the nonviolent kingdom or the razing of Jerusalem. Today Jerusalem has become the world."[6] Eschatology, then, looks to that choice of Christian nonviolence, and chooses with Jesus to proclaim God's reign of nonviolence coming to humanity right this very moment, for all people, for all time and beyond into eternity.

The Nonviolent Coming of God and God's Reign

Jesus proclaimed that the reign of God is at hand. This realm of God's nonviolence, he declared, has come and is coming to humanity on earth. It includes justice, peace, mercy, reconciliation and unconditional, universal love. The Second Vatican Council spoke of Jesus' reign as "the consummation of the earth and of humanity," "a new dwelling place and a new earth where justice will abide, and whose blessedness will answer and surpass all the longings for peace which spring up in the human heart.[7] The signs of this nonviolent reign include the healing of the sick, the liberation of the oppressed, a new era of justice and peace, the beating of swords into plowshares and the preaching of good news to the poor. As we see these signs, begun in the life of Jesus, happening even today, we know that the reign of God is among us.

To imagine, ponder and proclaim the nonviolent coming of God invites its coming. As Douglass notes, Jesus confronted the violence of the world and its destructive potential through his way of nonviolence. That way of nonviolence still holds within it the seeds of God's reign, which can grow and transform humanity and earth itself. With Christ, Douglass suggests, we are invited to envision and to experience the nonviolent coming of God:

> We can live out the imperative of transformation by acting on a faith in the nonviolent coming of God. Being precedes action. Our nonviolent God initiates the changes we have not yet fully chosen. Nothing is predetermined. Yet our transformation is underway; it is our deepest reality; it is beginning to surface in nonviolent movements everywhere. If we open our eyes, as Martin Luther King did, we can still see the beloved community coming into being. We can see peacemakers, justice-makers, giving their lives to God, in an earth-encircling Love that will transform even the carnage of the Persian Gulf war. We do have the capacity to destroy ourselves. But our very freedom is so profoundly an expression of Compassionate Love . . . that we can have faith in our ultimately choosing the beloved community. God's upside-down kingdom for the poor and the oppressed is at hand—a kingdom where we love our enemies and are saved by them as the Jew in the ditch, in Jesus' parable, was saved by the enemy Samaritan. In the nuclear age that kingdom where we resist evil nonviolently and realize transformation through our enemy, must come. It will come. It is coming now.[8]

Jesus portrayed the coming reign of God through parables. Chapter 13 of Matthew's gospel, for example, paints several images of God's reign. Jesus likens that reign to a person who has sown good seed in his field, and while he sleeps, an enemy sows bad seed. He lets both the good wheat and the weeds grow, and then at harvest time, gathers the weeds to be burned and takes the wheat to his barn (Mt 13:23-30, 36-43). In the explanation of the parable at the end of the chapter, Matthew points out that after evildoers have been dismissed "into the fiery furnace," "the righteous will shine like the sun in the kingdom of their God." This fire can symbolize the divine holiness, which purifies the repentant and unrepentant. The thrust of the parable suggests that as we seek to live in God's reign, we are called to be patient and nonviolent, to repent and to trust in our nonviolent God to bring about the reign in God's good time.

Second, the reign is characterized as a mustard seed, the tiniest of seeds, which grows into a large bush where birds can live (Mt 13:31-32). Elsewhere Jesus likens himself to a seed that falls and dies and then grows again, thus identifying himself with the nonviolent reign of God. The parable suggests that we nurture the seed, but that ultimately its growth lies in God's hands, not ours. The reign of God grows on its own.

Third, God's reign resembles a woman mixing a small amount of yeast with three measures of wheat flour (the equivalent of fifty pounds of flour). A small ingredient within a huge mass transforms the whole and makes it what it should be. The nonviolence of Christ in the mass of humanity also can transform the whole. We are called to be such nonviolent, transforming yeast in today's world.

Fourth, Matthew writes of the reign in terms of a person who sells everything and buys a field with buried treasure (Mt 13:44). He has nothing left; he has sold everything to buy that treasure. This fanatical devotion to the buried treasure symbolizes our commitment to God's reign, which, the scripture tells us, will cost everything we have.

Fifth, a merchant who finds a pearl beyond all others sells everything and buys it; he too stands as a symbol of God's reign (Mt 13:45). The reign of God is like the pearl of great price, which the merchant sells everything to possess. So, too, we give everything for God's way of nonviolence, God's reign. It consumes our very life.

Sixth, God's reign "is like a net thrown into the sea, which collects fish of every kind." The good is collected while the bad is thrown away. At the end of the age, "angels will separate the wicked from the righteous" (Mt 13:47-50). Once again, the writer stresses the urgency to turn toward God's way.

Seventh, in the parable of the workers in the vineyard (Mt 20:1-16), Jesus speaks of a landowner who hires workers throughout a day and pays them each the same final wage. This points out that "the last will be first and the first will be last" in God's reign. God's nonviolence is embraced late in life by some, but the life of nonviolence bestowed on us by God remains the same for all.

Finally, in the parable of the wedding feast (Mt 22:1-15), Jesus likens God's reign to a wedding feast in which the invited guests do not show up; thus the poor and outcast are brought in to enjoy the feast. "Many are invited, but few are chosen."

All these images speak of a God who longs to bring us all together in peace, a God who struggles with our refusal to join this divine peace movement and a God who nonetheless loves us and wishes for complete reconciliation.

From both the perspective of the poor and the perspective of nonviolence, such images of the reign of God invite our own conversion and the transformation of the world. They can be understood most fully in the context of Jesus' teachings on love. The Jesus who announces the reign of God and the nonviolent coming of God invites us to love this God, our neighbors, ourselves, the poor, and, at the height of God's unconditional love, our enemies.

Jesus invites us to practice the love of God, who loves unconditionally both the just and the unjust. Jesus summons us to that perfect love. As he describes this great love in the Sermon on the Mount, he declares, "Seek first the reign of God and God's justice and all these things will be given you besides" (Mt 6:33). A theology of nonviolence interprets these images of the reign of God within this context of nonviolent love. God is luring us into this reign of peace right now. As we are transformed, we will participate in God's transformation of humanity. As we enter into this peacemaking, unconditional love, we too will experience the urgency of Jesus and the struggle to share God's reign with all people so that everyone will wake up and know God's reign. This love, this new life in the reign of God, commits us to a lifelong struggle, which culminates in crucifixion and resurrection. As we join in that struggle, we share in the nonviolent coming of God and God's reign.

Death, Judgment, Heaven and Hell

Eschatological nonviolence upholds the vision of life after death, of the resurrection that follows persecution, arrest, torture and execution for holy, active nonviolence on behalf of God's justice and peace. It understands that death opens the way to new life. Indeed, the nonviolent Christ teaches that the way to life goes through death. "If anyone wishes to come after me," Jesus teaches, "you must deny yourself and take up your cross daily and follow me. For whoever wishes to save their life will lose it, but whoever loses their life for my sake will save it" (Lk 9:23-24). Dietrich Bonhoeffer translates this invitation, "When Christ bids us come and follow, he bids us come and die." This journey of active nonviolence risks suffering and crucifixion and takes us into the resurrection and eternal life of Christ.

In the light of Christ's nonviolence, we can take a new look at our traditional understandings of judgment. The gospels speak strongly about God's judgment of the world and the last judgment, which every human being faces. The judgment we face comes from the incarnation of nonviolence, the One who has identified completely with the poorest of the poor, who taught and practiced nonviolence and who suffered execution for that active life. We may recall three teachings that shed light on this judgment of nonviolence. John writes of judgment as the revelation of God's unconditional love that demands a choice. The Spirit, which Jesus will send, will "convict the world in regard to sin and righteousness and condemnation: sin, because they do not believe in me; righteousness, because I am going to the Father and you will no longer see me; condemnation, because the ruler of this world has been condemned" (Jn 16:8-11). The judgment of Jesus will prove to be true, and this judgment, we learn, is rooted in love.

After instructing us in the Sermon on the Mount on the way of nonviolence and the love of enemies, Jesus notes, "Do not judge and you will not be judged. For as you judge, so will you be judged, and the measure with which you measure will be measured out to you" (Mt 7:1-2). In other words, as we practice the nonviolent love that Jesus teaches, so too will we experience ever more fully the nonviolent love of God for us. In Matthew's final parable of the last judgment we read how we will be measured by this active love, a love which stands in solidarity with the poor and oppressed:

> When the Son of Humanity [or "Human One"] comes in his glory and all the angels with him, he will sit upon his glorious throne, and all the nations will be assembled before him. And he will separate them one from another, as a shepherd separates the sheep from the goats. He will place the sheep on his right and the goats on his left. Then the [Holy One] will say to those on his right, "Come, you who are blessed by my [God]. Inherit the kingdom prepared for you from the foundation of the world. For I was hungry and you gave me food, I was thirsty and you gave me drink, a stranger and you welcomed me, naked and you clothed me, ill and you cared for me, in prison and you visited me." Then the righteous will answer him and say, "Lord, when did we see you hungry and feed you, or thirsty and give you drink? When did we see you a stranger and welcome you, or naked and clothe you? When did we see you ill or in prison, and visit you?" And the [Holy One] will say to them in reply, "Amen, I say to you, whatever you did for one of these least brothers or sisters of mine, you did for me." Then he will say to those on his left, "Depart from me, you accursed, into the eternal fire prepared for the devil and his angels . . . What you did not do for one of these least ones, you did not do for me." And these will go off to eternal punishment, but the righteous to eternal life (Mt 25:31-41, 45-46, *NAB*).

This last judgment challenges us to the life of active nonviolence. It speaks harshly of heaven and hell, using the language of "fire" and "eternal punishment" to shake us into the life of nonviolent service and solidarity. It suggests that in the reign of God, everything as we know it will be upside-down. The last shall be first, the poor shall be rich, the outsiders shall be inside, those in the back will be brought up front to the place of honor, and God will be recognized in the poor and marginalized. Those who assume they are headed straight to heaven after their deaths may have it all wrong; those condemned by society (in Jesus' day, the poor, the prostitutes, the tax collectors, the prophetically nonviolent) will enter God's reign first. Judgment, then, is the challenge and gift to live in God's own peace with justice, to seek God's nonviolent reign, and to serve God present in suffering, marginalized humanity. How we meet and treat that nonviolent God, individually and corporately, determine our own judgment. Our choices will decide our fate, for what we do or do not do, we do and do not do to God. Our apathy, indifference and hostility to a suffering, nonviolent God present in suffering, nonviolent humanity will have spiritual consequences.

In this light, the words, actions and, ultimately, the nonviolence of Jesus demonstrate already God's judgment on humanity, for us personally and collectively. God judges with nonviolence. This judgment may be easier for us to face than our own judgments toward ourselves and other human beings, judgments rooted in violence. The challenge lies in getting beyond ourselves and our violence, and thus our harmful judgments, and into the judgment, the nonviolence, of God.

Our nonviolent God invites us to become people of nonviolence who love justice, make peace and serve God in the poor and oppressed. As we ponder God's nonviolence and try to delve into it with all our hearts and lives, we discover the boundless mercy of God and find ourselves longing more and more for the reign of God, what scripture and tradition call heaven. Like Jesus, we pray for the heaven of justice and peace to be present now on earth. In this light, with the passion and urgency of Jesus calling us to practice his nonviolence and walk with him among the poor, we may conclude, as contemporary theologians are beginning to assert, that God is drawing everyone into the heaven of justice and peace, into God's realm of nonviolence. Though we live in an urgent moment, when justice cries out to heaven, still we can walk in the light of faith that we shall be united in heaven, and more and more, on earth, here and now, to the extent that we give over our lives to Christ's nonviolent struggle for justice. Heaven then marks the perfection and completion of our present union with God in a community of nonviolent love.

In this light the church has proposed the possibility of purgatory as a process of purification or conversion and transformation to the heavenly community of love. Such a purgatory can happen in this life; we can be transformed and participate in God's nonviolent transformation of the earth for justice and peace. Indeed, this transformation stands at the center of Jesus' urgent, pleading invitation. The question of hell is a speculation that may not be helpful to ponder, except to push us further into the risky nonviolence of Christ. Hell, we could say, speaks of the totality of the world's hatred and violence, where we have become completely closed to God and vulnerable to all the forces of evil. The word *hell* never appears in the Jewish scriptures; instead, we read of Gehenna, the place of the dead. The Christian scriptures speak of hell to convey the ultimate urgency and seriousness of conversion to God and God's way of life; Jesus does not want us to turn away from God and to be forever alienated from God. The Second Vatican Council never mentions hell. If we choose not to love God and God present in suffering humanity, we choose to be separated from God. We choose our own isolation, alienation and perhaps annihilation. God allows our free choice but hopes that we will choose God and God's way of peace. God does not so much punish us as respect our lifelong choice. Such nonviolence still gives over its life even unto death so that others will choose that Love. And as nothing is impossible with God, perhaps all humanity may one day be finally transformed and reconciled, even freely, into our loving God. Jesus urgently calls us to that moment, beginning with the present moment. Instead of speculating upon such matters to the neglect of our suffering sisters and brothers, Jesus challenges us to get on with relieving the misery of the poor, ending the hell on earth and joining in the nonviolent coming of God right now.

A theology of nonviolence calls us not so much to focus on these ultimate questions of heaven and hell, but rather to live them out now with our lives, to risk our lives in gospel nonviolence, so that the poor and oppressed may be relieved from the hell of systemic violence and injustice they are suffering. Nonviolence asks, If God is nonviolent—and we believe God is—can there be a hell, and would this God send people there? It notes that God is unconditionally merciful, that God practices clemency, as Jesus demonstrated at the moment of his death on the cross. Yet it points out that heaven and hell are at hand. The suffering masses of humanity experience hell on earth in a day-to-day struggle to survive war, poverty, degradation, hunger, disease, imprisonment, torture, racism, sexism, classism and oppression. The God of nonviolence calls us to join in liberating them from the hell they suffer. This God declares that we have the power of nonviolence in our hands; we can help God liberate them from that hell, to transform that hellish life into the heavenly, nonviolent realm of justice and peace for them, with them, right now. We have our work cut out for us; thus we need not linger on the speculation of life after death. We can trust and believe in the Nonviolent One and get on with his life mission, the task of proclaiming the reign of heaven and its justice and peace for the poor and oppressed, indeed, for all humanity. Indeed, with the still possible hellfire of nuclear war and global destruction, we have an urgent mission to transform the heart of humanity and the structures of the world to prevent the final hell of nuclear war, institutionalized violence and environmental destruction from destroying us all.

Theologian Rosemary Radford Ruether urges that instead of focusing on an "unrealized future," we base our theological reflections on conversion. She writes:

> The concept of social change as conversion to the center, conversion to the earth and to each other, rather than flight into the unrealizable future, is a model of change more in keeping with the realities of temporal existence. To subject ourselves to the tyranny of impossible expectations of final perfection means to neglect to do what can and must be done for our times . . . It is this shaping of the beloved community on earth, for our time and generation to bequeath to our children, that is our primary responsibility as human beings . . . We can do nothing about the "immortal" dimension of our lives. It is not our calling to be concerned about the eternal meaning of our lives, and religion should not make this the focus of its message. Our responsibility is to use our temporal life span to create a just and good community for our generation and for our children. It is in the hands of Holy Wisdom to forge out of our finite struggle truth and being for everlasting life.[9]

True
(we
speculate
a lot.)

It is not our calling to be concerned about the eternal meaning of our lives. The eternal One has given us specific responsibilities for the temporal realities of suffering and violence which plague humanity. A theology of nonviolence calls us to get on with that human responsibility of divine nonviolence. It challenges us to enter the struggle for a nonviolent world without war and injustice, to choose to be part of that struggle, instead of choosing selfish isolation and complicity in systemic violence.

Resurrection and the Hope of Nonviolence

T & Hope

Eschatology bespeaks hope. It asks: Where is our hope? What do we hope for? If we are starving in Somalia, our hope may be quite concrete: food. If we are being bombed in Baghdad, our hope will be the end of the bombing, a life of peace and healing. If we live next to a nuclear silo, our hope may be in the dismantling of all nuclear weapons and a world where we can trust one another and live in peace with justice. Christian nonviolence calls us to be a people of hope who enact our hope by doing hopeful things for suffering humanity.

Jesus lived a fervent hope in the coming of God's reign. He was convinced that this reign is at hand, that God invites us into the new life of nonviolence and justice, and that this new life has been offered to us if we choose to accept it. This hope led him to Jerusalem; to his nonviolent, direct action in the Temple; and to his arrest, torture and execution on the cross and resurrection three days later. In the resurrection, the gospels point to the hope that awaits us all—the gift of Christ's own peace as eternal life with God.

What does the resurrection mean in a world of total violence? Scripture and church tradition teach the resurrection of the body, the spirit, and the whole person, into God's reign of nonviolence and justice. It illustrates the total transformation in God after death that brings to perfection our transformation in God in this life. The resurrection of Jesus, the nonviolent peacemaker, the Crucified One, reveals to humanity the reality of risen life, the resurrection of humanity into God's reign of unconditional love. In his resurrection account Mark speaks of the hope for transformation beginning again in the remnant community of nonviolence in Galilee, which will take the nonviolent struggle of justice and peace to Jerusalem, back where Jesus began.[10] As Ched Myers explains Mark's resurrection account, the disciple/reader is invited to take that same journey from Galilee to Jerusalem and the cross, a journey of active nonviolence for God's reign on earth:

> The disciple/reader is being told that that narrative, which appeared to have ended, is beginning again. The story is circular! The full revelation of the Human One has resulted in neither triumphal victory for the community (as the disciples had hoped), nor the restored Davidic kingdom (as the rebels had hoped), nor tragic failure and defeat (as the reader had feared). It has resulted in nothing more and nothing less than the regeneration of

the messianic mission. If we have eyes to "see" the advent of the Human One we will be able to "see" Jesus still going before us . . . We do not entirely understand what "resurrection" means, but if we have understood the story, we should be "holding fast" to what we do know: that Jesus still goes before us, summoning us to the way of the cross. And that is the hardest ending of all: not tragedy, not victory, but an unending challenge to follow anew. Because that means we must respond.[11]

The good news of resurrection declares that death does not have the last word; it proposes that nothing is impossible with God. Our nonviolent God cannot be destroyed but lives on and invites us into eternal peace through giving up our lives in risky peacemaking. The implications of this hope are foreshadowed in Jesus' vision of the fall of Satan from heaven. "I saw Satan fall like lightning from heaven," Jesus tells us (Lk 10:18). Douglass comments that this vision of the fall of Satan heralds the good news that God will be victorious and nonviolence will bear fruit for all:

Because Satan had fallen, Jerusalem need not fall. Jerusalem and Israel could be transformed. Rome could eventually be transformed. The key to this prophetic hope was Jesus' own experience of Satan's fall like lightning from heaven, his certain sense of evil's fall from power. Satan's fall from heaven is a mythological way of seeing good's victory over evil on earth. It is the other side of the presence of God's kingdom. Satan's fall and the kingdom's presence express Jesus' hope for nonviolent change. Satan, or evil, is not in control of the earth. Caesar is not in control. The Roman legions are not in control. The Temple authorities are not in control. Multinational corporations are not in control. The nuclear powers are not in control. God alone is in control, to the extent that we realize, as Jesus did, the truth of God's kingdom—a nonviolent kingdom of infinite power. Jesus realized that truth in his evil-shattering vision of Satan's fall like lightning, then in his living out that vision and the presence of the kingdom in response to his people's crisis of violence. Because Satan had fallen, Jerusalem did not have to fall, however desperate the situation. The kingdom of God was at hand, is at hand. Its power is no farther away than your and my hands. Gandhi realized the same transforming truth in his doctrine of satyagraha, or truth-force. Satan's fall, the kingdom of God and satyagraha are all ways into an infinite power of change that is always present, yet seldom realized. This nonviolent God of Love is the forgotten factor in every apparently hopeless conflict.[12]

In his letter to the Romans, Paul proclaims the hope that we have because of the reconciliation granted to all humanity (with each other and with God) because of Christ. Our hope in the way of nonviolence is indeed the way out of our madness:

> Since we have been justified by faith, we have peace with God through our Lord Jesus Christ, through whom we have gained access by faith to this grace in which we stand, and we boast in hope of the glory of God. Not only that, but we even boast of our afflictions, knowing that affliction produces endurance, and endurance, proven character, and proven character, hope, and hope does not disappoint, because the love of God has been poured out into our hearts through the holy Spirit that has been given to us. For Christ, while we were still helpless, yet died at the appointed time for the ungodly. Indeed, only with difficulty does one die for a just person, though perhaps for a good person one might even find courage to die. But God proves God's love for us in that while we were still sinners Christ died for us. How much more then, since we are now justified by his blood, will we be saved through him from the wrath. Indeed, if, while we were enemies, we were reconciled to God through the death of God's Son, how much more, once reconciled, will we be saved by his life. Not only that, but we also boast of God through our Lord Jesus Christ, through whom we have now received reconciliation (Rom 5:1-11).

Paul concludes that "neither death, nor life, nor angels, nor principalities, nor present things, nor future things, nor powers, nor height, nor depth, nor any other creature will be able to separate us from the love of God in Christ Jesus our Lord" (Rom 8:38). Similarly, the book of Revelation, a testimony of nonviolent resistance to imperial violence, culminates in a vision of reconciliation, mercy and heavenly renewal:

> I saw a new heaven and a new earth. The former heaven and the former earth had passed away, and the sea was no more. I also saw the holy city, a new Jerusalem, coming down out of heaven from God, prepared as a bride adorned for her husband. I heard a loud voice from the throne saying, "Behold, God's dwelling is with the human race. God will dwell with them and they will be God's people and God will always be with them as their God. God will wipe every tear from their eyes and there shall be no more death or mourning, wailing or pain for the old order has passed away." The one who sat on the throne said, "Behold, I make all things new" (Rv 21:1-5).

I experienced this transforming, hopeful Spirit of nonviolence calling us to a new earth as I joined a dozen friends at dawn on October 12, 1992, the five-hundredth anniversary of Columbus's arrival in the Americas. We climbed the fences around the nuclear weapons storage centers at the Concord Naval Weapons Station near Concord, California. The Concord Naval Weapons Station ships weapons for war around the world (including one third of all the bombs dropped on Iraq during the Persian Gulf war) and stores hundreds of nuclear weapons. Carrying signs that read "From Columbus to Concord, 500 years of domination is enough!" and "We want 500 years of nonviolence," we climbed three eight-foot-tall, barbed-wire fences, walked through fields and finally approached the main nuclear weapons bunker. Suddenly, two tanks and several marines (with machine guns pointed at us) appeared at the bunker and told us to halt or they would "shoot to kill." With a large wooden cross we knelt in a circle and prayed for the transformation of humanity into God's reign of nonviolent love and justice. As we faced this center of death, which could literally spark the end of the world in a global firestorm of nuclear destruction, we offered ourselves to the God of peace to spark a spiritual explosion of nonviolent transformation which we hoped would result in the dismantling of all weapons at Concord and elsewhere and the shipment of food and medicine to all those in need around the world. In that moment of risky nonviolence, as we faced guns aimed at us by fellow human beings, I experienced hope that the God of nonviolence would indeed lead us all into a global transformation for peace. The hope of nonviolence, the hope of resurrection and transformation, I discovered, is given through the action of nonviolence. As more and more of us choose to experiment with God in this way of nonviolence, God indeed will reign on earth as God reigns in heaven.

This same experience of hope was felt by the Plowshares Eight as they hammered on unarmed nuclear nosecones at the General Electric Plant in King of Prussia, Pennsylvania, on September 9, 1980. "In confronting General Electric," their statement read, "we choose to obey God's law of life, rather than a corporate summons to death. Our beating of swords into plowshares is a way to enflesh this biblical call. In our action, we draw on a deep-rooted faith in Christ, who changed the course of history through his willingness to suffer rather than to kill. We are filled with hope for our world and for our children as we join this act of resistance."[13] "For us, the deepest meaning of this act surpasses all ideologies and tactics," Daniel Berrigan told a gathering of Jesuits later. "The meaning also surpasses the plenary punishment meted out to us. Simply, we wanted to taste the Resurrection. We wanted to test the Resurrection in our bones, to see if we might live in hope, instead of in the 'silva oscura' of nuclear despair. May I say we have not been disappointed."[14]

In this nonviolent activity practitioners of Christian nonviolence experience hope and taste the resurrection. We glimpse the nonviolent coming of God, the reign of God in our midst. The church calls the fulfillment of this reign a reconciled "communion of saints" that rests in a "beatific vision" with God. Martin Luther King, Jr., spoke of this communion as the beloved community of humanity, finally reconciled, at one in the nonviolent love of God, where we live eternally at one with each other, Christ and God. Daniel Berrigan wrote of that day of reconciliation as the coming together of all humanity around the Lord. His poem concludes with an image of the poor, the prisoners and the martyrs—those practitioners of gospel nonviolence—taking center stage before the reconciling God:

> The prisoners for justice's sake   the martyrs   the naysayers
> the intractable ones   the irreformable   unrehabilitatable ones
> those who under every sun   every political flag   every spasm
>   of crowds of jut-jawed bemedaled monsters
> keep a kind of Last Day Cool
> an unswipeable smile
> a passionate distance
> from Blah and Blight and   The Next Hard Riding Messiah
>   Over the Hill
> Let us accord honor   let us make way for these   as they filed
>   toward the center
> where they truly belong
> in rags and stripes and newly struck chains . . .
> See!   after endless years
> sons   sisters   friends
> from exile delivered   from gulags   from kangaroo courts
> from torture   from unjust sentence
> from seizure of fortune   from Devil's Islands
> from Siberias   from tiger cages
> from interrogation centers   from ghettoes   reserves
> from colonels and shahs and juntas and sheriffs delivered
> from starvation delivered
> and above all   beyond all   miracle of all
> from death delivered!
> See now
> in the grey face   and skinny bones
> and silence long as the spool of the fates—
> here the human venture vindicated!
> Here the philosopher's stone and
> Lost Atlantis and   Shangri-la and
> modest utopia!
> They near
> The Lord looks up   the multitude folds in   like living dough
> How long O Lord how long?   has been their plaint
> Now   This moment   His look   somber   self collected
>   the look of one who   endures   comes through (but
>   barely)—
> that look breaks the glacial will of God
> They embrace   one after another
> Tears   laughter   two weathers contending in one
>   sky.[15]

Daniel Berrigan
" The Discipline of The Mountain "

Eschatological nonviolence calls us to enact that moment of the Last Day, the first Day of Nonviolence, right now with all our lives in this world's systemic violence. "We live in both the time of the end—the time of nuclear weapons, mass starvation, global warming, and the hole in the ozone layer— *Douglass* and the time of the beginning, the time of God's coming in violence-transcending ways we could not have imagined only a short time before," Douglass concludes. Even "massive US intervention in the Middle East and Soviet repression in the Baltics can both be seen as desperate, last-ditch attempts to reassert a reign of violence that has been losing ground in the world to its alterative, a nonviolent transformation of humanity."[16]

In a world of violence and death our deepest human hope dreams for a world of nonviolence, peace and justice, a world without pain, hunger, injustice and death, a world where we can be ourselves with one another and with God in peace. The new "far-reaching interpretation of the content of hope as Jesus preached it," Monika Hellwig concludes, is nothing less than "the conversion of the world to the reign of God."[17] For such a hope to be realized, we need to sacrifice our lives in a nonviolent struggle for justice and peace. We have to imagine and choose that vision of hope and live in it now, so that one day it can become reality for all humanity. As we live into that hope and enflesh it with our very lives through an ongoing, active nonviolence, we will discover that our hope has become real. We will recognize that the nonviolent coming of God is arriving and will win everyone into a heaven of peace and love. We will realize the peaceful reign of God is at hand.

CHAPTER 10

An Anthropology of Nonviolence

The Human Family as a Community of Sisters and Brothers

On August 9, 1943, Franz Jägerstätter, an Austrian farmer, was beheaded in Berlin by the Nazi government for refusing to fight for Hitler's army. His refusal went against the wishes of his wife, three daughters, mother, pastor, bishop and friends. His decision and death were known only to his family, his small village, a few church people and Nazi officials. In the face of World War II and the Nazi war machine, his refusal to kill made little difference. Indeed, he died unknown, not seeing any fruit from his conscientious faith. But faith held the key to life for Franz Jägerstätter. He intended to obey the God of nonviolence, come what may. He placed all his trust in God and went to his death in peace. Now, over fifty years later, his story is told around the world and some recognize him as one of the great saints and martyrs of the century.

The poet Edna St. Vincent Millay once wrote, "I shall die but that is all I shall do for death." Jägerstätter gave his life refusing to take the lives of others. Like Gandhi, he came to the conclusion that noncooperation with evil is as much a duty as cooperation with good. "As a Christian," Jägerstätter wrote, "I prefer to do my fighting with the Word of God and not with arms." On another occasion he wrote, "I am convinced that it is still best that I speak the truth even though it costs me my life." "It is still possible for us, even today, to lift ourselves, with God's help, out of the mire in which we are stuck and win eternal happiness—if only we make a sincere effort and bring all our strength to the task. It is never too late to save ourselves and perhaps some other soul for Christ."[1]

To refuse to be violent, to kill and to participate in war in today's world of total violence stands out as an extraordinary, superhuman achievement. In a world of peace such a decision would be quite normal. Franz Jägerstätter, by all accounts, was an ordinary individual who possessed a steadfast determination to follow the nonviolent Jesus. As we look back on the age of the Nazi holocaust and the atomic bombings of Japan, his example models what

98

human life should be about. Each and every human being can refuse to kill and participate in war. As Jägerstätter wrote and testified with his life, every human being is called to such a refusal, to the life of nonviolence.

The witness of Franz Jägerstätter gets lost easily in today's world of massive violence. Nonetheless, it forces basic questions about human existence: What does it mean to be a human being in a world of violence and systemic injustice? What does a full human life mean in a world where so many kill and support systemic violence? In a world of anti-human violence, the nonviolence of Franz Jägerstätter stands as an example of what it means to be human. A theology of nonviolence explores the image of the human as a peacemaker, a person of nonviolence, revealed ultimately in the peacemaking humanity of Jesus.

An Anthropology of Nonviolence

Anthropology studies the human. It explores human life. It notes that we humans are free, intelligent and ultimately loving, even to the point of sacrificing our lives for others. As we introduce nonviolence into the field of anthropology, we recognize that human beings are created in community to love one another and God; thus they are created, within the framework of God's nonviolence, to be nonviolent toward one another. Nonviolence challenges traditional anthropology to uphold the vision of the human being as a person of nonviolence.

All humans are created in God's image, in body and spirit according to the God of nonviolence. An anthropology rooted in nonviolence may sound redundant, but given the violence of our world, it is necessary to state the obvious in such terms. An anthropology of nonviolence observes that human beings are created as the fulfillment of God's creative nonviolence. We are created as sisters and brothers, as God's own children, to love and serve God in each other in this life and for an eternity of peace.

In the light of nonviolence we see more clearly that humans are not created to dominate and kill one another but to serve and love one another. Though they are each unique and personal, humans are not created to live selfishly at the expense of others. Rather, humans are created in interdependence—to depend on God and one another in a never-ending circle of nonviolent love. We are created as a global community. With the God of nonviolence as our loving Parent, human beings are called to live together as a family where every single person in the world is our sister and brother, each a unique and beloved child of our nonviolent God. Together we are called to practice nonviolence, justice and peace toward one another. In this vision of a nonviolent humanity the weapons in our hands and the violence in our hearts fall aside. We pledge never to hurt and kill one another again, but to dedicate our lives in loving service for all humanity. Indeed, in this vision of a nonviolent humanity, we become who we already are; we fulfill our calling to be children of the God of nonviolence.

Human beings are created in the image of God. A theology of nonviolence holds that God is a God of nonviolence. Human beings, therefore, are created to be a people of nonviolence, children of the God of nonviolence. We are made for this God and, thus, for each other. Modelled after the peacemaking community of the triune God, we are made to live in the beloved and eternal community of nonviolence, in this life and into the next. When we commit acts of violence and actively support the institutionalized violence of our world, we divide the human family and fall short of the people we are called to be. In violence we fail to live up to our ordinary vocation to be human, that is, to be nonviolent. We are not called to dominate over others, to hurt or kill others, or to spend our lives making money at the expense of the starving masses; rather, we are invited to be human beings, to be a people of nonviolence who love and serve each other with all our hearts.

An anthropology of nonviolence, then, notes three basic points: 1) for a variety of psychological, sociological and historical reasons, humanity left to itself remains addicted to violence; 2) the gospel calls us to renounce that violence and to love one another; and 3) the grace of God heals, perfects and elevates human beings to live nonviolently, to become more human than if we were left to ourselves. As we discussed, the sin of violence breaks our relationship of nonviolent love with God and one another. When we sin, we fall short of our human potential; we become less than human. But God gives us grace to enable us to overcome sin, to become a people of nonviolence. We can choose to be the human beings we were created to be, indeed, the human beings we already are, if we simply cooperate with the grace of our nonviolent God in this ongoing transformation of love. To be fully human, then, to cooperate with the grace of God, requires a radical commitment, a wholehearted determination to live the way of nonviolence. As we cooperate with God, we discover not only that we can live with peace inside ourselves and at peace with one another and even become instruments of God's peace, but also that we are being led on a journey into God's own realm of peace. Death becomes then a deeper entrance into the reign of nonviolence, where the God of peace is known face to face by all humanity.

Jesus Christ, Model of the Nonviolent Human Being

Given our worldwide violence, most people, especially in North America, have concluded that it is impossible to become nonviolent, that we might as well not even bother. Cultural violence naturally leads to such rock-bottom despair. The spirit of violence tells us that we have no other alternative; it insists that violence is our very nature.

The God of nonviolence tells us otherwise. In the life of Jesus, God invites us to become the people we can be. Anyone can practice nonviolence; everyone is called to practice nonviolence. God would not have invited us to this life of peacemaking if it were impossible. The church, unfortunately, has often taught the ideal but at the same time insisted that the ideal is impossible to live and gone on to present an "interim ethic" of justified violence. But as Jesus revealed, God never calls us to violence. Over the centuries the church has done a great disservice to God and humanity by blessing violence and warfare. The gospel is much stronger. It insists that nonviolence is not just an option, it is a commandment. We are commanded by Jesus to practice nonviolence. Humanity is charged with the grace of God; our sin is the conscious choice not to act in the grace of nonviolence. Given our violence, we need to ask the God of nonviolence for the grace to become like God, to renounce our violence and join faith communities of nonviolence to help us live lives of active love. God has promised that the grace is ours for the asking.

Nonviolence is possible for every human being, for every violent person, if we but turn to God and ask for grace. To be fully human means to open up our hearts to the grace of God, to allow God to disarm our hearts, to transform our hearts and souls into instruments and channels of God's nonviolent love.

History is filled with people who learned God's way of nonviolence. From Gandhi and Dorothy Day, Martin Luther King, Jr., and Jean Donovan, to Wang Weilin (the Chinese student who stood before a column of tanks near Tiananmen Square in June 1989) and the thousands of Filipinos, Russians and Lithuanians who nonviolently resisted tyranny, our age is brimming with noble practitioners of nonviolence. They model what it means to be human in today's world.

These peacemaking people point us back to the peacemaking Christ. Jesus presents the fullest image of what it means to be human because he lived and taught nonviolence to the fullest. He models the God of nonviolence. He shows us what it means to be human in his nonviolence, that is, his love, compassion, mercy, truth-telling and nonviolent resistance to evil. He leads us in hope and fidelity to the God of peace.

Jesus is the model human being because he is nonviolent. He is just, faithful and unconditionally loving. He loves enemies; serves people; tells truth; builds community; prays to the God of peace; and risks his life in active nonviolence, even to arrest, torture and execution. Because of this steadfast nonviolence, God raises Jesus from the dead to uphold his life for all humanity to emulate.

Violence so dominates our world that it has corrupted our image of God. We have created God into our own image—into a god of violence who waits to destroy us all in an explosion of anger and violence. The reverse side of this perversion is our own desire for (violent) power—the desire to be God. In this mad attempt to be superhuman, to be divine, we assert our egos over one another and our national ego over other nations. We seek to become God when we are invited merely to be human.

The great irony of this error is that while we seek to be God, God desires to become human. In Jesus, God fulfills this desire and demonstrates to us how to be human. God becomes one of us and lives humanly. As Walter Wink explains:

> The essence of sin is the desire to be God, which is in effect
> to enter into mimetic rivalry with God . . . We are meant to
> imitate God . . . but sin enters when imitation turns to envy and

God becomes the ultimate rival. Desire thus transforms God into an idol on whom human beings not only project their own violence and hatred, but whom they also depict to themselves as the sanctifier of the violence at the heart of all religious systems. To desire to usurp the place of God inevitably leads a person to create God after the image of a jealous rival, and fosters an unconscious death wish against God. The human desire to be God is countered by the divine desire to become human. God reveals the divine weakness on the cross, leaving the soul no omnipotent rival to envy, and thus cutting the nerve of mimetic desire . . . Jesus absorbed all the violence directed at him by people and by the Powers and still loved them. But if humanity killed the one who fully embodied God's intention for our lives, and God still loves us, then there is no need to try to earn God's love. And if God loves us unconditionally, there is no need to seek conditional love from the Powers who promise us rewards in return for devotion. When the early Christians proclaimed that "there is salvation in no one else" (Acts 4:12), this should be taken as literally true: only through Jesus is the scapegoat mechanism exposed and the spiral of violence broken. "Salvation" here is an anthropological, not a theological term. It simply states a fact about human survival in the face of human violence . . . The problem is that, once the gospel has deprived a society of the scapegoating mechanism, that society is defenseless against the very violence in which it trusts. For us today, the only alternative to love and nonviolence is apocalypse. And it is not a vengeful God who ushers in apocalypse, but ourselves. The "wrath" or judgment of God is precisely God's "giving us up" to the consequences of our own violence (Rom 1:18-32). It is now a race between the gospel and the effects of the gospel: either we learn to stop mimetic violence and scapegoating, or having been stripped of the scapegoating mechanism as an outlet for our violence, we will consume ourselves in an apocalypse of fire. In a world of nuclear weapons, even more urgently than in that of the Roman empire, scapegoating must be exposed and eradicated, or we will destroy ourselves.[2]

In Jesus, we see "God in trouble for being human," as Daniel Berrigan writes. It is precisely God's humanity—God's nonviolence—that gets God into trouble. Jesus is executed by the empire for his nonviolent resistance to evil, for his love for his fellow humans.

"The only vocation to which a Christian is called," William Stringfellow observed, "is to be a mature human being."[3] An anthropology of nonviolence asks, in light of today's global violence, What does it mean to be a human being? It concludes that a human being is a person of nonviolence, a peacemaker in a world of war, a seeker of justice in a world of injustice, a channel of compassion in a world of apathy. A mature human being worships the God of nonviolence by living at peace with every other human being. It asks: What does it mean to be alive in the nuclear age? In light of the peacemaking Jesus, an anthropology of nonviolence answers that a full human life worships the God of life and gives over its own life so that all humanity may live in peace with justice without the threat of violence. To be human is to be nonviolent.

CHAPTER 11

An Ecclesiology of Nonviolence

The Church as a Community of Peacemakers

In the middle of brutal military repression and revolutionary violence on the island of Negros in the Philippines, a small group of church people declared their rural village, Cantomanyog, a zone of peace. Following the guidelines of nonviolence, they announced, one day during a Mass for peace, that no weapons would be allowed in their village.

In the summer of 1990, representing Pax Christi USA, the national Catholic peace movement, a friend and I traveled to that zone of peace and met the courageous Christians who had dedicated themselves to the nonviolent Jesus and thus risked their lives for peace. The high point of the visit occurred one evening when we joined one of the base Christian communities for prayer and bible study. We met in the two-room, bamboo hut of a pregnant mother of seven children. Though she and her children, like all the local people, were suffering from malnutrition, they served a fish that they had caught in our honor. Their hut was located right in the middle of a war zone, several hundred yards from a rebel stronghold on one side and several hundred yards from a government military fortress on the other side. We listened to the gospel of John and shared our reflections on the biblical call to love. During our faith-sharing, a group of armed guerrillas passed through and questioned us. Thirty minutes later, Filipino soldiers carrying US-made weapons also disrupted the meeting, questioned us, and eventually left.

I was impressed by the community's simple witness to gospel nonviolence. Afterward, the community of twenty people broke into song. "We are the church, we are the church," they sang. "We are the community of peace and love." As I listened to these suffering, starving, third-world peasants (most of them women), victims of military repression and revolutionary violence, and watched their ongoing witness to the nonviolent Christ, it occurred to me that indeed they are the church, for they are a community of peace and love. They are the heart of the church—the poor of the world, gathered in Christian community, proclaiming the nonviolence of Christ with their very lives. They model to the entire world what Jesus and the early Christian communi-

104

ties were all about: loving and serving one another in the Spirit of nonviolence that says no to imperial and revolutionary death and relies on God alone for justice and peace.

Throughout the world similar base communities of the poor and marginalized gather regularly to pray and reflect on the gospel call to make peace and follow Jesus. These communities comprise the church at its best—a community of disciples and peacemakers struggling to proclaim God's nonviolent reign of justice and peace in today's world. Meanwhile, many institutional church leaders continue to justify war and bless powerful regimes that oppress and dominate people around the world.

Ecclesiology is the study of the church, the theological self-understanding of the Christian community. In a world of total violence an ecclesiology of nonviolence asks: What does it mean to be church? What does it mean to be gathered in community as followers of Jesus? How would the church as a community of nonviolence look? A theology of nonviolence envisions the church as just such a community, as a community of peacemakers.

From a Church of Martyrs to an Imperial Church

In the first three centuries the church consisted of a loose collection of communities centered around the risen Jesus, united in the Spirit of nonviolent love and determined to resist the violence of imperial Rome. The early church was pacifist and, thus, became a church of martyrs.[1] Thousands of Christians were publicly killed for not worshipping the emperor or killing for him."The nonviolent resistance offered by thousand of Christians to Roman society . . . showed faithfulness to Christ's command to love one's enemies," church historian Ronald Musto writes. The thousands of Christians who were martyred for their adherence to Jesus manifested "the ideal of nonviolence." "The history of the early church demonstrates the principles of active peacemaking," Musto concludes.[2]

With the conversion of Emperor Constantine to Christianity in 312, the church was coopted by imperial Rome and, over time, abandoned gospel nonviolence and took up imperial warmaking. By the Middle Ages, it openly waged war in the name of Jesus. Though pockets of peacemaking Christian communities survived through the centuries (from monastic communities to the later Society of Friends and the Mennonites), the church has continued to support warfare and systemic violence down to the present day. "I rebel against orthodox Christianity, as I am convinced that it has distorted the message of Jesus," Gandhi once commented about the institutional church. "Jesus was an Asiatic whose message was delivered through many media and when it had the backing of the Roman emperor, it became an imperialist faith as it remains to this day."[3]

"The only people on earth who do not see Christ and his teachings as nonviolent are Christians," Gandhi observed.[4] Theologian Walter Wink explains what happened:

This is what I what unveils [handwritten marginalia]

When the church that had stood up nonviolently to the brutal repression of the Roman Empire found itself strangely victorious, it naively assumed the role of court chaplain to an empire eager for its support. It is as if Satan, unable to defeat the church by violence, surrendered to the church and became its ward. The price the church paid, however, was embracing violence as the means of preserving empire. But the removal of nonviolence from the gospel blasted the keystone from the arch, and Christianity collapsed into a religion of personal salvation in an afterlife jealously guarded by a wrathful and terrifying God—the whole system carefully managed by an elite corps of priests with direct backing from the secular rulers now regarded as the elect agents of God's working in history.[5]

Emperor Constantine assumed control of the Christian community, organized the Council of Nicaea (in 325), reimaged Jesus as Christ the King and Emperor, and restructured the grassroots Jesus movement into an imperial institution that supported warfare. In the year 303 Emperor Diocletian had forbidden any member of the Roman army to be Christian; by the year 416, no one could be a member of the Roman army unless he was a Christian.[6] Modelling itself on imperial Rome, institutional church leaders developed over the centuries what has become a nation-state (Vatican City) that holds diplomatic relations with other nations. They created an emperor (the pope), who was God's representative on earth; formed an army; set up an imperial system of representatives around the world (cardinals, archbishops, and priests, comprised primarily of white men); and eventually codified a legal system (canon law). Leonardo Boff comments:

> The important thing about the church of the first three generations was not its institutional character. Unity was guaranteed by the commonality of faith and by the courage of public martyrs, and not by institutional structures . . . The situation changed radically with the conversion of Constantine. From an illicit religion, Christianity became both the official religion and the sacred ideology of the empire . . . It took on great power, with all of the risks that such power implies . . . When the leaders of the empire joined the church, a paganization of Christianity took place, and not a christianization of paganism. The church, which until A.D. 312 was more of a movement than an institution, became an heir of the empire's institutions: law, organization by diocese and parish, bureaucratic centralization, positions, and titles. The church-institution accepted political realities and assumed inexorable uniformity. It began on a path of power that continues today and that we must hasten to end. The key category for understanding the church is in terms of power. The church understands itself primarily as the community invested with power

|| [handwritten marginalia]

(the hierarchy) together with the community deprived of power (the People of God, the laity). This church sees power as the greatest way in which the Gospel will be accepted, understood, and proclaimed. Christ becomes the emperor, the cosmic Lord, and not the Suffering Servant who confronted the powers of this world (including the empire of which the pope is now heir), not the Jesus who decidedly renounced all earthly power and glory.[7]

The Church's Need for Conversion to Nonviolence

Today, despite the teachings of Jesus, the communal vision of Paul, the history of the early community and the growing base community movement around the world, many institutional church leaders cling to the church as the hierarchical structure itself. In their model of church as institution, grace trickles down from top to bottom. That institutional, imperial church still justifies warfare and blesses the violence that tears apart the human community. "The church-institution functions as if it were a giant multinational corporation," Boff writes. "The headquarters where all ideological and tactical decisions are made is located in Rome with the pope and the curia. Dioceses, for all practical purposes, are branches located throughout the world. A relationship of dependence is established between the curia and the periphery on theological, pastoral, liturgical, juridical, and all other levels."[8]

The institutional church is more interested in its own survival than in giving its communal life for justice for the poor and for liberation of the oppressed. During the Nazi reign of terror the church did not speak out and act prophetically because of the danger of its being eliminated. Though millions of Jews and non-Jews were being exterminated, the institutional church preferred survival and remained silent, and thus became a participant in systemic violence. As Boff observes:

> There is a great difference between the church of the first three centuries and the later church which rose to power. The primitive church was prophetic; it joyfully suffered torture and courageously gave its life through martyrdom. It did not care about survival because it believed in the Lord's promise that guaranteed it would not fail. Success or failure, survival or extinction, was not a problem for the church; it was a problem for God. The bishops were at the forefront, convincing their brothers and sisters to die for the Lord. The later church was opportunistic; that it would not fail was a question of prudence and compromise that allowed it to survive in the midst of totalitarian regimes, at the expense of gospel demands. The bishop in this later church does not freely walk in witness to his death; rather, he pushes others, walking behind his flock and often as-

[handwritten margin note: Is this a proven fact?]

sisting in the death of its prophets, fearful and reticent, calling
for fidelity not to Christ but to the institutional church. Such practices of power in the church, generating ecclesial marginality,
tenuous and lifeless communication between its members, as well
as religious and evangelical underdevelopment, result in the image of a church almost neurotically preoccupied with itself and,
as such, lacking a real interest in the major problems facing humanity.[9]

"It is strange to see that the church institution has developed into exactly that
which Christ did not want it to be," Boff continues.[10]

Instead of modelling itself on imperial Rome, the church needs to be transformed into a community of nonviolence, where its spokespeople, animators
and facilitators immediately insert themselves in the world's violence in order to stop wars, end hunger and transform oppression. The hierarchical vision
of the church does not resonate with gospel nonviolence; indeed, for the poor,
for women, for the people of God, it often functions as institutionalized, systemic violence and models the oppressive structures Jesus called us to oppose
and transform. The church is not supposed to be dominating, powerful or
hierarchal. As the Second Vatican Council suggested, the church is the graced
people of God dependent on the Spirit of Jesus for guidance. When it focuses
on itself *as hierarchy*, and not on the nonviolent Jesus and the gospel mandate
to make peace in a world of war and injustice, it loses the Spirit of God and
disintegrates into another oppressive institution. It falls prey to the tempta-
tions of power, domination, wealth and imperial warmaking. Instead of being
a grassroots movement of practitioners of nonviolent resistance (like Jesus),
it becomes an imperial structure with no life in it. As the institutional church
today focuses on sex and ceremony instead of discipleship and the hard work
of peacemaking, it drifts farther apart from the life of Jesus and loses its integrity.

The church cannot authentically address the world's structures of violence
and advocate gospel nonviolence when it does not practice what it preaches.
The church needs to be converted into a community made up of communities
of nonviolence, where women and men share equally all the ministries of
service to humanity. The church needs to listen again to the words of the
nonviolent Jesus, who speaks directly to us today: "You know how those who
rule the nations exercise tyranny over them and they practice violence against
them. This is not to be among you: on the contrary, if one of you wishes to be
great, he or she must be your servant; and he or she who desires to be first
among you must serve all; because the [Human One] did not come to be served
but to serve and give his life for the redemption of many" (Mk 10:42-44; Lk
22:25-27). Today's church needs to become a church of the poor, a church of
nonviolent resistance to systemic violence, a church of peacemakers. This
church is called to oppose the world's violence, not to be coopted by it, not
to be involved in it, not to remain silent in the face of it, even if that means
its leaders will be martyred. It has to recall that its leader, Jesus, was martyred

for his nonviolent resistance to systemic violence. It has to become a freelance, global, grassroots movement of resisting communities, whose members risk their lives for God's nonviolent reign of peace with justice.

The church is much more than a set of buildings, a hierarchical structure with its ordained ministries. A theology of nonviolence holds that the church is a community made up of communities of active nonviolence. Indeed, renewed commitment to gospel nonviolence will lead us beyond power, domination, triumphalism, hierarchy and clericalism. The church will have to renounce its sexism, patriarchy, racism, elitism, oppression and sanctioning of war. Because the world's violence has led us to the brink of global annihilation, church people around the world, such as the base community Christians in Cantomanyog, are beginning to return to the gospel vision of church as community of peacemakers. The center of the church, from the perspective of the nonviolent Jesus, is among the poor who resist systemic violence through active nonviolence. Jesus is risen, not in those who cultivate power and domination in Christ's name, but in those who risk their lives for his gospel of peace. The church is the community of peacemakers, a community of people who put into practice the nonviolence of Jesus. Those who reveal Christ's peace and justice are the church. They illustrate what it means to be human in a world of inhuman violence. In a world of war the church gathers in the name of Jesus to witness to Christ's peace, to the gospel way of nonviolence, to reconcile humanity. Nonviolence challenges the church to be transformed by the nonviolent Jesus from an organization that supports war and systemic injustice to a peacemaking community of disciples. It invites all those who are baptized to embrace the nonviolence of Jesus, to refuse to hurt or kill others, and to spend their lives in loving service of humanity and nonviolent resistance to systemic violence. It suggests that whenever the church supports violence, it betrays the gospel and turns against the God of nonviolence.

The church is broader than any small local community and yet, at the same time, each local community is the fullest representation of the church. Through gospel nonviolence all Christians are united in love and solidarity with each other; thus, because there is no more rivalry, hostility, or enmity between Christians around the world (who should refuse to kill each other if they are true to their faith), the church unites us all. When Christians adopt nonviolence, as Jesus called us to, then our first act should be to refuse to kill or oppress one another. We should begin to love our enemies and refuse to kill them.

The church is called to model the redeemed human community. Its structures by definition need to be nonviolent, open, inclusive and liberating. It remains a community of sinful people who commit violence, but through the grace of the Holy Spirit it strives to practice the way of active nonviolence. The church has been missioned to prophetic nonviolence to transform the violent status quo into a haven of justice and peace.

To be truly catholic or universal, the church needs to embrace nonviolence. Pluralism can only thrive through nonviolence. Active nonviolence permits us to be free with each other, to disagree and to find the truth in every human being—but precisely without recourse to violence or oppression. A nonviolent, catholic, Christian community actively opposes killing and oppression. By doing so we become an image of nonviolent humanity, loving each other, at peace with each other, and dedicated to selfless service. In this way the church reflects the coming nonviolent reign of God.

A New Ecclesiology: Church as Community of Peacemakers

The Second Vatican Council spoke of the church as a mystery, as the body of Christ, as the people of God, as hierarchy, as laity, as holy, as religious and as a pilgrim community, indeed, as the sacrament of Christ on earth. In *Models of the Church* Avery Dulles upheld different models to help us reflect on the church. The church, he wrote, is generally understood in six different ways. First, some define it simply as an institution, as a hierarchical structure, a definition which has little biblical basis and was criticized by Christ. Second, others discern it as a mystical communion, as Paul's image of body of Christ, which can lead to a divinization of the church. Third, still others interpret the church as a sacrament, as a symbol of grace, which does not invite service. Fourth, many envision the church as a servant, a notion which fits well within the John 13 image of communal service. Fifth, many others assume that the church is a herald, a prophetic voice proclaiming the gospel to an unbelieving world. Finally, Dulles offers a last image of the church as simply a community of disciples.[11] Our theology of nonviolence sees the church as a community of peacemakers and nonviolent resisters, transforming the world's systemic violence into a realm of God's peace. The network of base communities in the Third World and the pockets of nonviolent resisting communities in the First World make up the Christian community as it seeks to liberate both oppressors and oppressed.

The church is not the center of salvation; it is a sign of God's reign coming among humanity. The church is called to transform its use of power from domination to the empowerment of others, especially the poor, and thus, to announce God's reign. "The church began on a path of power that continues today and that we must hasten to end," Leonardo Boff writes.[12] "The church cannot be indifferent to the justice or injustice of a cause nor can it be silent in the face of the obvious exploitation of people."[13] "Because of the church's ideals and origins (the dangerous and subversive memory of Jesus of Nazareth crucified under Pontius Pilate), its mission is revolutionary."[14]

"Peacemaking is not an optional commitment," the US Catholic bishops wrote in 1983. "We are called to be peacemakers, not by some movement of the moment, but by our Lord Jesus. The content and context of our peacemaking is set, not by some political agenda or ideological program, but by the teaching of his church."[15] The church is called to be a community of peacemakers who follow the active, nonviolent spirit of Jesus, moving us to risk our lives in nonviolent transformation of the world's violence into God's reign of justice and peace. To become a church of nonviolence we need to renounce our violence and our complicity with systemic injustice. At some point we will have to abandon the just war theory (as we shall discuss in chapter 15), seek full inclusion of women into all church ministries (as we shall discuss in chapter 16) and accompany the poor and oppressed of the earth. A North American church of nonviolence can be glimpsed in those Christians who live and work with the poor and speak out and act for justice and peace in the name of Christ. The Catholic Worker movement and the Plowshares movement pose two such images of the church of the future, a community of nonviolence.

In the lives of great peacemakers such as Martin Luther King, Jr., we see the rebirth of this church of nonviolence. On Good Friday 1963, Martin Luther King, Jr., was arrested in Birmingham, Alabama, for demanding racial justice. From his jail cell King wrote a historic essay on nonviolence and justice. In this "Letter from a Birmingham Jail" King responded to a group of white clergy who had publicly criticized him for disrupting Birmingham. In his long meditation he named his disappointment as well as his hope in the church. Between the "do-nothingism" of the complacent on the one hand, and the violent "hatred and despair of the black nationalist movement" on the other hand, King wrote, there is the "more excellent way of love and nonviolent protest. I'm grateful to God," he continued, "that, through the Black church, the dimension of nonviolence entered our struggle."[16] But, King confessed, he was greatly disappointed with the church—especially the white church leadership:

> I do not say that as one of the negative critics who can always find something wrong with the church. I say it as a minister of the gospel who loves the church . . . I had the strange feeling when I was suddenly catapulted into the leadership of the bus protest in Montgomery several years ago that we would have the support of the white church. I felt that the white ministers, priests and rabbis of the South would be some of our strongest allies. Instead, some have been outright opponents, refusing to understand the freedom movement and misrepresenting its leaders; all too many others have been more cautious than courageous and have remained silent behind the anesthetizing security of the stained-glass windows. In spite of my shattered dreams of the past, I came to Birmingham with the hope that the white religious leadership of this community would see the justice of our cause, and with deep moral concern, serve as the channel through which our just grievances would get to the power structure . . . But again I have been disappointed. I have heard numerous religious leaders of the South call upon their worshippers to comply with a desegregation decision because it is the law, but I have longed to hear white ministers say, "Follow this decree because integration is morally right and the black person is your brother and sister." In the midst of blatant injustices inflicted upon blacks,

I have watched white churches stand on the sideline and merely mouth pious irrelevancies and sanctimonious trivialities. In the midst of a mighty struggle to rid our nation of racial and economic injustice, I have heard so many ministers say, "Those are social issues with which the gospel has no real concern," and I have watched so many churches commit themselves to a completely otherworldly religion which made a strange distinction between body and soul, the sacred and the secular. So here we are moving toward the exit of the twentieth century with a religious community largely adjusted to the status quo, standing as a taillight behind other community agencies rather than a headlight leading men and women to higher levels of justice . . . In deep disappointment, I have wept over the laxity of the church. But be assured that my tears have been tears of love. There can be no deep disappointment where there is not deep love . . . Yes, I love the church . . . Yes I see the church as the body of Christ. But, oh! How we have blemished and scarred that body through social neglect and fear of being nonconformists.[17]

King went on to reflect the misdirected change that the church has taken in history, from a community of martyrs to a church that blesses the unjust status quo, and he pondered the critical transformation that it needs to undergo if it is to be faithful to the God of justice and peace:

There was a time when the church was very powerful. It was during that period when the early Christians rejoiced when they were deemed worthy to suffer for what they believed. In those days the church was not merely a thermometer that recorded the ideas and principles of popular opinion; it was a thermostat that transformed the mores of society. Whenever the early Christians entered a town the power structure got disturbed and immediately sought to convict them for being "disturbers of the peace" and "outside agitators." But they went on with the conviction that they were a "colony of heaven," and had to obey God rather than people. They were small in number but big in commitment. They were too God-intoxicated to be "astronomically intimidated." They brought an end to such ancient evils as infanticide and gladiatorial contest. Things are different now. The contemporary church is often a weak, ineffectual voice with an uncertain sound. It is so often the arch-supporter of the status quo. Far from being disturbed by the presence of the church, the power structure of the average community is consoled by the church's silent and often vocal sanction of things as they are. But the judgment of God is upon the church as never before. If the church of today does not recapture the sacrificial spirit of the early church, it will lose its authentic ring, forfeit the loyalty of mil-

> lions, and be dismissed as an irrelevant social club with no meaning for the twentieth century . . . Is organized religion too inextricably bound to the status quo to save our nation and the world? Maybe I must turn my faith to the inner spiritual church, the church within the church, as the true *ecclesia* and the hope of the world.[18]

In the same challenging Spirit, Archbishop Oscar Romero understood the prophetic, peacemaking mission of the church. "An accommodating church, a church that seeks prestige without the pain of the cross is not the authentic church of Jesus Christ."[19] "The church's good name is not a matter of being on good terms with the powerful. The church's good name is a matter of knowing that the poor regard the church as their own, of knowing that the church's life on earth is to call on all, on the rich as well, to be converted and be saved alongside the poor, for they are the only ones called blessed."[20] "The church, in its zeal to convert to the gospel, is seeing that its place is by the side of the poor, of the outraged, of the rejected, and that in their name it must speak and demand their rights."[21] "The church could not be the ally of the Roman Empire or of Herod or of any king on earth or of any political system or of any human political strategy."[22] "This is the mission entrusted to the church, a hard mission: to uproot sins from history, to uproot sins from the political order, to uproot sins from the economy, to uproot sins wherever they are. What a hard task! . . . The church must suffer for speaking the truth, for pointing out sin, for uprooting sin."[23]

Romero came to understand that the task of the Christian is to be a peacemaker. He sought a new kind of church and, with his life and death, gave birth to the possibility of such a new church. "The church cannot agree with the forces that put their hope only in violence."[24] "The church does not choose the ways of violence . . . The church's option is for what Christ says in the Beatitudes."[25] "The only violence that the gospel admits is violence to oneself. When Christ lets himself be killed, that is violence—letting oneself be killed. Violence to oneself is more effective than violence to others. It is very easy to kill, especially when one has weapons, but how hard it is to let oneself be killed for love of the people."[26] "I will not tire of declaring that if we really want an effective end to violence, we must remove the violence that lies at the root of all violence: structural violence, social injustice, exclusion of citizens from the management of the country, repression."[27]

Nearly ten years after his assassination, after tens of thousands of Salvadorans had died, six Jesuits along with the two women co-workers were massacred for the same peacemaking effort. In offering their lives in the struggle for peace and justice, they, like Romero, combatted the old warmaking church and the image of God as a warmaker. Afterward, one soldier confessed that a few minutes before the massacre took place, at midnight on November 16, 1989, the Salvadoran military commanders, US military advisors and soldiers (possibly with the Salvadoran president present) gathered at the military headquarters and prayed "to do God's will and to save the

*"violence" against the self has to be explained. There is: (1) the Gospel's "the violent bear [the K of G] away, and (2) masochism.

faith." They misunderstood that God never wills killing or injustice; they did not understand that faith in God calls for nonviolence, because God is a God of nonviolence and justice.

"The church has a vocation for nonviolence," Walter Wink writes. "That vocation is grounded in the teaching of Jesus, the nature of God, the ethos of the kingdom and the power of the resurrection."

> The church is called to nonviolence not in order to preserve its purity, but to express its fidelity. It is not a law but a gift . . . Those who today renounce the kingdom of death do so not because they are trying to please a deity who demands obedience, but because they have committed themselves to the realm of life. They refrain from killing, not because they are ordered to, but because they recognize something of God in everyone, and realize that what we do to the least of these—our enemies—we do to God. Nonviolence is not a matter of legalism but of discipleship. It is the way God has chosen to overthrow evil in the world. It is the praxis of God's system. Christians are to be nonviolent, not simply because it "works," but because it reflects the very nature of God (Mt 5:45; Lk 6:35).[28]

"Nonviolence is not a fringe concern," Wink concludes. "It is of the essence of the gospel. Therefore Jesus' nonviolent followers should not be called pacifists, but simply Christians."[29]

CHAPTER 12

Catholic Social Teaching and the Gospel of Peace

A New Attitude for a New Moment

Roman Catholic social teaching on justice and peace dates back over one hundred years. In the past thirty years this "new" tradition has opened the door to a theology of peace. A simple review of the church's social teachings on justice and peace may shed light on our theology of nonviolence. This new theology can learn from *Pacem in Terris*, the Second Vatican Council's stand on peace, recent social teachings, the US Catholic bishops' pastoral letter *The Challenge of Peace* and other recent statements on war and violence. With this background, we will be better able to examine how the church is moving beyond the age-old just war theory and back to the roots of gospel nonviolence.

Pacem in Terris: A Public Cry for Peace

A few months after the world came to the brink of nuclear warfare during the Cuban missile crisis, John XXIII issued the church's strongest plea for peace. His 1963 Easter tidings broke new ground immediately, because it was addressed "to all men and women of goodwill," not just the Christian community. The document took principles of traditional social doctrine, made them universal and rooted them in the gospel call for peace. *Pacem in Terris* suggests that peace is "founded on truth, built according to justice, vivified and integrated by charity, and put into practice in freedom" (no. 167). It declares that "every human is a person endowed with intelligence and free will, who has universal and inviolable rights and duties" (no. 9). Because of this foundation in human rights and justice, the peace proclaimed in *Pacem in Terris* questions all warfare and opens the door to a church of nonviolence:

> Justice, right reason and humanity urgently demand that the arms
> race should cease; that the stockpiles which exist in various coun-

115

tries should be reduced equally and simultaneously; that nuclear arms should be banned, and a general agreement reached for a progressive disarmament . . . All must realize that there is no hope of putting an end to the building up of armaments . . . unless everyone sincerely cooperates to banish the fear and anxious expectations of war with which men and women are oppressed.[1]

Pacem in Terris raised the questions of peace and disarmament before the whole world and invited humanity to reexamine its recourse to war. In doing so, it invited a theology of nonviolence consistent with its vision of peace with justice.

The Peacemaking Vision of *Gaudium et Spes*

Two years after *Pacem in Terris*, the Second Vatican Council took up the challenge of peace. The day before the Second Vatican Council was to address the threat of nuclear warfare, Pope Paul VI flew to New York City and issued a historic address at the United Nations calling for peace. "No more war! War never again!" he declared on October 4, 1965, the feast of Francis of Assisi. By speaking to the United Nations, the pope not only challenged the leaders of the world at the height of the Cold War, but he sent a strong message to the Council itself: he was serious about peace and, in particular, about the theme of the new document up for discussion, *Gaudium et Spes*. John XXIII's *Pacem in Terris* laid a momentous foundation for peace, and Paul VI wanted that groundwork taken seriously.

Gaudium et Spes ("The Pastoral Constitution on the Church in the Modern World"), ratified on December 7, 1965, issued a breathtaking new vision for the church. It threw wide the doors of the church, looked out on the world, affirmed humanity in its "joys and hopes, its griefs and anguishes," and called forth a new vision of love, human community and justice. It dealt with a plethora of topics: truth, conscience, freedom, death, atheism, the common good, the human person, social justice, solidarity, marriage, culture, economics, work and property. In particular, however, it issued the only condemnation of the Second Vatican Council, a condemnation of nuclear war.

Early on in *Gaudium et Spes*, Jesus' command to love enemies is restated as a foundational mandate. In its concluding chapter, "The Fostering of Peace and the Establishment of a Community of Nations," the challenge of peace is directly taken up. In its own words, the document "outlined the true and noble nature of peace, condemned the savagery of war, and earnestly exhorted Christians to cooperate with all in securing a peace based on justice and charity."[2]

The introduction to the concluding section on peace in *Gaudium et Spes* (no. 77) begins with praise for peacemakers and notes that these are critical times in human history. "In our generation, which has been marked by the persistent and acute hardships and anxiety resulting from the ravages of war and the threat of war, the whole human race faces a moment of supreme crisis in its advance toward maturity," the document declares. Then, peace is defined as "more than the absence of war."

> [Peace] cannot be reduced to the maintenance of a balance of power between opposing forces nor does it arise out of despotic dominion, but it is appropriately called the "effect of justice" (Is. 32:17). It is the fruit of that right ordering of things with which the divine founder has invested human society and which must be actualized by humanity thirsting after an ever more perfect reign of justice . . . Peace cannot be obtained on earth unless the welfare of humanity is safeguarded and people freely and trustingly share with one another the riches of their minds and their talents. A firm determination to respect the dignity of other peoples along with the deliberate practice of love are absolutely necessary for the achievement of peace. Accordingly, peace is also the fruit of love, for love goes beyond what justice can ensure (nos. 77-78).

"All Christians are earnestly to speak the truth in love (cf. Eph. 4:15)and join with all peace-loving men and women in pleading for peace and trying to bring it about," the document continues. Then those who act nonviolently in the tradition of Jesus are upheld as examples: "In the same spirit we cannot but express our admiration for all who forgo the use of violence to vindicate their rights and resort to those other means of defense which are available to weaker parties, provided it can be done without harm to the rights and duties of others and of the community."

Only by actively seeking peace and renouncing violence can Christians fulfill Isaiah's vision of people "beating their swords into plowshares," the Council declared:

> The savagery of war threatens to lead the combatants to barbarities far surpassing those of former ages . . . Any action which deliberately violates these principles [of natural law] and any order which commands such actions is criminal and blind obedience cannot excuse those who carry them out. The most infamous among these actions are those designed for the reasoned and methodical extermination of an entire race, nation, or ethnic minority. These must be condemned as frightful crimes; and we cannot commend too highly the courage of the men and women who openly and fearlessly resist those who issue orders of this kind (no. 80).

The Council upheld the right of conscientious objection, addressing the topic for the first time since the practice of conscientious objection was lauded during the age of the martyrs in the first three centuries: "Laws should make humane provision for the case of conscientious objectors who refuse to carry arms, provided they accept some other form of community service" (no. 80). The specifics of war were then analyzed:

> It is one thing to wage a war of self-defense; it is quite another to seek to impose domination on another nation. The possession of war potential does not justify the use of force for political or military objectives. Nor does the mere fact that war has unfortunately broken out mean that all is fair between the warring parties (no. 80).

The nuclear threat is then discussed in sober terms:

> The development of armaments by modern science has immeasurably magnified the horrors and wickedness of war. Warfare conducted with these weapons can inflict immense and indiscriminate havoc which goes far beyond the bounds of legitimate defense. Indeed if the kind of weapons now stocked in the arsenals of the great powers were to be employed to the fullest, the result would be the almost complete reciprocal slaughter of one side by the other, not to speak of the widespread devastation that would follow in the world and the deadly after-effects resulting from the use of such arms (no. 80).

With this specter of nuclear holocaust hanging over our heads, the Council made a modest but profound declaration: "All these factors force us to undertake an evaluation of war with an entirely new attitude." Then, the Council issued its only condemnation:

> People of this generation should realize that they will have to render an account of their warlike behavior; the destiny of generations to come depends largely on the decisions they make today. With these considerations in mind the Council, endorsing the condemnations of total warfare issued by recent popes, declares: Every act of war directed to the indiscriminate destruction of whole cities or vast areas with their inhabitants is a crime against God and humanity, which merits firm and unequivocal condemnation . . . [The arms race] is no infallible way of maintaining real peace and the resulting so-called balance of power is no sure and genuine path to achieving it. Rather than eliminate the causes of war, the arms race serves only to aggravate the position. As long as extravagant sums of money are poured into the development of new weapons, it is impossible to devote adequate aid in tackling the misery which prevails at the present day in the world. Instead of eradicating international conflict once and for all, the contagion is spreading to other parts of the world (nos. 80-81).

"Therefore," the document states in strong language, "we declare once again: the arms race is one of the greatest curses on the human race and the harm it inflicts on the poor is more than can be endured. And there is every reason to fear that if it continues it will bring forth those lethal disasters which are already in preparation . . . Providence urgently demands of us that we free ourselves from the age-old slavery of war. If we refuse to make this effort, there is no knowing where we will be led on the fatal path we have taken" (no. 81).

Then the path toward disarmament is outlined:

It is our clear duty to spare no effort in order to work for the moment when all war will be completely outlawed by international agreement . . . Since peace must be born of mutual trust between peoples instead of being forced on nations through dread of arms, all must work to put an end to the arms race and make a real beginning of disarmament, not unilaterally indeed but at an equal rate on all sides, on the basis of agreements and backed up by genuine and effective guarantees (no. 82).

After encouraging the education of young people about the priority of peace, the Council continued:

Every one of us needs a change of heart; we must set our gaze on the whole world and look to those tasks we can all perform together in order to bring about the betterment of our race . . . Unless animosity and hatred are put aside, and firm, honest agreements about world peace are concluded, humanity may, in spite of the wonders of modern science, go from the grave crisis of the present day to that dismal hour, when the only peace it will experience will be the dread peace of death. The Church, however, living in the midst of these anxieties, even as it makes these statements, has not lost hope. The Church intends to propose to our age over and over again, in season and out of season, the apostle's message: "Behold, now is the acceptable time" for a change of heart (no. 82).

To establish peace, the Council concludes, injustice must be eliminated, because it is the root cause of conflict and violence. "Not a few of these causes [of war] arise out of excessive economic inequalities and out of hesitation to undertake necessary correctives. Some are due to the desire for power and to contempt for other people, and at a deeper level, to envy, distrust, pride and other selfish passions. Humanity cannot put up with such an amount of disorder; the result is that, even when war is absent, the world is constantly beset by strife and violence between people."

Gaudium et Spes concludes by proposing concrete recommendations for international justice, solidarity, dialogue and the community of nations. The task of justice and peace "is all the more urgent now that the greater part of the world is in a state of such poverty that it is as if Christ himself were crying out in the mouths of these poor people to the charity of his disciples. Let us not be guilty of the scandal of having some nations, most of whose citizens bear the name of Christians, enjoying an abundance of riches, while others lack the necessities of life and are tortured by hunger, disease, and all kinds of misery" (no. 83).

The Second Vatican Council's Stand on Peace

With *Gaudium et Spes* the scriptural tradition may not have replaced the later sources of Roman law, natural law and Aristotelian logic as the basis for the church's action in the world, but it was placed on a par with those sources in such a way as to root all future teachings in the gospel of peace. Such a new biblical emphasis paved the way for a day in the future when gospel nonviolence will be embraced fully and the just war theory discarded once and for always.

Six basic areas need to be highlighted regarding the Second Vatican Council's stand on peace. First, although it opened the door for Christian nonviolence, it did not go far enough. This is the most important factor for any understanding of the Second Vatican Council. Second, and unfortunately, it upheld the just war theory instead of dismissing it as impossible to fulfill and fundamentally unchristian (as we shall discuss in the next chapter). Third, it gave too much support to allegiance to the nation-state, instead of primary allegiance to God. Fourth, it finally declared that conscientious objection is a valid option for Catholics—a major breakthrough. It prepared for the day when the church will uphold nonviolent resistance and conscientious objection to any and every war. Fifth, it began to make the connection between justice for the poor of the world and the questions of war and peace (and the billions of dollars spent for weapons while millions of people starve and suffer), giving an opening for the liberation theologies of the Third World. Finally, it promoted international dialogue and solidarity, essential ingredients if the world is one day to know peace.

After the Council, Jim Douglass summed up the strengths and weaknesses of the document in *The Nonviolent Cross*:

> The Constitution bases its praise of nonviolence on the reconciliation of all men and women through the Cross of Christ, by which Christ slew hatred in his own flesh and poured forth the spirit of love into the hearts of men and women (Eph.2:16; Col.1:20-22). It is both inspiring and reassuring to see the cross that was raised over Constantine's army, and over the crusades and pogroms of succeeding centuries, being returned finally to its Gospel meaning of reconciliation.[3]

Unfortunately, Douglass continues, the Council allows governments the right to a military defense in the nuclear age. "The question of whether a military rather than a nonviolent defense can long remain 'legitimate' for a modern nation, and will not become instead that total war which 'merits unequivocal and unhesitating condemnation,' is a question left open by the Council."[4] "Nor does it condemn total-war deterrent," he observes. "It still upholds the nuclear deterrent." Douglass concludes:

> What the Council succeeds in doing in effect, by way of any rigorous application of its total-war condemnation to current conditions, is to bring down the curtain on the just-war doctrine. All war in our time has been shown to involve "acts aimed indiscriminately at the destruction of entire cities" . . . Judged by the Council's declaration, modern war itself is a crime against God and humanity and merits unequivocal and unhesitating condemnation. If we wish to take the Council seriously in its central declaration, in spite of the Council's own evident hesitancy to face that declaration squarely throughout its statement, we must declare the just war dead. What the Council fails to do in lieu of the death of the just war, or does only slightly and hesitantly, is to reopen that scripturally founded tradition of nonviolence which has remained largely unexplored since the early age of the church but which now has Gandhi's, and King's experiments in truth as proof of its untapped power.[5]

Catholic Social Teaching after Vatican II

After the Second Vatican Council, Catholic social teaching called more and more for the justice that will make peace possible. In *Populorum Progressio* ("The Development of Peoples," 1967), Paul VI called for economic justice as the basis for peace. He urged the world to overcome the roots of oppression, misery, hunger and poverty. "The superfluous wealth of rich countries should be placed at the service of poor nations," he wrote (no. 49). "To struggle against injustice is to promote the common good. Peace is not the mere absence of war" (no. 83).

The Latin American Bishops' Conference (CELAM), which met in Medellín in 1968, called for "a preferential option for the poor" to combat the structural injustices that plague the Third World. "Structural justice is a prerequisite for peace," Medellín declared (no. 15). Just as people should not put their hopes in violence, the arms race and domination of the world's poor should be stopped. This solidarity with the poor was upheld in *Octogesima Adveniens* (Paul VI, 1971), *Justice in the World* (the Synod of Bishops, 1971), *Evangelii Nuntiandi* (Paul VI, 1975), and the CELAM conferences at Puebla (1979) and Santo Domingo (1992). In the first example of post-Vatican II episcopal collegiality, the bishops called for action that does justice:

> Action on behalf of justice and participation in the transformation of the world fully appear to us as a constitutive dimension

of the preaching of the Gospel, or in other words, of the church's mission for the redemption of the human race and its liberation from every oppressive situation (*Justice in the World*, no. 36).

In its demand for justice, the bishops called for the end to the arms race. Paul VI then invited a new evangelization, which would lead to liberation from oppression and to justice and peace. He clearly rejected violence and called for personal conversion.

In 1979 John Paul II upheld the vision of justice, human rights and the need to oppose injustice in his encyclical *Redemptor Hominis*. In *Laborem Exercens* (1981) John Paul II suggested that we take responsibility for injustice and encouraged the poor to overcome oppression. In *Sollicitudo Rei Socialis* (1988) he critiqued the "structures of sin"; the liberal capitalism of the West; the Marxist collectivism, which had made up much of the East; and called for conversion toward international solidarity, the option for the poor and a new concern for the environment.

The US Bishops' Challenge for Peace

The US bishops' pastoral letter *The Challenge of Peace* proposed a theology of peace, explored the scriptural basis of peacemaking, presented Jesus as a peacemaker and elevated nonviolence as a real Christian option. We are "in a new moment," the bishops wrote, because of Hiroshima and the bomb. For the first time in Catholic social teaching, church leaders used the term *nonviolence* to describe the gospel's way of peacemaking:

> In the centuries between the fourth century and our own day, the theme of Christian nonviolence has echoed and re-echoed, sometimes more strongly, sometimes more faintly . . . The vision of Christian nonviolence is not passive about injustice and the defense of the rights of others; it rather affirms and exemplifies what it means to resist injustice through nonviolent methods. In the twentieth century, prescinding from the non-Christian witness of a Mahatma Gandhi and its worldwide impact, the nonviolent witness of such figures as Dorothy Day and Martin Luther King has had a profound impact upon the life of the Church in the United States. The witness of numerous Christians who had preceded them over the centuries was affirmed in a remarkable way at the Second Vatican Council. Two of the passages which were included in the final version of the *Pastoral Constitution* gave particular encouragement for Catholics in all walks of life to assess their attitudes toward war and military service in the light of Christian pacifism [in paragraph 79, referring to conscientious objection, and praise for those who renounced the use of violence.][6]

Though the bishops did not reject nuclear deterrence, they did conclude that "our 'No' to nuclear war must be definitive and decisive" (no. 138).

> We need a "moral about-face." The whole world must summon the moral courage and technical means to say "no" to nuclear conflict; "no" to weapons of mass destruction; "no" to an arms race which robs the poor and the vulnerable; and "no" to the moral danger of a nuclear age which places before humankind indefensible choices of constant terror or surrender. Peacemaking is not an optional commitment. It is a requirement of faith. We are called to be peacemakers, not by some movement of the moment, but by our Lord Jesus (no. 333).

Ten years later the bishops released a statement on the anniversary of their peace pastoral. In *The Harvest of Justice Is Sown in Peace* the bishops write:

> Nonviolence implies both a philosophy and a strategy which shuns force and pursues a range of alternative actions (e.g., dialogue, negotiation, protests, strikes, boycotts, civil disobedience and civilian resistance) in order to bring law, policy, government itself or other armed parties in line with the demand of justice. Although nonviolence has often been regarded as simply a personal option or vocation, recent history suggests that in some circumstances it can be an effective public undertaking as well. Dramatic political transitions in places as diverse as the Philippines and Eastern Europe demonstrate the power of nonviolent action, even against dictatorial and totalitarian regimes . . . These nonviolent revolutions challenge us to find ways to take into full account the power of organized, active nonviolence . . . As a nation we have an affirmative obligation to promote research and education in nonviolent means of resisting evil. We need to address nonviolent strategies with much greater seriousness in international affairs. In some future conflicts, strikes and people power may be more effective than guns and bullets.[7]

While recognizing "the unprecedented impact of nonviolent methods in recent history," unfortunately the bishops continued their support of the just war theory, deterrence and the maintenance of nuclear weapons, instead of taking a strong stand for Jesus' way of nonviolence.

A Time to Renounce War and Embrace Nonviolence

"The arms race is to be condemned unreservedly," the 1976 "Vatican Statement on Disarmament" declared. "It is in itself an act of aggression against those who are the victims of it. It is an act of aggression, which amounts to a crime, for even when they are not used, by their cost alone, armaments kill the poor by causing them to starve."

Though the institutional church has hesitated to take a strong stand for nonviolence, it has begun to address the world's systemic violence and to call for an about-face. One year after becoming pope, John Paul II journeyed to Ireland and issued a dramatic plea for peace:

> Never before in the history of humankind has peace been so much talked about and so ardently desired as in our day . . . Peace is more and more clearly seen as the only way to justice; peace is itself the work of justice. And yet, again and again, one can see how peace is undermined and destroyed. Why is it then that our convictions do not always match our behavior and our attitudes? Why is it that we do not seem to be able to banish all conflicts from our lives? . . . Peace cannot be established by violence; peace can never flourish in a climate of terror, intimidation and death. It is Jesus himself who said: "All who take the sword will perish by the sword" (Mt 26:52). This is the word of God and it commands this generation of violent men and women to desist from hatred and violence and to repent. I join my voice today to the voice of Paul VI and my other predecessors, to the voices of your religious leaders, to the voices of all men and women of reason, and I proclaim, with the conviction of my faith in Christ and with an awareness of my mission, that violence is evil, that violence is unacceptable as a solution to problems, that violence is unworthy of humanity. Violence destroys what it claims to defend: the dignity, the life, the freedom of human beings. Violence is a crime against humanity, for it destroys the very fabric of society . . . To all of you who are listening I say: Do not believe in violence; do not support violence. It is not the Christian way. It is not the way of the Catholic church. Believe in peace and forgiveness and love; for they are of Christ. Communities who stand together in their acceptance of Jesus' supreme message of love, expressed in peace and reconciliation, and in their rejection of all violence, constitute an irresistible force for achieving what many have come to accept as impossible and destined to remain so. To all men and women engaged in violence, I appeal to you, in language of passionate pleading. On my knees I beg you to turn away from the paths of violence and to return to the ways of peace . . . Violence only delays the day of justice. Violence destroys the work of justice . . . In the name of God, I beg you: return to Christ, who died so that men and women might live in forgiveness and peace. He is waiting for you, longing for each one of you to come to him so that he may say to each of you: Your sins are forgiven; go in peace . . . True courage lies in working for peace.[8]

One year later, on February 25, 1981, John Paul II stood before ten thousand people at Peace Memorial Park in Hiroshima, Japan, and told them that "to remember Hiroshima is to abhor nuclear war. To remember Hiroshima," he continued, "is to commit oneself to peace . . . War is the work of humanity," he stated. "War is destruction of human life. War is death." He continued:

> Humanity is not destined to self-destruction. Clashes of ideologies, aspirations and needs can and must be settled and resolved by means other than war and violence. Humanity owes it to itself to settle differences and conflicts by peaceful means . . . Let us not repeat the past, a past of violence and destruction. Let us embark upon the steep and difficult path of peace, the only path that befits human dignity, the only path that leads to the true fulfillment of the human destiny, the only path to a future in which equity, justice and solidarity are realities and not just distant dreams . . . Let us pledge ourselves to peace through justice; let us take a solemn decision, now, that war will never be tolerated or sought as a means for resolving differences; let us promise our fellow human beings that we will work untiringly for disarmament and the banishing of all nuclear weapons; let us replace violence and hate with confidence and caring . . . To everyone I repeat the words of the prophet: "They shall beat their swords into plowshares and their spears into pruning hooks. Nation shall not lift up sword against nation, neither shall they learn war any more" (Is.2:4).[9]

Three decades after the Second Vatican Council spoke for peace, and despite the many Catholics who have come forward and taken a stand for peace, we still have a long way to go to move beyond the nuclear age into true Christian nonviolence. Today the church's teaching on war and peace lies dormant, as the North American church's silence during the 1991 US war in the Persian Gulf demonstrated. The majority of Catholics in the United States supported the US bombing raids over Iraq, which left nearly half a million people dead and nearly 300,000 sick and injured, mainly children. No new evaluation of war emerged. Three days before the United States began the slaughter of Iraq, John Paul II begged humanity to "outlaw war completely and cultivate peace as a supreme good."[10] Nonetheless, in the United States the same old patriotic warmaking prevailed. Christ's gospel was again betrayed.

The church needs more and more to renounce its complicity in the organized murder which is war and which still threatens to destroy the entire human race. We are called to "love our enemies" and to "not return evil for evil" (Mt 5:38). Christian nonviolence needs to be proclaimed not just as an option but as an obligation for every Christian. The time has come for the church to dismiss the just war theory, to embrace Jesus' way of active nonviolence and to call for its application on the national and international levels.

CHAPTER 13

From Just War to Nonviolence

Renouncing War and Embracing Peace

Though Jesus commanded his followers to love their enemies and though the early Christians went to their deaths rather than fight in battle, Christians over the centuries moved away from nonviolence and to the ways of war. Ironically, when the Roman empire legitimated Christianity, Christians put aside gospel nonviolence and took up the sword in direct contradiction to Christ's teaching. Christians were then obliged under penalty of excommunication to render military service; with the law of December 7, 415, pagans were not allowed to belong to the Roman imperial army. The Roman military forces were made up only of Christians. To explain this imperial co-optation of Christians into the work of mass murder, Augustine outlined a theory justifying war as a last resort. His work was later refined by Aquinas.

For the last fifteen hundred years, this just war theory has been used to justify the murder of millions and millions of people. To become a community of nonviolence, a peacemaking church, we need to reexamine and ultimately renounce the just war theory, which has long been the guideline for the church's attitude toward war.

A theology of nonviolence submits that there is no such thing as a just war, that there has never been a just war, that all wars are unjust. Nonviolence maintains that God does not justify warfare, that for God there is no victory in war, that for God war itself is the enemy. Nonviolence calls Christians to disavow the practice of war and return to the nonviolent Jesus.

The Just War Theory

Interestingly enough, the just war theory begins with a preference for peace and a presumption against war. From Augustine to Aquinas to recent moral theology, a so-called just war requires *all* of these conditions to be met before a decision to go to war is considered justified (*jus ad bellum*):

1. The war must be a "just cause."
2. It must be waged by "a legitimate authority."
3. It must be "formally declared."
4. It must be fought with "a peaceful intention."
5. It must be "a last resort."
6. There must be reasonable "hope of success."
7. The "damage" inflicted and the "costs" incurred by war must be "proportionate" to the good expected by taking up arms.

Three additional conditions must be met regarding the conditions for the permissible conduct of war (*jus in bello*):

1. Noncombatants must be given immunity.
2. Prisoners must be treated humanely.
3. International treaties and conventions must be honored.[1]

As Walter Wink notes, "these general rules can be extremely difficult to apply in concrete situations" and their use depends on "one's starting assumptions."[2]

Christian nonviolence, on the other hand, holds that killing is never just. Nonviolence suggests that no cause, competent authority, comparative justice, right intention, success or proportionality can ever justify the taking of human life. In their 1983 pastoral letter *The Challenge of Peace*, the US Catholic bishops reflected extensively on the just war theory and to a lesser degree on nonviolence.[3] They traced the history of Christian nonviolence to Jesus himself and those first three centuries of church history, when Christians refused to kill. "The vision of Christian nonviolence is not passive about injustice and the defense of the rights of others," they wrote. "It rather affirms and exemplifies what it means to resist injustice through nonviolent means" (no. 116). "While the just war teaching has clearly been in possession for the past 1500 years of Catholic thought," they suggested, "the 'new moment' [recognized in the Second Vatican Council] in which we find ourselves sees the just war teaching and nonviolence as distinct but interdependent methods of evaluating warfare" (no. 120).

With the rapid changes in the world, including the failure of communism, the collapse of the Soviet Union and the Persian Gulf war, more and more Christians are beginning to reject the just war theory as the aberration of the gospel that it is. Many are concluding that war is never just and that the just war theory is, in any case, obsolete with the weapons of mass destruction that the world now has. More to the point, people are beginning to recognize that the just war theory does not enable us to be faithful to the nonviolent Christ, who refused to kill anyone and who called us beyond deterrence and war to the love of enemies. The Catholic bishops hinted at this new understanding of the gospel and the rejection of the just war theory when they condemned the use of nuclear weapons "for the purpose of destroying population centers or other predominantly civilian targets" (no. 147). They declared that no situation "in which the deliberate initiation of nuclear warfare, on however restricted a scale, can be morally justified." They dismissed the possibility of a "limited nuclear war" (no. 160). Though the bishops still accepted the just war theory, the door was opened for a future day when nonviolence will ground all church positions.

La Civilta Cattolica's Stand against the Just War Theory

Perhaps the clearest sign of the reappraisal of the just war theory came after the Persian Gulf war, on July 6, 1991, when *La Civilta Cattolica*, the Italian journal which usually reflects Vatican positions on significant issues, came out strongly against the just war theory and for a deeper commitment to peace. Its editorial, "Christian Conscience and Modern Warfare," declared that the destructive force of conventional and nuclear weapons makes the just war theory "outdated" and that from now on, Christianity will stress that "modern war is always immoral." All war, including so-called holy wars, are condemned as immoral. This editorial points to a new understanding of peace in church teaching, to the day when the just war is officially abandoned and the gospel's way of peace is officially embraced.

The four thousand word editorial cites the Persian Gulf war as an example of the destructive power of modern weapons and the irrationality of wars, which create more problems than they solve. "Modern warfare is radically different from wars of the past," the editors write, "and therefore the theoretical categories and moral judgments which applied to past wars no longer seem applicable to modern warfare."[4] "War is always an evil. But its wickedness becomes so much more evident when one looks at modern warfare," *La Civilta Cattolica* notes. "If wars of the past, because of the relatively limited losses involved, could be justified—by some—as the lesser evil, this can no longer be said of modern warfare."

> Modern warfare is always "total." The Gulf war is a clear example. In that war, thermonuclear weapons were not used, though at times the employment of tactical nuclear weapons was being considered and it was feared that the Iraqis might have recourse to chemical weapons. But the weapons used were so terribly destructive and lethal that—according to reliable sources—175,000 soldiers [indeed, well over 200,000] and 30,000 [actually, more than 100,000] Iraqi civilians were killed. There was also the almost total destruction of the civilian infrastructure (roads, bridges, irrigation systems) as well as the economic and industrial complex of Iraq . . . Iraq has been pushed back into a pre-industrial era. Unquestionably, a dramatic change—indeed a radical reversal—in the very nature of war is taking place. "Modern warfare" is radically different from war in the past.[5]

"Today, Christian conscience must deal with the problem of war in a manner radically different from the past," *La Civilta Cattolica* continues. "A war cannot really be conducted according to the criteria required for a just war." The conditions are unattainable because modern war by its very nature is "waged with brutality." "It always produces harm that far exceeds any advantages that may accrue in terms of justice and right, and it tends to inflict on the enemy damages much more serious than the good which is being sought and which would otherwise make the war a just war."[6]

> In reality war has its own proper logic, which is to inflict on the enemy very serious damages so much greater than what is probably necessary to achieve the end for which the war is being waged. The motive of this cruelty, peculiar to war, is the unwillingness to be satisfied with simply achieving the end for which the war was declared; instead there is a desire to destroy the adversary in such a way that the adversary will be unable to recover and thus will no longer constitute a danger for the future.[7]

The just war theory is "indefensible and needs to be abandoned," *La Civilta Cattolica* declares. "Modern warfare unleashes a violence on which, given the use of modern weapons, it is impossible to place limits . . . Besides being immoral, warfare today is useless and harmful. On the one hand, it does not solve, even apparently and momentarily, the problems which it unleashes . . . On the other hand, not only does it not solve problems, it aggravates them, rendering a solution practically impossible and in fact creating yet more grievous problems. Thus it sows the seeds of future conflicts and wars."[8]

> War almost never ends with a true peace: it always leaves behind a remnant of hatred and a thirst for revenge, which will explode as soon as the opportunity offers itself. That is why the human story has been a series of unending wars. War initiates a spiral of hatred and violence, which is extremely difficult to stop. War is therefore useless, since it solves no problems, and damaging because it aggravates problems and makes them insoluble.[9]

Besides condemning war, the church is called now to promote peace in the world, *La Civilta Cattolica* concludes. The church "must announce the gospel, which is a gospel of peace."

> The proclamation and promotion of peace among people is part of the church's religious mission. Therefore when the church speaks of the necessity of involving herself in the cause of peace and declares herself against war, she is not invading the field of politics, but is staying within the sphere of her own proper religious and moral mission . . . Through Jesus, men and women are brothers and sisters of one another, because they are children of God. This means that they must rid themselves of the categories

of "stranger" and "enemy," categories so basic to the ideology of war. The church has only one intent, which is to strengthen the gospel call to brotherhood and sisterhood among God's people.[10]

The church "opposes war" and "wills peace," *La Civilta Cattolica* insists. This new understanding of the Christian mission places new concrete priorities in our day and age upon us as followers of Jesus.

> In practical terms, it means opposing the idea that war is able to resolve the problems which are at the root of conflicts. It means opposing the idea of war as the last resort, because in practice there is no last resort, because it is impossible to prove that all the means to avoid war were considered and put into action. More than that, the one who decides that there is no alternative but war is the very person who really wants to wage war and is simply waiting for an opportune time to begin. Being against war and for peace also means opposing the idea that war is "necessary" or "inevitable" and that peace is not possible. Finally, it means opposing the idea that wars are waged for noble motives: to restore a universal order of justice and peace or simply to make amends for injustices. These noble motives—which may be present in a few people—in most cases serve as a juridical and moral cover-up for the true motives of war, which are motives of political domination and economic interests. In other words, to oppose the "ideology of war" is to do what is needed to unmask war by showing it as it really is: to uncover its motives and its results. It means to show that it is always the poor and the weak who pay for war, whether they wear a military uniform or belong to the civilian population.[11]

The peace that the church "wills" is a peace "founded on justice, solidarity and mutual trust."

> The church maintains that there can be no peace, where situations of grave injustice persist and where the just aspirations of people—for freedom, for self-determination, for a homeland of their own, for the right to live a life worthy of human dignity—are frustrated by force and violence. There can be no peace where feelings of frustration and hatred and vengeance are fostered among peoples and nations and continents. There can be no peace where mutual trust is lacking and peace is based on "an equilibrium of terror" and is sustained by an on-going arms race, whether conventional arms or nuclear ones. That is why the church—decisively proclaiming herself for peace and against any war—asks that remedies be found for situations of injustice which exist in today's world and which otherwise will be the forerun-

ners of new wars. Above all, solutions must be found for the radical injustice which has created dramatic conditions of growing poverty in the Southern half of the planet.[12]

Applying Nonviolence to International Conflict

Following the advice of *La Civilta Cattolica*, Christians are called to renounce war and to apply nonviolence in national and international conflicts. This means that we take seriously Jesus' mandate of universal love, even love of enemies. If we genuinely love our enemies, we will not kill them; we will not even threaten or prepare to kill them.

Nonviolence on an international scale has rarely been attempted but holds enormous possibilities. It requires a distinctly different way of organizing international relations, with greater reliance on the nonviolent intervention of the United Nations, nonviolent peacekeeping teams, and international solidarity campaigns such as embargoes aimed at transforming repressive or warmaking governments. Such a commitment to nonviolence on national and international levels will seek to root out the causes of war by addressing the world's injustice and poverty, by relieving hunger and misery, and by creating nonviolent structures which serve humanity and promote life. Such nonviolent conflict resolution will learn from the massive movements of nonviolence that forced the departure of imperial Britain from India in 1947, resisted Hitler in Norway and Denmark and brought down the Berlin Wall and totalitarian communism in the Soviet Union.[13]

To the charge that nonviolence does not work, theologian John Howard Yoder responds that the time has come to apply the same serious effort, talent, money and energy that we have used to wage war for thousands of years to nonviolent alternatives. We need to commit ourselves as nations and cultures to the way of nonviolence and to the justice that nonviolence presumes.

> Those who move, either immediately or less rapidly, to the claim that in a given situation of injustice there are no nonviolent options available, generally do so in a way that avoids responsibility for an intensive search for other options . . . The military option for which they reach so soon involves a very long lead time; it demands the preparation of leadership people by special training, educational institutions, and experiences; it demands financial and technical resources dependent on extensive government funding in a situation of defense; and it demands broad alliances. It includes the willingness to lose lives and to take lives, the willingness to sacrifice other cultural values for a generation or longer, the willingness of families to be divided. Yet the decision that "nonviolence will not work" for analogous ends is made without any comparable investment of time or creativity, without comparable readiness to sacrifice, without serious

projection of comparative costs. The American army could not "work" if we did not invest billions of dollars in equipping it and in preparing for its effective use. Why should it be fair to measure the moral claims of an alternative moral strategy by setting up the debate in such a way that that other strategy must produce comparable results at incomparably less cost?[14]

Rejecting War and Pursuing a Nonviolent Peace

To illustrate the irrationality of the just war theory, theologian and peace activist Richard McSorley proposes a corresponding "just adultery theory," responding respectively to God's commandments, "Thou shall not kill," and "Thou shall not commit adultery." "A Christian minister or priest who openly preaches the just adultery theory would be run out of church, but not so with the just war theory."[15] Applying the conditions of last resort, good intention, protection of the innocent and proportionality, McSorley concludes that a just adultery theory would be absurd. The just war theory, he writes, is equally absurd. It gives license to the killing of millions of people. "Why is it," McSorley asks, "that most Christians understand the weaknesses of the just adultery theory, but are blind to the weaknesses of the just war theory? . . . Do we put the authority of the government above that of God? If a president, king, dictator or general says an action is necessary for the defense of a country, do we say a Christian may do it and not be guilty of sin? . . . If the leaders says, 'rape,' the Christian rapes. If the leaders says 'kill,' the Christian kills . . . Can we serve both God and government when the government orders what God forbids?"[16]

McSorley's question gets at the heart of the matter: Do Christians serve governments and their military forces or God and God's mandate of nonviolence? If the answer is that Christians are called to be faithful to God and thus to live according to the moral imperative of nonviolence, then Christians can never justify war. They will refuse to bless war, refuse to fight in war, and disobey governments which wage war.

A theology of nonviolence based on the gospel necessarily rejects killing, warfare and the very existence of nuclear weapons. It calls us to reject the just war theory once and for all and to embrace gospel nonviolence in all areas of life, including international conflict resolution. It responds to the call of the US Catholic bishops for "a moral about-face." "The whole world must summon the moral courage and technical means," they write in *The Challenge of Peace*, "to say 'no' to nuclear conflict; 'no' to weapons of mass destruction; 'no' to an arms race which robs the poor and the vulnerable; and 'no' to the moral danger of a nuclear age which places before humankind indefensible choices of constant terror or surrender. Peacemaking is not an optional commitment. It is a requirement of our faith. We are called to be peacemakers, not by some movement of the moment, but by our Lord Jesus" (no. 333).

Given this new assessment of the just war theory and the Christian imperative to live nonviolence, the time has come, as Carroll Dozier, the late bishop of Memphis, once said, to discard the just war theory in the same file as the flat earth theory. The time for nonviolence has clearly arrived.

CHAPTER 14

Feminism and Nonviolence

Women, Christ and the Transformation of the World

More often than not, systemic violence strikes women. Somewhere in the world a women is beaten every three minutes. In the United States, a woman is beaten every eighteen seconds. Somewhere in the world a women is raped every five minutes; in the United States, a woman is raped every three minutes. Every ten minutes a little girl is molested, somewhere, by some man.[1] In two-thirds of all marriages women are beaten at least once; one-fourth of the women in the United States are beaten weekly.[2] Worldwide, women bear the brunt of poverty. Men dominate women everywhere, everyday. This institutionalization of sexism or patriarchy is best described as a male power structure in which all relationships are understood in terms of superiority and inferiority and social cohesion is assured by the exercise of dominative power. This same patriarchy justifies racism, ageism, classism, colonialism, clericalism and nuclearism as well as sexism.

In a patriarchal society God is an almighty father, "the first patriarch and the legitimator of all others."[3] By and large, men wage war and inflict death, while women make peace and give birth to new life. Men have structured sexism and so ingrained it into society that women everywhere routinely suffer from the violence of men.

To address the reality of violence in the world, we need to face the violence of men against women. The nonviolence of God, we will then discover, calls us to a nonviolent liberation of women, which liberates both oppressed and oppressors, which transforms us all, women and men, into God's own children, daughters and sons. Only then can we recognize each other as sisters and brothers and together give birth to a new humanity rooted in nonviolence, equality and justice.

What Is Feminism?

Feminism maintains that all women and men are equal. It insists that women have the same rights as men, that they are just as much human beings as men, and therefore that the violence and the unjust structures that oppress and kill women need to be dismantled and transformed to promote equality and dignity for all. Christian feminism does not seek the domination of women over men; it does not replace the violence of patriarchy with that of matriarchy. It is more revolutionary. It calls for the equality of all, and does so from the perspective of women, who suffer the oppression of patriarchy and sexism.

Christian feminism roots this insistence on the equality of women and men in the gospel of Jesus, who was himself a feminist. Jesus lived the equality of women and men. In a sexist, patriarchal world Jesus affirmed the dignity of women, healed women, associated with women, taught women and took women as his friends and disciples. Followers of Jesus, Christian feminism asserts, uphold this dignity of women by proclaiming their equality with men. It insists that we are already one, already reconciled, that in Christ-God there is neither male nor female but one Spirit of nonviolent love.

Sadly, the institutional church does not reflect the feminism of Jesus. Instead, men and men alone have structured the church as hierarchy and patriarchy. Two thousand years after the life and death of Jesus women are still not permitted into all the ministries of the church. They are not treated as equals. The violence and oppression from which women around the world suffer is not addressed by the institutional church, because church leadership consists solely of men. Christian feminism calls for the transformation of patriarchy, including and especially the patriarchy and male domination within the church, so that the entire human family can live as it was created to live, in justice and peace.

How Do Feminism and Nonviolence Connect?

Nonviolence maintains the equality of all human beings and insists that every human being is a daughter or a son of God. With this spiritual insight, nonviolence urges us never to hurt one another, kill one another, wage war, oppress others or threaten to destroy the human race. It understands that we are all called to live together in justice and peace, as equals, and thus it calls us to pursue that struggle for justice and equality, but to do so through the way of unconditional love, relentless insistence on truth and persistent reconciliation. Such a vision of peace coincides with feminism. Christian nonviolence and Christian feminism emerge as two sides of the same slice of bread.

Nonviolence and feminism are two ways of articulating the gospel truth of human life. Given the sexism and patriarchy of today's world, a theology of nonviolence clearly must address this violence, especially within the Chris-

tian community, and embrace the Christian feminism that calls for the transformation of the world into a nonsexist, nonpatriarchal, nonviolent world of
justice and peace. Such Christian nonviolence would highlight the machismo
which builds structures of oppression and leads to war and would seek to
disarm and transform that masculine aberration into a holistic, nonviolent
approach to life. It would give peace a chance by encouraging nonviolent
women to take the lead in church and society, so that a more compassionate
world might be born.

The Feminine Image of God

Christian feminism tears down the walls of male domination. It points back
to the scriptures and reads between the lines of sexism in the biblical texts to
reveal the image of a nonviolent, feminist, peacemaking Jesus and the feminine face of God.

God is not sexist, Christian feminism proclaims. God is not patriarchal.
God is more than "two men and a bird," as one feminist theologian observes.
God can have the face of a woman as well as that of a man. As feminist theology is revealing more and more, God is not only masculine; She is also
feminine.

"Theological tradition has never assigned sex to God," theologian Sandra
Schneiders declares.[4] Gregory of Nazianzus, for instance, writes, "The terms
'Father' and 'Son' as applied to the persons of the Trinity were not names of
natures or essences but of relations and even in this case the terms are used
metaphorically."[5] Early Christian writers understood the metaphorical nature
of their language, Schneiders explains, and "never intended to impute actual
sexuality to the God whom scripture affirms is pure Spirit (Jn 4:24)."[6] "Theological tradition has virtually always maintained that the maleness of Jesus is
theologically, Christologically, soteriologically and sacramentally irrelevant."[7]
The maleness of Jesus, Schneiders observes, has been used to support the
claim that maleness is normative for humanity. The "fatherhood" of God is
used to justify patriarchy, and the masculinity of God and Jesus has been used
to deny the likeness of women to God and to Christ and thereby to exclude
them from full participation in the church.[8] Such misinterpretations of God
are falling by the wayside, thanks to many women who have remained faithful to the God of all.

A Feminist Reading of Scripture

Though the scriptures were by and large written by men, for men, about
men and about God as a man, we can dig deep and discover a different God,
a God of peace and equality, a God who gives birth to and mothers us with
love. If we wrestle with the Word and take the text seriously, we encounter a
God who is in many ways feminine. In this new feminist reading of scripture,

we discover as well the powerful testimony of women who were faithful to this mother/father God.

Schneiders outlines four different types of language used regarding God in the Jewish scriptures. First, there is literal language, which describes God, for example, as the liberator who brings the Hebrews out of Egypt or the covenant-maker who bound Israel and its God together at Sinai. These images of the God of the Hebrews have no gender. Second, names are given for God; most important, a name which is really a non-name—"I am who I am" (Ex 3:14). Again, we have no clue in such names of the gender of God. Third, the Jews had two personifications of God, as wisdom and "shekinah" (from the Hebrew root meaning "to dwell"). Such names are definitely feminine, both grammatically and rhetorically. Fourth, the scriptures use metaphor to describe God. For example, God is described as sun (Ps 84:11), rock (Dt 32:15), fire (Dt 4:24), lion (Hos 5:14) and mother eagle (Dt 32:11-12). Human metaphors for God include God as potter, builder, hero, midwife, mother, father and husband. "While there is no question that male metaphors outnumber feminine ones," Schneiders notes, "feminine metaphors have definitely been neglected in the tradition because of patriarchal self-interest."[9] In an analysis of the Jewish metaphors for God, Schneiders concludes:

> God is not presented in the Old Testament in exclusively male terms. Even the two necessarily male metaphors, father and husband, are balanced by maternal imagery and the presentation of marital love as a relation of mutuality between equals. It is true that male imagery for God predominates, but this should serve to draw our attention to the unexpected feminine imagery which is perhaps more revelatory precisely because it cannot be adequately explained by the culture. Any literalizing of God metaphors results not only in an impoverishment and distortion of the religious imagination but in a blasphemous assimilation of God to human categories and an idolatrous divinizing of human maleness.[10]

The biblical texts also speak of women who were faithful to the God of the Hebrew people. From Sarah and Esther to Ruth and Naomi, women are part of the faithful people of God. Joan Chittister points out, for example, the role of Moses' mother and Pharaoh's daughter in the liberation of God's people:

> Moses' mother and Pharaoh's daughter lived in a society where "men were men" and differences were solved by destruction, and might made right and the innocent were sacrificed for the sake of the powerful. Moses' mother and Pharaoh's daughter wanted no part of the domination and destruction that characterize the male power paradigm. Moses' mother and Pharaoh's daughter believed in compassion instead of conflict, and collaboration instead of coercion, and cooperation rather than competition. And

together, secretly, those two women—one inside the destructive
system and one outside the destructive system—reach across the
boundaries of their lives to subvert it by refusing to be enemies,
by saving the child and therefore saving the race . . . [But] there
is no doubt about it, the agenda of Moses' mother and Pharaoh's
daughter has definitely not been satisfied. The theology of domination and machomania is with us still and threatens now not a
people but a globe.[11]

The Feminism of Jesus

Millions of women are leaving the church because of its entrenched sexism and patriarchy. Many women are discarding their image of a male God.
Such women have renounced the institutional church's patriarchal image of
God. Many of them find it hard to separate the Jesus of the gospels from the
institutional church's patriarchy. The Jesus demonstrated to them dominates,
oppresses and blesses sexism and patriarchy. Because of this presentation of
a Jesus who approves of the dominant patriarchal order, many women have
difficulty with a male savior and are leaving the church. Thanks to Christian
feminism and the theology of feminism, a clearer picture of Jesus is developing. In this new image of Jesus we discover not only his steadfast feminism
and liberating spirit, but a new image of God and a new vision of the church
and the world.

The gospels reveal a drastically different Jesus from the Jesus of institutionalized patriarchy. The Jesus of the Christian scriptures was nonviolent
and revolutionary. His gentle revolution included a dramatic feminism that
broke the chains of sexism and patriarchy. It is clear from the gospels that
Jesus was a feminist. He advocated the equality of men and women, he be-
friended women in a society that relegated women to worse than second-class
citizenship, and he invited women to discipleship.

Though the gospels use male metaphors and images for the God of Jesus,
they also use female metaphors and images, such as "the divine mother of
whom believers are born [who] is the one God who is Spirit" (Jn 3:1-7).[12]
Jesus also envisions God as a woman householder (Lk 15:8-10) and a baker
woman (Mt 13:33; Lk 13:34). At one point in Matthew's gospel (Mt 23:27;
see Lk 13:34), Jesus describes himself as a mother hen longing to shelter her
chicks under her wing. As Virginia Mollenkott points out, this self-descrip-
tion of Jesus is "not a reflection of his earthy self-understanding but of his
messianic identity as representative of God."[13] "By placing on the lips of Jesus
himself several important feminine metaphors for God," Sandra Schneiders
writes, "the Gospels make quite clear that the male metaphors are not to be
literalized or absolutized."[14]

The cultural constraints of patriarchy take responsibility for Jesus' primary experience of God as father. But this fatherhood did not mean absolute
power and authority over humanity.[15] Jesus' description of God as Abba, a
tender, loving parent, not a powerful patriarch, breaks with his culture and

presents a different image of God. Jesus' God breaks through the patriarchal standards of society, as the parable of the prodigal son demonstrates.[16]

Jesus' maleness does not reveal anything about the sex of the Godhead, Schneiders suggests.[17] The God of the Jewish scriptures "which most comprehensively influenced the understanding of Jesus in the early church was the feminine figure of Wisdom, so if Jesus reveals anything about the gender of God, it is certainly not that God is masculine."[18] Schneiders argues that given the patriarchy of the world, "Jesus had to be a male in order to reveal effectively the true nature of God and of humanity."[19] As she notes, Jesus revealed by his preaching and his life the inadequacy of the masculine definition of humanity in terms of competition, domination and violence. His behavior and teaching, in fact, called for a reform of male-female relationships (Jn 4:4-42; 20:11-18). Finally, Jesus undermined patriarchy by not marrying, thereby not taking possession of a woman and so remaining free to relate to all women as equals.[20] Schneiders concludes:

> Today we would call Jesus a feminist, that is, a person who believes in the full personhood and equality of women and who acts to bring that belief to realization in society and church. It is hard to imagine how Jesus' challenge to revise the oppressive relations between women and men could have been presented by a woman. The most effective denunciation of injustice is that which comes from within the ranks of the oppressors . . . Jesus accepted membership in the oppressor class of society in order, from within, to demonstrate the bankruptcy of the dominative social system. Only as a man could he have subverted the accepted definition of masculinity, validated the so-called feminine virtues despised by men but dear to God, redefined the relationship between women and men as one of equality and mutuality, and destroyed patriarchy's claims to divine sanction.[21]

Jesus is the nonviolent liberator of women and men. This nonviolent Christ redeems us all, beginning with the women who suffer the brunt of patriarchy. A story from the gospel explains this liberation:

> On a Sabbath day, Jesus was teaching in one of the synagogues. There was a woman there who for eighteen years had been crippled by a spirit which drained her strength. She was bent over, completely incapable of standing erect. When Jesus saw her, he called to her and said, "Woman, you are free of your infirmity." And he laid his hands upon her and immediately she stood up straight and began thanking God (Lk 13:10-12).

Mary of Bethany, the Samaritan woman, Mary Magdalene, the women at the tomb and other women play crucial roles in the life and witness of Jesus. Mary of Bethany refused to stay in the kitchen with Martha and broke the rules of patriarchal etiquette by sitting with the men at the feet of Jesus, the spiritual master. Jesus affirmed Mary by saying that she had chosen the better part. In the patriarchal world of Jesus' culture, even in our own world, such words are revolutionary.

According to John's gospel, the first person Jesus freely tells that he is the messiah is a woman, a non-Jew from an enemy territory. This Samaritan woman, not Paul, becomes the first apostle to the Gentiles, for she tells all her people about Jesus and thousands follow him because of her.

One woman, perhaps Mary of Bethany, anoints Jesus when the others deny his way of nonviolent resistance, and Jesus affirms her. "She is doing what you are not doing," he declares to the men. "She is preparing me for my burial." She had accepted Jesus' way of the cross; the men had yet to understand it.

Perhaps most significantly Mary Magdalene, not Peter, is profiled as the most faithful disciple. She remains with Jesus from Galilee into Jerusalem, to his crucifixion and the tomb. Mary Magdalene first encounters the risen Jesus. She is missioned to proclaim to the world the good news of resurrection. In John's gospel Jesus appears to Mary Magdalene and specifically says to her, "Do not remain here. Go and tell my brothers that I have risen" (Jn 20:17). Mary, we read, did what she was asked to do. She went "and announced to the disciples, 'I have seen the Christ'" (Jn 20:18).

Throughout the story of Jesus we read about the three male disciples of Jesus—Peter, James, and John—who were privy to Jesus' most significant teachings and experiences. Yet these men, we are told in each gospel, consistently failed to understand what Jesus was talking about and doing. Set against the blundering discipleship of the men stands a faithful group of women, who remain with Jesus from beginning to end, from Galilee to the cross and to the resurrection. We are told of three women who lurk first in the background, who follow Jesus throughout his public ministry and who stand with Jesus at Calvary, publicly supporting him in his time of need. When Jesus confronts the systemic injustice of the Temple, is arrested and executed as a revolutionary, the male disciples flee. Jesus' close friend Peter publicly denies three times that he even knows Jesus. Yet there at the foot of the cross, looking up at the bloody, crucified Jesus, are three women: Mary Magdalene, Mary the mother of the younger James and of Joses (probably, Mary, the mother of Jesus, now portrayed as a disciple, not just his mother) and Salome (15:40). These women escort the body to the tomb (Mk 15:47). Mark specifically points out that they are Galilean disciples of Jesus (15:61). "These women had followed Jesus when he was in Galilee and ministered to him. There were also many other women who had come up with him to Jerusalem" (Mk 15:41). Not only are these women model disciples, not only did they follow Jesus, not only were they present in his agony and death, but, we are told, they served Jesus.[22] The story ends with women serving Jesus just as the gospel begins with a woman serving Jesus (Mk 1:31). Ched Myers observes:

> Not only did the women "follow," but they "served" Jesus throughout the Galilee ministry. Here at the end, as at the very beginning of the story, Mark tells us that it is women who serve, as if to say that they alone understand the true vocation of lead-

ership. These women came up with Jesus to Jerusalem, and have stayed with him to death. In other words, not all deserted Jesus at Gethsemane. The women now become the "lifeline" of the discipleship narrative. The women have done the two things that the males in the community found impossible: they have been servants, and they continued to follow Jesus even after he was arrested and executed . . . Whoever the three women are, Mark presents them as an alternative to the three men of the former inner circle (Peter, James, and John): they are the true disciples.

Nice !

This is the last—and, given the highly structured gender roles of the time, surely the most radical—example of Mark's narrative subversion of the canons of social orthodoxy. The world order is being overturned, from the highest political power to the deepest cultural patterns, and it begins within the new community. It will be these women, the "last" become "first," who will be entrusted with the resurrection message.[23]

Women are the witnesses to the resurrection. Even in resurrection Jesus challenged sexism. The risen Christ appears to women, according to every gospel, and sends them to proclaim the gospel to men. In Mark's gospel the angel tells the women, "Go and tell his disciples and Peter, 'Christ is going before you to Galilee; there you will see him, as he told you.'" The women flee in fear and trembling, for they understand the truth of this gospel pronunciation, that the disciples are now invited to take up the journey of nonviolent resistance to systemic, patriarchal injustice, even unto martyrdom. Despite their fear and trembling, they go to tell the men, who dismiss the report as ludicrous. Luke's gospel explains: "The women returned from the tomb and announced all these things to the eleven and to all the others. The women were Mary Magdalene, Joanna, and Mary the mother of James; the others who accompanied them also told this to the apostles, but their story seemed like nonsense and they did not believe them" (Lk 24:9-11). As Joan Chittister points out, just as the male disciples did not believe Mary Magdalene, so, today, two thousand years later, men still do not believe women who proclaim the good news of Christ's resurrection. Yet, because so many women have remained faithful and have continued to proclaim the good news of resurrection, we still know the good news today.

The Christian scriptures challenge the institutional patriarchy of the church. From chapter one of Mark's gospel, which reveals that Peter was married and thus undercuts the entire structure of male celibacy as a criterion for church leadership, to the women who encounter the risen Christ and are missioned to announce the greatest intervention of God in human history, the scriptures call us to a transformed humanity. In the letters of Paul we realize that in the early community bishops were married and women were leaders. Paul mentions Prisca, his "co-worker in Christ Jesus who risked her neck for my life" (Rom 16:3). "I commend to you Phoebe our sister, who is a minister of the church at Cenchreae," Paul writes to the Romans, "that you may receive her in the Lord in a manner worthy of the holy ones, and help her in whatever she may need from you, for she has been a benefactor to many and to me as well" (Rom 16:1-2). Despite patriarchy's insistence otherwise, the women of the gospels were equals. They pointed out the way to the nonviolent, peacemaking Christ.

Jesus the liberator breaks down the walls of patriarchy when understood in the light of Christian feminism. Christ begins the transformation of humanity, as Rosemary Radford Ruether notes:

> Jesus as the Christ, the representative of liberated humanity and the liberating Word of God, manifests the *kenosis of patriarchy,* the announcement of the new humanity through a lifestyle that discards hierarchical caste privilege and speaks on behalf of the lowly. In a similar way, the femaleness of the social and religiously outcast who respond to him has social symbolic significance as a witness against the same idolatrous system of patriarchal privilege. This system is unmasked and shown to have no connection with favor with God. Jesus, the homeless Jewish prophet, and the marginalized women and men who respond to him represent the overthrow of the present world system and the sign of a dawning new age in which God's will is done on earth.[24]

"Christ, as redemptive person and Word of God, is not to be encapsulated 'once-for-all' in the historical Jesus," Ruether concludes. "The Christian community continues Christ's identity. As vine and branches, Christic personhood continues in our sisters and brothers. In the language of Christian prophetism, we can encounter Christ in the form of our sister."[25]

The Feminist Vision of Nonviolence

Christian feminism holds clear implications for our life of Christian discipleship and for a theology of nonviolence.

Christian feminism challenges us to a new image of a God who is a feminist; a God who rejects sexism and patriarchy; a God who hears the cry of women and is transforming the world into a new reign of equality, justice and peace. The feminine face of God, which we are now recognizing, leads us to a fuller picture of the face of humanity.

Christian feminism challenges theology with a hermeneutic of suspicion. It questions any sexism, domination or hint of patriarchy in all reflections on God. It calls us to root our theology in the vision of a new humanity, where women and men are seen as sisters and brothers, equal children of a loving God who is both Father and Mother. As Schneiders notes, Christian feminism demands that "language must be purified of patriarchal overtones, male exclusive references to God, and the presentation of male religious experience as normative."[26]

Christian feminism leads us to read the scriptures with new eyes, from the perspective of women. It calls us to hear the story of women today and to participate in their nonviolent struggle for equality and justice. It invites us to transform the structures of our church, to break down the walls of patriarchy, to welcome Christian women to all the ministries of the church (including leadership roles of priest, bishop, and pope). Indeed, Christian feminism calls us to a new model of church that goes beyond hierarchy to service, where the poor and the marginalized are at the center of the church. Christian feminism calls us to construct not empires or nations, but communities of service which uphold the dignity of men and women, equally.

Christian feminism charges us all to let go of any power that dominates and to be part of God's Spirit that empowers us all, women and men alike. Christian feminism invites us to a new way of understanding power; it invites us to the powerful powerlessness of nonviolence, a power which empowers others and does not oppress. Christian feminism calls us to a dramatic paradigm shift, from the world view of patriarchy and domination, which leads to oppression, imperial violence and weapons of death, to the world view of nonviolence, which leads to partnership, equality, sharing, peacemaking, justice, dignity and respect for all. The Christian feminism of nonviolence can help us give birth with God our Mother to a new world of peace, the reign of God.

CHAPTER 15

Liberating Nonviolence
and Institutionalized Violence

Making Peace with Liberation Theology

The theology emerging in recent decades from Latin America and the southern regions of the world stresses God's liberating action for the poor and oppressed. This liberation theology has revolutionized theology—and the world itself. Though some first-world theologians and religious authorities have tried to dismiss and denigrate it, liberation theology has emerged from and spoken deeply to the people of God themselves, proclaimed anew the gospel's hope for the poor in light of the world's injustices, and sparked a transformation for justice and liberation that is only just beginning.

How does liberation theology connect with a theology of nonviolence? What are the similarities, common ground, and differences that could strengthen and challenge each theological movement? A theology of nonviolence, which speaks of a peacemaking God in a world of total violence, needs to listen to the voice of liberation theology, the voice of the poor and the voice of their liberating God, in order to contribute to true social change. Likewise, the struggle for liberation in the Third World can learn from those movements and theologies of active nonviolence, which are transforming war and injustice into greater peace and justice. Together, they can point the way to a liberating nonviolence which can transform our world by rooting out the causes of violence, dismantling the structures of injustice and bearing fruit in true peace with justice for reconciled humanity.

Liberation Theology as Critical Reflection on Praxis
for Justice

Liberation theology, posed initially by Gustavo Gutiérrez in his groundbreaking work, *A Theology of Liberation*, speaks about God from the perspective of the world's poor and oppressed and about God's desire to liberate the poor from that oppression. Though liberation theology emerged primarily from Latin America, today it can encompass any theological movement that condemns specific forms of oppression and seeks true liberation (and thus includes Asian, African and African-American, as well as feminist theologies). It begins among the poor as a theology of the poor, for the poor, and by the poor. It starts with the inhuman experience of poverty, which kills millions of people around the planet. It declares that the violence of poverty is not the will of God, that God wants every human being to have life to the full, not to die in misery. Liberation theology declares that God is actively involved in the struggles of the poor to end the violence of poverty around the world. It points to the God who liberates, beginning with the biblical story of Exodus and culminating in the liberating life and message of Jesus Christ, the liberator, who continues to liberate the poor today. It explores the gospel as good news for the poor and challenges Christians to act for justice on behalf of the poor and oppressed.

When asked to define liberation theology, Gustavo Gutiérrez responded:

> Theology is a way to speak about God, a way to look at life from a faith perspective. Thus, liberation theology is an attempt to speak about God from the perspective of the poor and for the poor of Latin America. Theology is always marked by a certain point of view, a way to understand things. Our way is marked by poverty. We often say that this theology comes from this question: How to say to the poor, the oppressed, the insignificant person, "God loves you"? Ultimately, this is the question for our Christian commitment, our preaching and our theology as well. But how to say this? This question is crucial because the daily life of poor persons seems the negation of "God loves you." In other words, liberation theology addresses how to speak about God (because theology is always a way to speak about God) from the suffering of the innocents, the suffering of poor persons. I would like to say honestly that this question is larger than our capacity to answer it. It's a very deep, permanent question. Ultimately, we have no intellectual answers except to be with the poor.[1]

"Behind liberation theology, there is a spiritual experience of a liberating God, the experience of innocent suffering, the experience of the hope of the poor," Gutiérrez observes.[2] The good news of liberation theology announces the good news of the gospel, that God struggles with the poor for justice. Such news is catching fire around the world as poor people are standing up and demanding an end to injustice and a share in true justice.

In *A Theology of Liberation* Gutiérrez called for "a new way to do theology." He envisioned theology as "critical reflection on historical praxis," thus, "a liberating theology, a theology of the liberating transformation of the history of humanity and also therefore that part of humanity—gathered into *ecclesia*—which openly confesses Christ. This is a theology," he wrote, "which does not stop with reflecting on the world, but rather tries to be part of the process through which the world is transformed."[3] Liberation theology cannot simply be pondered in the classroom; it is lived among the poor who seek justice. This praxis for justice combines "both the goal and criterion" of liberation theology.[4]

The biblical reflection which accompanies the praxis of liberation theology has refocused traditional theology to view God as a God of the poor, a God who takes sides with the poor, a God who calls us to live a "preferential option" for the poor and oppressed. "For the Christian," Gutiérrez teaches, "the option for the poor is centered in God—the God of Jesus Christ who prefers the 'last.' The preference for the poor wants to take very seriously the gospel expression, 'The last will be first.' Thus, our option is not rooted in the quality of the poor, but in the nature of God. We don't need to romanticize the poor to be committed. We are committed because we believe in God. It's a theocentric option."[5] Liberation theologians see Jesus precisely as the liberator of the oppressed. This Jesus is present among the poor, marginalized, oppressed and voiceless peoples who live and die on the streets and in the slums of Latin America and throughout the world. This liberating Jesus fulfills God's work of liberation and gives over his life in the struggle of justice for the poor, even to the point of dying on a cross, executed as a revolutionary for justice. Today, the liberating Christ continues that struggle of liberation for the oppressed people of the world. Indeed, the risen Christ lives on wherever people struggle for human liberation and justice.

Theology rooted in the world of the poor sees the injustices, oppression and death that the poor of the world are subjected to in each concrete situation and context. It understands that in a world of violence, the poor are belittled not just as people without resources, but as "non-relevant persons" or "non-persons," as Gutiérrez writes. This theology pushes us forward in our action for justice with the poor so that the poor will be able to live fully human lives with basic justice and human dignity. It uses social analysis combined with biblical reflection in basic Christian communities to transform the realities of injustice and oppression. It encourages us to join God in liberating the poor so they can be fully alive and fully human. It works with the poor in their faith in a liberating God for all the justices and dignities that God created for everyone, including food, decent housing, education, health care, peace and a future for all children. In this light the great icon and martyr of the poor, Archbishop Oscar Romero, assassinated in El Salvador on March 24, 1980, rephrased the age-old insight of St. Irenaeus to declare that God is not just glorified in the fullness of human life, but given our world, specifically, "the glory of God is the poor person fully alive!"[6]

Liberation theology does justice. It both *denounces* the systemic, social sins of violence and injustice, which kill millions of poor people throughout the world, and it *announces* the good news of God's liberation for justice and peace, for the creation of a new world where everyone knows the fullness of life. Liberation theology insists on the gospel imperative to do justice, accompany the poor and liberate all who suffer under oppression. It speaks to a faith life that struggles for justice for and with the poor, that labors to break free from the oppressive structures which oppress the Third World. Such theology is necessarily, as Gutiérrez points out, the "second act." The "first act" involves commitment, the personal decision we make with our whole being to be available to God and the poor of the world for the transformation of the world.[7]

The Biblical Images of Liberation

Liberation theology correctly highlights the primordial demand for justice for the poor which is at the core of the scriptures. Thousands of base Christian communities gather every day around the Third World to study this scripture in light of the poverty and injustice they suffer. The poor are now reading the scriptures from their perspective of injustice. They bring a new hermeneutic of suspicion to the text, questioning first-world interpretations that justify and bless the structures of injustice which oppress the poor.

From Exodus to Isaiah, from the gospel of Matthew to the Book of Revelation, we read about a God who takes sides with the poor in their struggle for liberation. The God of Exodus led the suffering people out of oppression (Ex 1:8-14; 2:23-24; 3:7-10ff); this same God became incarnate among the poor, journeyed to Jerusalem and underwent crucifixion to offer a resurrection gift of peace that brings justice and liberation to all humanity. This liberating God is the same God liberating the poor of today's world. Walbert Bühlmann comments on this new insight to the biblical understanding of the God of the poor:

> Too long had we preached a piety that was individualistic (you and your Jesus), spiritualistic (save your soul!), and supernaturalistic (make no account of the goods of this world; strive rather for those of eternity). [Now] we rediscovered the fact that the God of the Bible gets very involved in politics, takes sides with the poor, hears the cry of the beloved people, and leads them out of the Egypt of their political and economic misery. God can do very well, thank you, without incense and animal sacrifices. God wants a commitment to the poor, and the prophets said so in no uncertain terms. Jesus, too, wrought signs of God's power and love for all women and men, especially the poor, the sick, the starving, and sinners. And so we Christians have come to know once more that it is not enough to cry, "Lord, Lord!"[8]

"To know God is to do justice," the prophet Jeremiah proclaimed to an unjust world (22:13-16). Our very religion is the doing of justice, for the God we worship liberates the poor and brings justice to the poor. Indeed, as Jeremiah and the prophets proclaimed, to worship God is to join God in bringing justice and liberation to the poor and oppressed. As Robert McAfee Brown explains, "To know God is not to engage in private piety or subscribe to certain orthodox statements or worship correctly on the Sabbath. To know God is to do justice. Conversely, the sign of not knowing God is to do injustice."[9] The prophet Amos, as another example, cried out God's same message of justice and liberation:

> Yes, I know how many are your crimes, how grievous your sins: oppressing the just, accepting bribes, repelling the needy at the gate! . . . Seek good and not evil, that you may live; then truly will the Lord, the God of hosts, be with you as you claim! Hate evil and love good, and let justice prevail at the gate, then it may be that the Lord, the God of hosts, will have pity on the remnant of Joseph . . . I hate, I spurn your feasts, I take no pleasure in your solemnities; your cereal offerings I will not accept, nor consider your stall-fed peace offerings. Away with your noisy songs! I will not listen to the melodies of your harps. But if you would offer me holocausts, then let justice roll down like waters and goodness like an unfailing stream (Amos 5:12-15, 21-24).

The concluding chapters of Isaiah put forward the case of God's liberating work in no uncertain terms:

> Is this the manner of fasting I wish, of keeping a day of penance: that a person bow his head like a reed and lie in sackcloth and ashes? Do you call this a fast, a day acceptable to the Lord? This, rather, is the fasting that I wish: releasing those bound unjustly, untying the thongs of the yoke; setting free the oppressed, breaking every yoke; sharing your bread with the hungry, sheltering the oppressed and the homeless; clothing the naked when you see them, and not turning your back on your own. Then your light shall break forth like the dawn, and your wound shall quickly be healed; your vindication shall go before you, and the glory of the Lord shall be your rear guard. Then you shall call, and the Lord will answer, you shall cry for help and God will say: Here I am! If you remove from your midst oppression, false accusation and malicious speech; if you bestow your bread on the hungry and satisfy the afflicted; then light shall rise for you in the darkness, and the gloom shall become for you like midday, then the Lord will guide you always and give you plenty even on the parched land (Is 58:5-11).

According to the gospel of Luke (4:16-30), Jesus began his public ministry by choosing Isaiah's bold appeal for liberation from oppression and justice for the poor. Quoting Isaiah 61:1-2, Jesus opened the scroll and read:

> The Spirit of the Lord is upon me; because God has anointed me to bring good news to the poor. God has sent me to proclaim

liberty to captives and recovery of sight to the blind, to let
the oppressed go free, and to proclaim a year acceptable to
the Lord.

After sitting down, Jesus announced to the congregation, "Today, this scripture passage is fulfilled in your hearing." Though they were initially "amazed" at his words, it only took a few minutes before they were so offended and threatened by his revolutionary message that they tried to kill him by throwing him off the cliff outside the synagogue. In a sense, the people of God still have trouble accepting Jesus' revolutionary announcement. Jesus' whole life summons us on a mission of liberation and justice, a ministry to the poor and oppressed for a radical transformation and restructuring of the world. For the comfortable, such an announcement can be bad news, because it requires a political and economic conversion toward the struggle of liberation for the poor and oppressed. For the poor, this event announces God's active solidarity in their struggle for justice and liberation.

The good news which Jesus preached to the poor has been summed up by Matthew in the Sermon on the Mount (Mt 5:1-7:28) and by Luke in the Sermon on the Plain (Lk 6:21-49). This message is addressed to the poor gathered around Jesus and begins with a blessing toward those poor. Blessed are the poor, the beatitudes proclaim, for the reign of God is yours. As Gutiérrez points out, this blessedness proclaims the coming of God's liberation of the poor; indeed, the fulfillment of God's reign of justice is at hand and specifically for them:

> "Blessed are you poor for yours is the kingdom of God" does not
> mean, it seems to us: "Accept your poverty because later this
> injustice will be compensated for in the kingdom of God." If we
> believe that the Kingdom of God is a gift which is received in
> history, and if we believe, as the eschatological promises—so
> charged with human and historical content—indicate to us, that
> the Kingdom of God necessarily implies the reestablishment of
> justice in this world, then we must believe that Christ says that
> the poor are blessed *because* the Kingdom of God has begun:
> "The time has come; the Kingdom of God is upon you" (Mk
> 1:15). In other words, the elimination of the exploitation and
> poverty that prevent the poor from being fully human has begun;
> a Kingdom of justice which goes even beyond what they could
> have hoped for has begun. They are blessed because the coming
> of the Kingdom will put an end to their poverty by creating a
> world of brotherhood and sisterhood. They are blessed because
> the Messiah will open the eyes of the blind and will give bread to
> the hungry. Situated in a prophetic perspective, the text in Luke
> uses the term *poor* [to mean] . . . poverty is an evil and therefore
> incompatible with the Kingdom of God, which has come in its
> fullness into history and embraces the totality of human existence.[10]

The Sermon on the Mount (and the Plain) trumpets good news of liberation and justice aimed specifically to the poor and oppressed peoples of the earth. It calls forth the reign of God's justice and peace, which is at hand, and affirms them in their struggle, God's struggle, for justice and liberation. But the culmination of the Sermon on the Mount (and the Plain) outlines a mandate more revolutionary than any of us have been prepared to hear; it invites us to nonviolence, the unconditional love of God at work in us through the love of enemies, which can bring down imperial systems of war, injustice and oppression. The proclamation of nonviolence in Jesus' teachings caps his good news of liberation to the poor.

The gospels make clear that Jesus understood the connection between liberation for justice and peacemaking through nonviolent love. Indeed, Jesus challenged the theologians of his day for neglecting both justice and peace. "Alas for you Pharisees," Jesus said at the house of a Pharisee. "You who pay your tithe of mint and rue and all sorts of garden herbs and overlook justice and the love of God! These you should have practiced" (Lk 11:42). Seek justice for the poor and practice the love of God, what I call the way of active nonviolence, Jesus tells the comfortable theologians of his day. Liberation and nonviolence are the number one priorities for Jesus' theology and they must be put into action before anything else.

How seriously we take Jesus' command to seek justice and practice the nonviolent love of God, to connect his message of liberation with his way of resisting evil through active nonviolence and the love of enemies, will measure our discipleship. Entrance into the poor's struggle for liberation and nonviolent transformation will unlock the door into God's reign of justice and peace. An exploration into this connection between liberation theology and a theology of nonviolence may help us connect the movements for justice and the movements for peace. When these theologies and movements connect, when theologians join the poor in practicing justice and nonviolence, then the reign of God's justice and peace will indeed be at hand.

Connecting Liberation Theology and a Theology of Nonviolence

The gospel message of liberation the poor are teaching us affects our theology of nonviolence. Instead of a "passive" nonviolence, which first-world Christians sometimes advocate, a nonviolence which actually is no nonviolence at all, liberation theology challenges us to root our theology in the poor's struggle for justice and liberation. It calls us to a risky, active nonviolence that takes on and transforms the structures and institutions of injustice and oppression which kill the poor around the world. Our hermeneutic of suspicion needs to hear the perspective of the poor as they invite us into their life struggle for justice, a struggle which will require further change of lifestyle, conversion of heart and a deeper solidarity.

Meanwhile, a theology of nonviolence challenges liberation theology not to give in to the despair of revolutionary violence, but to hear and practice the challenging, revolutionary nonviolence of Jesus and the Sermon on the Mount which, when practiced, conveys good news of liberation to the poor. Indeed, a theology of nonviolence calls us beyond every form of violence, whether institutionalized structural violence, repressive military violence or revolutionary violence. It bestows the weapon of God on the poor and oppressed, the weapon of nonviolent resistance to evil and the love of enemies which can transform us all, liberating both the oppressed and the oppressors into God's reign of justice and peace.

Fundamentally, liberation theology names a theology of the poor. This theology characterizes their claim in the reign of God's justice as a gift that belongs to them. Thus, the poor of the world are not waiting for white, first-world North Americans to liberate them; they are moving ahead in their own faith journey into God's reign. The challenge to North American peacemakers lies in not just being for the poor, but resisting the forces of destruction that are killing the poor around the world. Thus, a preferential option for the poor professed by the North American solidarity movement expresses a commitment to resist institutionalized violence, low-intensity conflict, and the militarism that holds the poor of the world hostage to first-world greed. A liberation theology of North America becomes then a theology of disarmament, transformation, nonviolence and resistance.

In this connection of justice and peace Gutiérrez writes that all Christians are invited to join the class struggle of the poor and oppressed for justice. We are called to take sides as God does. "Neutrality is impossible. It is not a question of admitting or denying a fact which confronts us; rather it is a question of which side we are on."[11] As we follow Christ and become people of nonviolence, we need to begin among the poor and oppressed, as Jesus did, in their journey of nonviolent resistance and transformation. As we join the victims of the world's institutionalized violence, we will be undertaking a true nonviolence, the nonviolence of God, who sided with the poor by becoming incarnate among them. Gutiérrez expresses this connection of nonviolence and liberation:

> The universality of Christian love is only an abstraction unless it becomes concrete history, process, conflict; it is arrived at only through particularity. To love all men and women does not mean avoiding confrontations; it does not mean preserving a fictitious harmony. Universal love is that which in solidarity with the oppressed seeks also to liberate the oppressors from their own power, from their ambition, and from their selfishness . . . One loves the oppressors by liberating them from themselves. But this cannot be achieved except by resolutely opting for the oppressed, that is, by combatting the oppressive class. It must be a real and effective combat, not hate. This is the challenge, as new as the gospel: to love our enemies . . . It is not a question of having no enemies, but rather of not excluding them from our love. But love does not mean that the oppressors are no longer enemies, nor does it eliminate the radicalness of the combat

against them. "Love of enemies" does not ease tensions; rather it challenges the whole system and becomes a subversive formula.[12]

Both theologies need to listen to the experience of the poor and to those who struggle to become a people of nonviolence in a world of imperial violence. This listening will spark a deeper faith and new directions for both; it will lead to a deeper liberation, a deeper nonviolence, a global transformation for justice and peace. In this deepening, liberation theology and a theology of nonviolence will lead Christians to protest and resist every form of violence, oppression and injustice, from institutionalized violence, repressive violence and revolutionary violence, to systemic injustice, fascism, nuclear war, hunger, disease and every form of poverty.

Liberation theology calls a theology of nonviolence to be rooted in the experience of the poor and oppressed, in the struggle of the poor for justice, so that our nonviolence has integrity, passion and action. It will be, like Jesus, a nonviolence that liberates.

Three twentieth-century figures who fully integrated the struggle for liberation and the way of nonviolence are Gandhi, King and Day. In his movement for the suffering masses of India, Gandhi encouraged the liberation of India from the brutal British oppression, but he did so specifically along the principles of nonviolence. Martin Luther King, Jr., followed Jesus and Gandhi by sparking a liberation movement against the racial injustice that oppresses African-Americans throughout the United States. King was both a liberation theologian and a theologian of nonviolence; both a practitioner of liberation and nonviolence. Indeed, King enacted a liberating nonviolence which caught the imagination of the world. Perhaps more than anyone in this century, King spoke for the poor, for justice and for peace. Similarly, Dorothy Day lived the connections between God's justice for the poor and God's movement for peace. In her Catholic Worker houses of hospitality she accompanied the homeless poor with her very life. At the same time she taught and practiced the gospel nonviolence that said no to every war and proclaimed Christ's way of nonviolence. Her life witness for justice and peace continues to bear fruit not only in the church but throughout North America. Her life suggests the real connection between liberation and nonviolence, a solidarity with the poor and the peacemaking peoples of the world. Dorothy Day called for both a preferential option for the poor and a preferential option for peace. With Gandhi, King, Day—and the thousands of others around the world who are making the connections—the liberating, nonviolent reign of God is at hand.

These connections are already being made by the poor and oppressed peoples of the world, from repatriating Guatemalan refugees to the indigenous peoples of Ecuador. "Our village is open to everyone whose intentions are good," said Natividad Epalan as she declared the village of Cantomanyog on the island of Negros the first zone of peace in the Philippines. "We wish to be free from the danger of weapons of war and death. Therefore, whoever enters this zone of peace should not bring any guns with them."[13] The residents have no weapons to enforce their zone of peace, but the publicity of their stand and the moral force of nonviolence behind it has kept the violence away. Their declaration caught the imagination of the nation and gave people new hope in their nonviolent struggle for justice and liberation.

A Theology of Liberating Nonviolence

Liberation theology and a theology of nonviolence blend together into a liberating nonviolence, the active peacemaking that Jesus lived, taught and practiced. Liberation challenges nonviolence to side with the poor, to risk our first-world privileges, indeed our very lives in a nonviolent struggle for liberation and justice for the poor. The call of liberation and nonviolence to the Christian community of the First World is Jesus' call to the rich official in Luke's gospel: "Sell all that you have and distribute it to the poor, and you will have a treasure in heaven. Then come, follow me" (Lk 17:22). When the man went away sad, Jesus turned to his disciples and told them: " How hard it is for those who have wealth to enter the reign of God! It is easier for a camel to pass through the eye of a needle than for a rich person to enter the reign of God" (Lk 17:24-25). After asking who can be saved, Peter told Jesus, "We have given up our possessions and followed you," to which Jesus responded, "There is no one who has given up house or wife [or husband] or brothers or sisters or parents or children for the sake of the reign of God who will not receive back an overabundant return in this present age and eternal life in the age to come" (Lk 17:28-29). Like the rich official, North American Christians are called to sell our possessions, give them away to the poor and follow Jesus to the cross in his nonviolent struggle for justice and peace. If our lives are to be good news of liberation to the poor and oppressed of the world, we have to enter as closely as possible into solidarity with them. In other words, we have to change our lifestyles to be serious about nonviolence. Indeed, in order to resist the institutionalized violence which the US economy wages against the world's poor (including the poor in the United States), we need to withdraw from this economic system, resist the culture's mad rush of consumerism and begin a living solidarity with the poor. Then our nonviolence—and our theology—will be more authentic. We will be given new eyes to read the scriptures and see the vision of God's reign coming to us all.

"Christian poverty, an expression of love," as Gutiérrez concludes, "is solidarity with the poor and is a protest against poverty."[14] The life of active nonviolence, liberation theology teaches us, includes a life of Christian poverty as an expression of love, a solidarity with the poor and the nonviolent protest against the poverty inflicted on the poor. This Christian solidarity of voluntary poverty and simple lifestyle joins the poor in their struggle for justice. It seeks the conversion of the First World's spending, away from billions spent on weapons of war and global annihilation to money spent for food, medicine and housing for the world's poor. Such active solidarity with the poor will push us forward to speak out the truth of justice in a spirit of nonviolence, to break the silence of our complicity with systemic injustice from which we benefit economically. As we befriend the poor we will find ourselves more and more able to risk our lives for those we love, the poor and oppressed who suffer and die under the brutalities of the world's governments. The poor, our friends, will convert our hearts, fill us with love and help us to know the forgiveness of God through their forgiveness of us. As we change our lives and our lifestyles, we will be converted; we will begin to understand the depth with which many poor people love their enemies and practice nonviolence; we will experience this love firsthand. This solidarity will help us risk civil disobedience to imperial violence and willingly take on suffering without retaliation because our hearts will be on fire for the liberation of those we love, those oppressed by the system. As we join in the struggle for liberation, our nonviolence will become more provocative, more creative, more public—more nonviolent—because it will be grounded in the suffering peoples of the earth. Finally, as we enter into greater solidarity with the poor and oppressed, we will be given the gift of hope. The poor have great hope in God, and hope is granted to those who believe and place all their trust in God and God's way of nonviolent action for justice. The poor can liberate us from our first-world despair and teach us to hope.

A steadfast, liberating nonviolence will struggle to liberate the poor from the oppressive violence of poverty that our culture inflicts on them, as well as to liberate us from our own violence. Because this task is so great, we can only do it through the liberating grace of a nonviolent God. An active, liberating nonviolence will help us renew our Christianity and take our gospel more seriously. Indeed, we will become nonviolent revolutionaries seeking not just the overthrow of the status quo but the transformation of society and human hearts as well. Such solidarity will require a deeper commitment to the poor and oppressed around the world. As we accompany, befriend and love the poor, we will realize the depths of the world's violence and understand finally that we can no longer stand idly by. We need to commit our entire lives to their liberating, nonviolent struggle for justice.

Oscar Romero reflected a theology of liberating nonviolence that struggled for the liberation of the oppressed poor and an end to institutionalized violence, as well as the repressive violence and revolutionary violence that sowed further seeds of destruction. Romero's liberating nonviolence called for conversion, demanded a real accompaniment (and defense) of the poor and an outspoken proclamation of the truth, even if such truth-telling cost him his life. "Like a voice crying in the desert, we must continually say No to violence and Yes to peace," Romero urged. His pastoral letter of August 1978 called for an active nonviolence and new justice for the poor, which would root out the causes of violence. He outlined the evils of "institutional violence," begged for the conversion of the repressive forces and advocated "the power of nonviolence that today has conspicuous students and followers." "The counsel of the gospel to turn the other cheek to an unjust aggressor, far from being passive or cowardly," he wrote, "is the showing of great moral force that leaves the aggressor morally overcome and humiliated . . . There is an unshakable moral principle that says one cannot do evil in order to achieve good," he concluded.[15] Romero committed himself to that nonviolent struggle for the liberation of the poor and continues, like Jesus, to invite us into that poor's struggle for justice with an active love.

Like Romero, Dom Helder Camara of Brazil has long linked the struggle of liberation with the movement of nonviolence that resists structured violence. Camara is credited with forming Brazil's base community movement, which today has over 100,000 communities; he is also considered a founding father of liberation theology. As the primary organizer of the 1968 Latin American Bishops' Conference in Medellín, he was the first to promote the preferential option for the poor for the church of Latin America and the worldwide church. He speaks as one of the church's greatest proponents of gospel nonviolence. "When I give food to the poor, they call me a saint," he has observed, "but when I ask why there are poor, I am called a communist." Though he has survived death threats and assassination attempts for his call for nonviolent conversion, liberation and revolution, he still holds a deep unconditional love for all people. Indeed, Camara loves his enemies, and that has made all the difference. "In the heart of every human being there are faults and sins, but there is always love," Camara told me once. "I think for human eyes, it is not easy to discover love in certain hearts, but God is able to discover love."[16] Camara appeals to the love in every human heart to join in the struggle for justice for the poor and the nonviolent witness for Christ's peace.

Similarly, Adolfo Perez Esquivel of Argentina, founder of Latin America's SERPAJ movement (Service for Peace and Justice), a movement of active nonviolence for the end of poverty and war, calls the poor of Latin America and the Third World to an active nonviolence. As he explained when he accepted the 1980 Nobel Peace Prize:

> For this continent where I live, the choice of the evangelical power of nonviolence presents itself, I am convinced, as a challenge that opens up new and radical perspectives. It is a choice that gives priority to a value essentially and profoundly Christian—the dignity of the human being, the sacred, transcendent, and irrevocable dignity that belongs to the human being by reason of being a child of God and a brother or sister in Christ, and therefore our own brother or sister. In these long years of struggle for our organization—the Service for Peace and Justice in Latin America—we have walked by the side of the poorest and most disadvantaged . . . We have much to share in order to achieve, by means of the nonviolent struggle, the abolition of injustices and the attainment of a more just and humane society for all. It is a walking side by side with our brothers and sisters—with those who are persecuted, those who hunger and thirst for justice, those who suffer because of oppression, those who are anguished by the prospect of war, those who suffer the cruel impact of violence or see constantly postponed the achievement of their basic rights . . . Despite so much suffering and pain, I live in hope

because I feel that Latin America has risen to its feet. Its liberation can be delayed but never denied. We live in hope because we believe, like St. Paul, that love never dies. Human beings in the historical process have created enclaves of love by their active practice of solidarity throughout the world, and with a view to the full-orbed liberation of peoples and all humanity. For me it is essential to have the inward peace and serenity of prayer in order to listen to the silence of God, which speaks to us, in our personal lives and in the history of our times, about power of love. Because of our faith in Christ and humankind, we must apply our humble efforts to the construction of a more just and human world. And I want to declare emphatically: Such a world is possible.[17]

"We know that peace is only possible when it is the fruit of justice," Esquivel told the gathering in Oslo. "True peace is the result of the profound transformation effected by nonviolence which is, indeed, the power of love."[18]

In 1986, when I asked Perez Esquivel about the connections between liberation for justice and active nonviolence, he turned first to the gospel. "The gospel itself is revolutionary," he said. "It is a liberating force."

When one begins to read the gospel from this perspective, everything becomes a liberating message, everything follows a coherent line of liberating action. Many Christians see the call to pacifism in the gospels. The Sermon on the Mount is where all the strength and power of this nonviolent liberating message is concentrated and synthesized. When Jesus says, "If someone strikes you on one cheek, turn the other," he's not telling us to be stupid. He's calling us to change the situation, to act in a different manner, to change bad into good, to return good for evil, to respond to injustice in a new way. Under no circumstances does that mean weakness. [The work before us] is to assume a deeper understanding of the liberating message of the gospel. The work is to break the structures of dominance through the force of nonviolence and through a personal commitment (such as a vow of nonviolence). Public demonstrations and confrontative actions, too, are important. Nonviolence needs to be directed toward social transformation, creating new alternatives in the economic situation, in the relations of power, and in the political and cultural situations.[19]

With Gandhi, King and Day, Helder Camara and Perez Esquivel symbolize those disciples who have integrated the struggle for liberation with the gospel mandate of nonviolence. They reject violence, even for revolutionary causes. They practice the revolutionary, liberating nonviolence of Jesus.

A theology of liberation and nonviolence, if adopted by Christians around the world, can unleash the gospel's power to liberate the poor from the lethal structures of poverty, injustice and war. For North Americans, living in a culture of unparalleled violence, this new, active theology will lead us to resist the corporate and military structures which kill the poor at home and abroad. The combination of liberation for justice and active nonviolence leads to a subversive, revolutionary theology, indeed, to the gospel itself, which we discover is both liberating and nonviolent. In this new link we can discover God's way to justice and peace. Indeed, we will encounter the risen Jesus, who leads the poor in a movement of nonviolent liberation.

The True practice of LT must work from a person's inner heart to her or his outer behaviors. LW is exactly this

CHAPTER 16

The Seamless Garment
of Nonviolence

A Consistent Ethic of Life

As we explore the various manifestations and inconsistencies that violence takes, we begin to notice the consistency of nonviolence. Eileen Egan, a founder of Pax Christi and associate of Mother Teresa and Dorothy Day, first coined the phrase "seamless garment of life" in order to speak of a consistent ethic of life. In light of a theology of nonviolence, we might rename this new insight the *seamless garment of nonviolence* or *the consistent ethic of nonviolence*. As we begin to move from theological reflection into action for justice and peace, we need to note how nonviolence connects to all issues and every variety of violence in a theological framework of grace and peace.

The Consistency of Nonviolence

The image of a seamless garment harkens back to the cloak woven as one cloth for which the soldiers threw dice after they crucified Jesus. A seamless garment approach to ethics links all the issues in the one vision of Jesus. It maintains that we cannot be selective in our ethics. It claims a logical method to every instance of violence and injustice. It upholds a unity and integrity for our ethical practices. It notes that Jesus' life, like his garment, was one, whole, integrated piece and challenges his followers to preserve that unity of vision with consistent practice. It criticizes those who practice an ethic of convenience, which in reality is no ethic at all. True ethics, based on the moral practice of Jesus, is not about pragmatism but rather about fidelity and consistency. It understands that we cannot have both morality and immorality; for example, we cannot be against killing in certain circumstances and for killing in other situations.

Nonviolence is consistent. By definition, nonviolence holds that violence is never justified, that killing another human being is always immoral, and that no violence is ever acceptable. For a consistent ethic of nonviolence, all issues are linked together in the question of life and death. All human life is understood as sacred, thus anything that hurts others or takes life is opposed to the consistent ethic of life. Nonviolence calls for obedience to the God of life who says, "Thou shalt not kill." This God does not say, "Thou shalt not kill the innocent, but thou shalt kill the guilty." We are told, "Thou shalt not kill"—period. A seamless garment of nonviolence holds, therefore, that all forms of violence—including war, poverty, structured violence, repressive violence, revolutionary violence, nuclear weapons, the death penalty, abortion, hunger, racism, sexism and classism—are to be resisted and transformed.

Just as it says no to every form of violence, a consistent ethic of nonviolence says yes to every form of life and justice. For the Christian, the ethic recognizes that Christ-God is present in every human being. Christ lives in the unborn, the imprisoned, the marginalized, the homeless, the poor and the enemy.

In this nonviolent approach to life we cannot oppose one manifestation of violence, such as abortion, and support another, such as the death penalty. We cannot be pro-life regarding abortion and yet support violence against women, war or the death penalty. Such inconsistencies are, by definition, pro-death. If we support violence in any form, we cannot be considered authentically pro-life. Thus, when George Bush claimed to be pro-life regarding abortion, but ordered and supervised the slaughter of nearly half a million Iraqis in the Persian Gulf war, he proved that he was in reality pro-death. Nonviolence maintains that we cannot support life for some people but not for others. To be nonviolent, we have to be for life for each and every human being, including enemies, criminals, the unborn, murderers, and oppressed and marginalized peoples. A consistent ethic of nonviolence stands against every form of violence.

The political divisions over abortion clearly highlight the inconsistency of violence. To claim to be against abortion and yet say nothing about the sexism, patriarchy, racism, and classism which are often at the root of abortion, or to fail to make the connection between abortion and the Pentagon, is to be inconsistent and not truly pro-life. Life itself is consistent; a theology of nonviolence demands the same consistency. Elizabeth McAlister, Coretta Scott King and Shelley Douglass are among the women who, as feminists, make the connections among abortion, the death penalty, nuclear war and poverty, thereby demonstrating what a consistent ethic of nonviolence is all about. As Jim Douglass explains it:

> As long as we prepare each day in our research institutes, corporations, and military bases to incinerate millions of children and adults abroad, why should we be surprised at an acceptance of the killing of unborn children in America? Abortion is the domestic side of the nuclear arms race. The people who believe in abortion as a necessary evil are often very different politically.

* "a little child shall lead you"

But what we all seem to hold in common in America, from pro-life weapons technicians to pacifist abortionists, is a willingness to take human life on a massive scale for the sake of a particular freedom. Human life is not held sacred in this country . . . Patriarchy (the systematic, institutionalized control of women by men) and its consequence, unwanted pregnancies, are the reasons why women get abortions . . . Abortion is a threefold violence. The first two stages of abortion's violence are a patriarchal violence done by men to women and the violence which a woman inflicts on herself in abortion. The third stage of abortion's violence is the killing of an unborn child . . . In a patriarchal society whose overall respect for human life can be measured by its nuclear stockpile, abortion is a desperate counter-violence seen as a form of self-defense by women, in much the same way as some Third World people see terrorist violence as a means of survival. The killing done through terrorist violence will not be stopped by the use of greater force by affluent nations. Killing by Third World revolutionaries will end when justice for them and their people is no longer blocked by the rich and powerful nations. Killing done through abortions, in a patriarchal society fortified by nuclear weapons, will not be stopped by anti-abortion laws but by a double conversion in the American people: a conversion to the underlying sacredness of human life and a conversion to a view of women equal to men in their rights and dignity. The destruction of life in their wombs by desperate women will cease as their society becomes one in which women are respected, life is recognized as sacred, and men assume equal responsibility with women for the care of their children . . . Our support of patriarchy and the Pentagon makes abortion inevitable.[1]

An important ingredient in the nonviolent approach to abortion will be shared dialogue and prayer among people on all sides of the issue. Such conversations have begun in quiet retreat settings around the country. They hold the potential for healing the roots of our divisions, ending the violence and sowing seeds for justice and peace.

Gandhi understood the consistency of nonviolence, that it requires an even distribution in every area of life, from the private and the personal to the public and the political. "Nonviolence is not a garment to be put on and off at will," Gandhi said. "If one does not practice nonviolence in one's personal relations with others and hopes to use it in bigger affairs, one is vastly mistaken. Nonviolence is the law of life."[2]

Martin Luther King, Jr., wrestled with the consistency of nonviolence as the United States sent troops to Vietnam. When he spoke out squarely against the Vietnam war, linked the civil rights and peace movements and criticized the violence perpetrated upon blacks in the United States and the Vietnamese people, he demonstrated a consistent ethic of life. He beheld a full vision of nonviolence. As he declared, he could not "segregate his conscience."

The profound affinity between racism, economic injustice and war that called forth King's undeviating nonviolence challenged an old friend who stopped by King's Atlanta house one day in 1967 to ask about his opposition to the Vietnam war. King responded with a commitment to nonviolence that cut across all issues with breathtaking consistency:

> You've never really given this organization full credit for what it really stands for . . . It's a nonviolent organization, and when I say nonviolent, I mean nonviolent all the way . . . Never could I advocate nonviolence in this country and not advocate nonviolence for the whole world . . . That's my philosophy. I don't believe in the death and killing on any side, no matter who's heading it up—whether it be America or any other country, or whether it be blacks . . . Nonviolence is my stand, and I'll die for that stand.[3]

"At that time, I understood for the first time in my life what was meant by nonviolence," King's friend later confessed.[4]

The Human Dimension

"The real concern is for human life," writes Elizabeth McAlister. "We need to move toward a re-valuing of human life, beginning with the point at which it is most threatened and dipping deeply into the connections that exist between poverty and the military budget."[5] A position of steadfast nonviolence, which rejects every form of violence and death, is bound to draw opposition in today's divided, violent world. Because of the political overtones of such issues as abortion and the death penalty, our basic opposition to killing often gets lost in the translation. But a consistent ethic of nonviolence transcends politics and reaches beyond to the human. Nonviolence, as Thomas Merton noted, strives for "the human dimension." It aims to uplift life for every human being, including the unborn, those in prison, enemies and those are who different from us. Merton wrote:

> The basic problem is not political, it is a-political and human. One of the most important things to do is to keep cutting deliberately through political lines and barriers and emphasizing the fact that these are largely fabrications and that there is another dimension, a genuine reality, totally opposed to the fictions of politics: the human dimension which politics pretend to arrogate entirely to themselves. This is the necessary first step along the long way toward the perhaps impossible task of purifying, humanizing and somehow illuminating politics themselves.[6]

Merton's own consistent ethic of nonviolence called him to speak out against every form of violence, most specifically the institutionalized violence that relegates the majority of the world's population to poverty and hopelessness. Merton continued:

> It is my intention to make my entire life a rejection of, a protest against the crimes and injustices of war and political tyranny which threaten to destroy the whole race of humanity and the world. By my monastic life and vows I am saying No to all the concentration camps, the aerial bombardments, the staged political trials, the judicial murders, the racial injustices, the economic tyrannies, and the whole socio-economic apparatus which seems geared for nothing but global destruction in spite of all its fair words in favor of peace.[7]

The Nonviolent Reign of God

The consistent ethic of nonviolence flows from the gospel vision of Jesus and its image of the God of nonviolence. It models the consistent ethic and practice of Jesus, who healed the ill, served those in need, reconciled the divided and challenged all to live the unconditional love of God. It asks, with Jesus, "Is it lawful to do good . . . rather than do evil, to save life rather than to destroy it?" (Mk 3:4). It declares, with Jesus, "Let the one without sin be the first to cast a stone" (Jn 8:7). It knows, with Jesus, that "those who take up the sword will perish with the sword" (Mt 26:52). Indeed, it enfleshes Jesus' "narrow gate," an image he proposed in the Sermon on the Mount:

> Enter through the narrow gate; for the gate is wide and the road broad that leads to destruction, and those who enter through it are many. How narrow the gate and constricted the road that leads to life. And those who find it are few (Mt 7:13-14).

A consistent ethic of nonviolence, like a narrow gate or constricted road, insists on life for all people and opposes death in any form so that all may realize the fullness of life. While most people grudgingly accept, permit or even support systemic violence, the narrow ethic of nonviolence, like Jesus, consistently says no, a voice that cries out above the din of violence.

Nonviolence helps us understand the reign of God. Jesus envisions God's reign as a place where all killing and all violence cease, where life reigns freely in peace, justice and unconditional love. To understand a consistent ethic of nonviolence we need to review the basic tenets of God's reign, including justice, a preferential option for the poor, compassion, nonjudgment, forgiveness and unconditional love.

First, a consistent ethic of nonviolence demands that justice be a priority. It recognizes the evils of racism, sexism, classism, greed, apathy and fear that pervade our world and lead us to killing. It acknowledges that we need to dismantle all structures of injustice, every system of violence, in order to weed out the roots of violence among us. We need to create alternative, nonviolent structures of justice, so that everyone will have adequate food, housing, health care, education, opportunity and dignity.

Second, this new ethic practices compassion toward all those who are suffering. It literally "feels with those who suffer," whether victims of violent crime, relatives of those victims, those on death row, the unborn, women who resort to abortion, victims of starvation or war. The ethic seeks to enflesh the compassion of God.

Third, from this heartfelt compassion nonviolence takes a preferential option for the poor, which includes all those who are threatened by systemic violence, from the unborn to those on death row, to the hungry and the homeless, to those who live in poverty and degradation. From this perspective of a preferential option for the poor we seek justice and peace for everyone—but we start with those on the bottom of society, the marginalized, the poor, the unborn and all those threatened with death.

Fourth, nonviolence does not judge others. As we seek justice in a spirit of compassion we do not judge those who commit acts of violence, whether rich oppressors or nuclear weapons manufacturers or suffering inner-city women who seek abortion or third-world revolutionaries who fight for freedom. Our compassion transcends political lines, opposing the killing and the injustice rather than specific people, and thus reaches out in a spirit of love to call all to the fullness of life.

Fifth, nonviolence practices unlimited forgiveness, even toward those who commit the most atrocious crimes of violence. The gospel of Jesus calls us to forgive "seventy times seven times," a metaphor for the infinite forgiveness of God. Thus, we are even called to forgive anyone who kills, without resorting to the violent retaliation of the death penalty. We are called to forgive those who wage war against us, calling them to a change of heart by our insistence on justice and our invitation to reconciliation. We are called to forgive those who support systemic violence. With this grace of forgiveness God promises to give us new strength and to lead us further into God's reign of nonviolence and justice.

Finally, a consistent ethic of nonviolence is rooted in unconditional love, a love even for enemies, as Jesus taught (Mt 5:43-48). If we practice unconditional love on a systemic level, then we cannot wage war against other nations; we cannot drop bombs on others; we cannot build nuclear weapons; we cannot send satellites into space for laser-beam warfare; we cannot allow others to starve to death or live in misery; we cannot participate in systemic injustice; we cannot but help to welcome the unborn and protect those who take life from others. The love of God becomes the standard by which we measure our own actions.

* LW: "The poorer you are, the more Jesus will love you."

The Consistent Ethic of the Cross

The consistent ethic of life and nonviolence finds its fullest expression on the cross, where Jesus suffered and died because he insisted on the truth of God's reign. He died a victim of the death penalty, but he refused to retaliate or to give in to hatred; instead, he forgave those who killed him and offered a heartfelt prayer of mercy. He witnessed to the spirit of unconditional love and invited us all to practice that transforming love in our lives and in our world. Jesus' steadfast nonviolence culminated in his resurrection, when God affirmed his consistency, revealing to humanity the possibility of a new way of life, the way of nonviolence.

This new ethic, then, chooses not to inflict death on others but, like Jesus, embraces the poor and oppressed, who are victims of the world's violence, in a spirit of unconditional love, steadfast truth and a commitment to nonviolence. It refuses to retaliate and accepts suffering while insisting on justice and life for all people everywhere. The cross presents the fullest expression of the consistent ethic of nonviolence. The gospels invite us all to take up that cross and walk the way of nonviolence. In today's complex world, making ethical decisions in accordance with the gospel and our conscience continues to be difficult. We need communities of faith and nonviolence to reflect and discern together how to make decisions and respond to violence within the consistent ethic of Jesus' nonviolence.

A theology of nonviolence upholds the consistent ethic of life, not naively or simplistically, but with an honest look at reality, at human life and at the gospel invitation to nonviolence. It seeks to understand the God who is consistent, the God of life who gives us life and calls us to the fullness of life. This God clearly is a God of nonviolence, who calls us to become a people of nonviolence. In order to be that people, we need to become consistent, to make the hard choices and to choose the narrow path of nonviolence. If we do, we pave the way to that new world where all can live life to the full.

This is why Thérèse welcomed suffering. For her, suffering was LOVE - OVERCOMING - VIOLENCE.

CHAPTER 17

Spirituality and Nonviolence

The Contemplative Roots of Nonviolence

"Nonviolence is the greatest force at the disposal of humanity," Gandhi once wrote. "It is mightier than the mightiest weapon of destruction devised by the ingenuity of humanity."[1] When we begin to plumb the depths of nonviolence, when we explore the spiritual dimensions of active nonviolence both within our own hearts and souls and among our sisters and brothers in humanity, we enter God's ongoing transformation of the world from the self-destructive chaos of violence into God's reign of nonviolence, justice and peace.

Underlying the life of Christian nonviolence is a spirituality which is an awareness of the abiding, loving presence of God in us and everywhere in the world. Indeed, this spiritual awareness of God's presence burns at the heart of nonviolence and a theology of nonviolence. Let us first attempt to define what we mean by spirituality and then examine the roots of a spirituality of nonviolence. These roots include a recognition of our unity in God; the underlying ground of love; and the prerequisites of prayer, contemplation, silence, solitude, community, fearlessness and hope.

Spirituality: Life in the Presence of God

A trap that has blocked people of faith from entering more fully into God's nonviolent transformation of the world is the all too frequent separation of our "spiritual" lives from our "real" lives, the separation of everything contemplative and prayerful from things active and public. Gandhi tried to get at this unfortunate division when he said that religion and politics are not two separate entities but the same life of service to God and humanity. He wrote, "I am endeavoring to see God through service of humanity, for I know that God is neither in heaven, nor down below, but in every one . . . The whole gamut of humanity's activities today constitutes an indivisible whole. You cannot divide social, economic, political and purely religious work into watertight compartments. I do not know any religion apart from human activity."[2]

In this spirit Gandhi acted in the world for the liberation of the oppressed peoples of India. His political work, his solidarity with the poor, his arrests and his years in prison, all were part of a continuum of nonviolence, a spirituality of nonviolence, a faith rooted in his heart that overflowed into nonviolent activity on behalf of suffering humanity. For Gandhi, nonviolence was spirituality, indeed, the only true spirituality.

Spirituality, then, is not separate from active nonviolence. The way of nonviolence maintains that spirituality is at the core of Christian peacemaking. With its roots in the gospel, Christian spirituality requires doing justice, accompanying the poor, loving enemies, making peace and living in the nonviolent Spirit of God. As followers of the greatest practitioner of nonviolence, Jesus, our spirituality is rooted in the Spirit of nonviolence. Thus, for many, Christian spirituality designates the life of Christian nonviolence.

Spirituality has been defined in many ways. For many, "spirituality refers to the way people lead their lives; it includes the deepest purpose toward which a life is directed and the values and goals that underlie motivation," Roger Haight writes. "All persons have some form of spirituality insofar as they consciously direct their lives. Christian spirituality refers to the way Christians actually live."[3] Given the world's violence, such a definition no longer suffices. Spirituality now encompasses peaceful resistance to violence and active nonviolence. Richard McBrien defines spirituality as "our way of being religious" and Christian spirituality as "one's way of experiencing God and of shaping one's life on the basis of that experience." Spirituality, he continues, is "the cultivation of a style of life consistent with the presence of the Spirit of the Risen Christ within us and with our status as members of the Body of Christ . . . [it is] our way of being Christian."[4]

William Stringfellow emphasized that spirituality must be biblically based and thus rooted in the world of violence, that is, within the framework of the fall:

> Biblical spirituality concerns living in the midst of the era of the Fall, wherein all relationships whatsoever have been lost or damaged or diminished or twisted or broken, in a way which is open to transcendence of the fallenness of each and every relationship and in which these very relationships are recovered or rendered new. This transformation wrought in biblical spirituality includes one's relationship with oneself, in the most self-conscious and radically personal sense, but it simultaneously implicates one concretely in reconciliation with the rest of creation and is thus the most profoundly political reality available to human experience. From a biblical perspective, therefore, the assertion of some species of so-called spirituality which is privatized and nonpolitical or antipolitical is, simply, nonsense.[5]

"Politics refers comprehensively to the total configuration of relationships among humans, institutions, other principalities and the rest of created life in this world," Stringfellow continues. "Politics describes the work of the Word of God in this world for redemption and the impact of that effort of the Word of God upon the fallen existence of this world, including the fallen life of human beings and that of the powers that be . . . Spirituality represents the ordinary experience of discerning and partaking in these politics ."[6] Thomas Merton describes nonviolence in a similar vein. "The chief difference between violence and nonviolence is that violence depends entirely on its own calculations. Nonviolence depends entirely on God and God's Word."[7] Our understanding of a Christian spirituality of nonviolence needs to be equally grounded in the Word of God.

Christian spirituality could be defined, then, quite simply as the way of nonviolence. Spirituality is a lifestyle of nonviolence, rooted in God, rooted in love, rooted in resistance to evil and rooted in compassion for all humanity, especially those who suffer. Christian spirituality is the life of Christian nonviolence, a life of active peacemaking rooted in the Spirit of the nonviolent, risen, peacemaking Christ.

"Nonviolence is a matter of the heart," Gandhi often said.[8] For Gandhi, to enter into God's nonviolent transformation of the world, into God's reign of justice and peace here on earth, we need first undergo that inner transformation of nonviolence. We need to plumb the spiritual depths of nonviolence within us so as to cooperate in God's nonviolent transformation of the world. This does not mean that nonviolence is for individuals only, that it is a private matter for the private soul. Nonviolence is a spiritual matter that touches individual hearts and souls, but simultaneously touches all of us together. It is a spirit that unites.

Nonviolence is the Spirit of God that disarms our hearts so that we can become God's instruments for the disarmament of the world. This nonviolent Spirit of God transforms us so as to transform the world. Spirituality, then, is the life of transformation from violence to nonviolence. It speaks of the way we enter into God's transformation of our hearts and God's transformation of humanity. It denotes the process of becoming God's instruments of peace and ultimately, the process of the entering into God's peace, indeed, into God.

Christian Spirituality and the Unity of Life

Thomas Merton spent his life exploring the roots of Christian nonviolence and practicing that way of life as best he could. He lived a spirituality of nonviolence and shared his refections on that way of life in his many writings. Shortly before he died from accidental electrocution in Bangkok in the fall of 1968, he spoke at a conference on prayer and spirituality in Calcutta. At that conference he pointed to a basic truth of nonviolence, the underlying reality of our common unity in the Spirit of God. "My dear brothers and sisters," he said, "we are already one. But we imagine that we are not. And what we have to recover is our original unity. What we have to be is what we are."[9] Asked to offer a closing prayer, Merton said:

We have to [be] aware of the love that unites us, the love that
unites us in spite of real differences, real emotional friction. The
things that are on the surface are nothing, what is deep is the
Real . . . Concentrate on the love that is in you, that is in us all . . .
O God, we are one with you. You have made us one with you.
You have taught us that if we are open to one another, you dwell
in us. Help us to preserve this openness and to fight for it with
all our hearts. Help us to realize that there can be no understanding where there is mutual rejection. O God, in accepting one
another wholeheartedly, fully, completely, we accept you, and
we thank you, and we adore you, and we love you with our whole
being, because our being is in your being, our spirit is rooted in
your spirit. Fill us then with love and let us be bound together
with love as we go our diverse ways, united in this one spirit
which makes you present in the world and which makes you witness to the ultimate reality that is love.[10]

In a letter to friends Merton wrote: "Our real journey in life is interior: it is
a matter of growth, deepening, and of an ever greater surrender to the creative action of love and grace in our hearts. Never was it more necessary for
us to respond to that action."[11]

The spirituality of nonviolence flows from a deep realization that, as Merton
said, we are all one. Every human being is equal; we are all children of God,
sisters and brothers of one another. As we continue to delve into this basic
spiritual truth—and act within and from this spiritual conviction—we begin
to realize that we can never hurt any human being or creature, much less kill,
wage war, plan the destruction of the planet or collude in institutionalized
violence. This spiritual dimension is the root of all nonviolence. It is the depth
which understands God as Spirit and Truth; it affirms that all human life is
intended to dwell in peace and justice. Within this spirituality of nonviolence
we discover, then, not just a tactic or method of resisting evil but an entirely
new way of seeing the world: from the underlying unity of all life.

Since all life is united in God, we recognize that it is God who is behind
every act of nonviolence. God is the fullest expression of nonviolence. This
nonviolent God seeks to disarm our own hearts and thus to disarm and transform our communities, our nation and the world into a world without war, a
world of justice and peace, the nonviolent reign of God on earth.

Martin Luther King, Jr., often spoke of the unity which unites all humanity
as one. Just as every act of violence affects others and leads to further violence, he pointed out, so too every act of nonviolence, every act of love, affects
others and leads to further nonviolence, to a deeper love and justice for all.
Our actions have spiritual consequences, King declared. As we journey into
the nonviolence of God we realize that we are called to be part of the spirit of
nonviolence that moves in the world, and so we allow our lives to bear the
fruit of justice and peace in the world.

Thomas Merton knew that this spiritual unity was at the heart of Gandhi's
nonviolence. Merton understood that nonviolence in action was the "living

out of a nonviolence of the heart, an inner unity already experienced in prayer."[12] Writing about Gandhi, Merton observed:

> The spirit of nonviolence sprang from inner realization of spiritual unity in himself. The whole Gandhian concept of nonviolent action and satyagraha [holding on to truth] is incomprehensible if it is thought to be a means of achieving unity rather than as the fruit of inner unity already achieved . . . The first thing of all and the most important of all was the inner unity, the overcoming and healing of inner division, the consequent spiritual and personal freedom, of which national autonomy and liberty would only be consequences.[13]

Faith in the transforming power of nonviolence is rooted in the complete oneness of God and humanity, as Gandhi wrote:

> I believe in the absolute oneness of God and therefore of humanity. What though we have many beliefs? We have but one soul. The rays of the sun are many through refraction. But they have the same source. I cannot, therefore, detach myself from the wickedest souls nor may I be denied identity with the most virtuous.[14]

"I believe in the essential unity of humanity and for that matter, of all lives," Gandhi declared. "Therefore, I believe that if one person gains spiritually, the whole world gains with that person and if one person falls the whole world falls to that extent."[15]

This attitude of nonviolence begins in the heart as God works and dwells within us. The spirit of nonviolence within then flows out into our entire lives. This spirit of nonviolence—the presence of God—touches those closest to us, our families and friends, our co-workers and communities, and from there, our neighborhoods and cities, and finally, our nation and the world. "One person who can express nonviolence in life exercises a force superior to all the forces of brutality," wrote Gandhi.[16] Spirituality is the daily, conscious struggle to live and move from the base of this essential unity of all humanity.

Christian Spirituality and the Hidden Ground of Love

The spiritual awareness of our unity in God calls us to become incarnations of God's nonviolent love in the world, where everything we do and say, indeed our very being, is loving. We see that all life is sacred, and we act from this perspective with a stance of holy love toward everything. This spirituality, rooted in love, leads inevitably to action for justice. The spirituality of nonviolence, therefore, is a life of nonviolent action, a life of active love.

Nonviolent love grows also from the awareness of God's unconditional love for each and every one of us, even though we are all sinners, all violent, all capable of killing, all able to push a button that could start a nuclear war. As we accept God's unconditional love for us, we recognize the sinfulness within ourselves and see the same violence in others. Then our hearts widen with compassion so that we reach out in active nonviolence to be God's instruments of liberating love for both oppressors and oppressed, for the entire human family.

The everyday spirituality which is the way of nonviolence blossoms with love for others concretely and personally, especially toward the poor and those perceived as enemies. Nonviolent love means renouncing every grain of retaliation in our hearts and cultivating a spirit of forgiveness and compassion for every human being.

"It is no nonviolence if we merely love those that love us," Gandhi wrote. "It is nonviolence only when we love those that hate us. I know how difficult it is to follow this grand law of love. But are not all great and good things difficult to do? Love of the hater is the most difficult of all. But by the grace of God even this most difficult thing becomes easy to accomplish if we want to do it."[17]

Nonviolence is rooted in an active love. "Gandhi believed that the central problem of our time was the acceptance or the rejection of a basic law of love and truth which had been made known to the world in traditional religions and most clearly by Jesus Christ," Thomas Merton wrote. "Gandhi himself expressly and very clearly declared himself an adherent of this one law. His whole life, his political action, finally even his death, were nothing but a witness to his commitment."[18] As Gandhi himself noted, "If love is not the law of our being, the whole of my argument falls to pieces."[19]

Further, this active, nonviolent love requires a conscious acceptance of suffering in the struggle for justice and peace without even the desire for retaliation. "Nonviolence in its dynamic condition means conscious suffering," Gandhi repeated over and over again. "It does not mean meek submission to the will of the evildoer, but it means the pitting of one's whole soul against the will of the tyrant. Working under this law of our being, it is possible for a single individual to defy the whole might of an unjust empire to save his honor, his religion, his soul and lay the foundation for that empire's fall or its regeneration."[20] A life of nonviolence is a life lost in unconditional, active love that is even willing to suffer and to die for the coming of God and God's reign of justice and peace.

Christian Spirituality and Contemplation

To maintain the spirit of nonviolence we have to believe in the God of nonviolence. "Nonviolence succeeds only when we have a living faith in God," Gandhi wrote.[21] "A living faith in nonviolence. . . is impossible without a living faith in God. A nonviolent person can do nothing save by the power and grace of God."[22] To be nonviolent in a world of violence requires listening to the God of nonviolence. Only in daily contemplation, turning to the

T's own words! (handwritten)

God of peace, do we grow in the spirit of nonviolence and become transformed.

"My greatest weapon is mute prayer," Gandhi said. "Prayer from the heart can achieve what nothing else can in the world."[23] In order to live in this everdeepening awareness of God's presence and the truth of nonviolence, we need to turn daily in prayer and contemplation to the God of nonviolence, our source of strength for lives of nonviolent action. By daily centering ourselves in God and dwelling in the very peace of God, we can walk forward into our violent world with a disarming love that touches the hearts of our sisters and brothers, allowing God to transform us all into people of nonviolence. Moreover, the regular contemplation of the God of nonviolence is our safeguard against discouragement, burnout, self-righteousness, judgmentalism and despair.

The first fruit of this daily, prayerful interaction with the God of nonviolence is a deep spirit of peace within, a spirit of humility, hope, love and trust in the God who disarms us every time we pray. "Nonviolence is not an easy thing to understand, still less to practice, weak as we are," Gandhi wrote. "We must all act prayerfully and humbly and continually ask God to open the eyes of our understanding, being ever ready to act according to the light as we daily receive it."[24]

St. Francis put it this way: "While you are proclaiming peace with your lips, be careful to have it even more fully in your heart."[25] Contemplative prayer is the way to maintain a peaceful heart. It is therefore a prerequisite of nonviolence.

This statement cannot stand alone without danger of being misunderstood. (handwritten)

Christian Spirituality and Detachment from Results

One of the greatest challenges from Gandhi's experience of nonviolence is detachment from all results. To enter into the depths of nonviolence, to develop a true spirituality of nonviolence, we have to renounce the fruits of our actions, even as we are pursuing those results in the name of nonviolence. True nonviolence is centered in God alone, fully aware that all results are in God's hands. In this way we do the good and live the truth of nonviolence, not for results, but simply because it is good and true. Thus we become more and more centered in God.

Very T (handwritten)

This attitude, so central to all Eastern religions, is very difficult for Westerners to grasp. We Westerners pride ourselves on results, effectiveness and efficiency. The entire culture of North America is built around the principle of achieving success. Nonviolence for us, then, is countercultural. It lets go of all success and leaves the outcome completely in God's hands.

This insight can be found throughout the gospels. We find it in Jesus' words in the Sermon on the Mount: "Every good tree bears good fruit and a rotten tree bears bad fruit . . . By their fruits you will know them" (Mt 7:18-20). "Your light must shine before others, that they may see your good deeds and glorify your heavenly God" (Mt 5:16). Jesus' message is not centered on re-

✱ Need to mention this in Chap. 5... (handwritten)

sults; it is centered on allowing God to bring forth the consequences of goodness in our lives.

Thomas Merton spoke directly to this challenge in his now famous letter to Jim Forest, who was organizing a Catholic peace group to resist the Vietnam war during the mid-1960s:

> Do not depend on the hope of results. When you are doing the sort of work you have taken on, essentially an apostolic work, you may have to face the fact that your work will be apparently worthless and even achieve no result at all, if not perhaps results opposite to what you expect. As you get used to this idea you start more and more to concentrate not on the results but on the value, the rightness, the truth of the work itself. And there too a great deal has to be gone through, as gradually you struggle less and less for an idea and more and more for specific people. The range tends to narrow down, but it gets much more real. In the end . . . it is the reality of personal relationships that saves everything . . . As for the big results, these are not in your hands or mine, but they can suddenly happen, and we can share in them: but there is no point in building our lives on this personal satisfaction, which may be denied us and which after all is not that important . . . All the good that you will do will come not from you but from the fact that you have allowed yourself, in the obedience of faith, to be used by God's love. Think of this more and gradually you will be free from the need to prove yourself, and you can be more open to the power that will work through you without your knowing it . . . The great thing after all is to live, not to pour out your life in the service of a myth: and we turn the best things into myths. If you can get free from the domination of causes and just serve Christ's truth, you will be able to do more and will be less crushed by the inevitable disappointments . . . I see nothing whatever in sight but much disappointment, frustration, and confusion.[26]

Gandhi's Hindu tradition called this detachment from results, this sole concentration on the goodness and the truth in the act of nonviolence, *nishkama-karma*, which, roughly translated, means "action without desire" or "doing what one must do regardless of the results."[27]

The goal, then, is purity of heart. For such purity of heart we need to be free, free even from the results of our work. The way of nonviolence does not concentrate on being effective. The outcome is in God's hands, not ours, and so we focus on living and practicing nonviolence from the core of our beings into the public arena of violence. Jim Douglass writes about this aspect of nonviolence:

> The Way [of nonviolence] is not effective. It is free. Jesus lived and died for no self-determined end but to fulfill God's will at

the center of his being. Gandhi, following the teaching of the Bhagavad-Gita, continually renounced the fruits of his actions, in contrast to his political allies, and remained free of the struggles for power which divided and almost destroyed independent India. The Way is free because it is a way not of technique and self but of openness and Being. The Way of Jesus and Gandhi is the way of liberation because, in being responsive to the suffering and injustice of the human family, it is faithful in every stage of its response to that creative truth of Being which loses itself for the life of all. Being is one. Those who live in its Way are radically free through the gift of themselves in Being's fundamental act of self-emptying love. The Way re-creates in the soul of those who walk it, through the gift of themselves, the union of all creation in the fullness of God.[28]

In this light, then, the active nonviolence of civil disobedience, which might land us in prison is, in Douglass's words, both "technically ineffective and spiritually explosive."[29] Tapping into the spiritually explosive nonviolence of God becomes the focus of our lives. We long simply to do God's will, and we try to do it. That is the spirituality of nonviolence. With A. J. Muste we discover that "there is no way to peace; peace is the way."

Christian Spirituality and Communities of Nonviolence

The spirituality of nonviolence, by definition, involves the entire human family. It is not lived in isolation. It is discovered among other human beings, with our sisters and brothers, among friends, as we come together to transform violence, injustice and war. Nonviolence thrives in the soil of community as we come together to pray, study and reflect so that we can live and practice nonviolence in the world of violence. Because none of us will ever be perfectly nonviolent, we need one another to share our struggles and to support each other as we act publicly for justice and peace.

As the Twelve Step model of Alcoholics Anonymous has shown us, community is essential to overcoming addiction. In a world addicted to violence and injustice we need to gather together, to confess our addiction and powerlessness in the face of violence, and to hand over our lives to a greater Power, the God of nonviolence. Then, together, we can support one another in becoming a sober people of nonviolence, followers of the nonviolent Christ. Following the Twelve Step method we can reform our lives and be transformed like the early apostles into communities of nonviolence. We will be able to break through the widespread denial that afflicts the culture and help each other deal with our violence and become God's nonviolent children. Together, then, we can address the massive violence which threatens to destroy us all.

Community, then, is more than a noble option; it is a requirement of nonviolence. Community life models the community life of God, the Trinity. Jesus understood the primacy of community. Jesus' first public act was to form a community of nonviolence. He did not walk alone, at least not until he was arrested and his community betrayed, denied and abandoned him. After his resurrection he regathered his community and missioned them to continue his life of active nonviolence together.

Along with nonviolent resistance, community living was the hallmark of the early church. The Acts of the Apostles twice emphasizes the communal life of Jesus' followers:

> They devoted themselves to the teaching of the apostles and to the communal life, to the breaking of the bread and to the prayers. Awe came upon everyone, and many wonders and signs were done through the apostles. All who believed were together and had all things in common; they would sell their property and possessions and divide them among all according to each one's need. Every day they devoted themselves to meeting together in the temple area and to breaking bread in their homes. They ate their meals with exultation and sincerity of heart, praising God and enjoying favor with all the people (Acts 2:42-47).

> The community of believers was of one heart and mind, and no one claimed that any of his possessions was his own, but they had everything in common. With great power the apostles bore witness to the resurrection of the Lord Jesus, and great favor was accorded them all. There was no needy person among them, for those who owned property or houses would sell them, bring the proceeds of the sale, and put them at the feet of the apostles, and they were distributed to each according to need (Acts 4:32-35).

The early church, known for its peacemaking martyrs, resembled the loose network of base Christian communities that gathers throughout the Third World today.

Similarly, both Mohandas Gandhi and Dorothy Day understood the centrality of community for lifelong nonviolence. Gandhi founded his first ashram or rural community near Durban, South Africa, in 1904, and lived in an ashram until his death in 1948. Dorothy Day's Catholic Worker movement is based in community life, a community of nonviolence, service and worship that welcomes the poor and marginalized. "The only solution is love and love comes with community," Day wrote in the concluding lines of her autobiography, *The Long Loneliness*.

It is practically impossible today to resist systemic violence through committed nonviolence without the support of community. Nonviolent resisters and peacemakers at the Jonah House community in Baltimore, Maryland (home of Philip Berrigan, Elizabeth McAlister and several plowshares activists), and the Sojourners community in Washington, D.C., for example, point to the strength and support they find in community life. Such peacemaking communities push their members to break free from egotism and individualism to a shared faith and a communitarian conscience. Communities of nonviolence not only model a more just and peaceful society, but they help people to be more human. Christian communities need to be rooted in regular bible study, faith-sharing sessions, forgiveness of one another and Eucharist to be authentic. From this communal foundation, people of faith are better equipped to make peace and resist injustice nonviolently.

A Spirituality of Nonviolence: A Way of Life

If the spiritual depths of nonviolence are plumbed, as Jesus experienced them and invites us to experience them, if we journey into the powerless power of our nonviolent God, as did Gandhi, Day, Merton, King, the Jesuit martyrs of El Salvador, and so many others, we can be partners in God's active transformation of the world. We can help transform the worldwide chaos of violence and injustice that has led us to the brink of nuclear and environmental destruction, creating instead a haven of God's justice, peace and nonviolent love. That transformation, as Jim Douglass writes, "would be a lightning east to west, the energy equivalent and alternative to a nuclear fire ending the world."[30] It would be the unleashing of God's spirit of nonviolence everywhere, marking the reign of God on earth.

Living in the spirit of the God of nonviolence is a lifelong journey. To put it in gospel terms, it requires renouncing ourselves daily, taking up the cross of nonviolence and following Jesus. The life of nonviolence renounces the false spiritualities of violence and practices the true spirituality of Jesus' nonviolence. Then our lives become transparent, and God moves freely through us to touch others and transform our world.

People of nonviolence are open to God's disarming action in their hearts and in our world. These peacemakers have been disarmed by God and are constantly being disarmed by God. Their lives and actions flow from the silent action of God in their hearts. Therefore, a spirituality of nonviolence means consciously living in the presence of God, growing ever more aware of God's presence in our hearts, disarming us, moving us ever deeper into God. From this base of God's action in us we reach out with love toward everyone. We walk with our brothers and sisters in community. We practice forgiveness toward all who hurt us, and we renounce the use of all violence, no matter how apparently noble the cause. We refuse even the desire for retaliation. Similarly, we stand up to every form of violence and seek to transform it with nonviolence, with truth and love. Our spirituality of nonviolence, therefore, is often a spirituality of resistance. Nonviolence rocks the boat of violence, the ship of state. It turns over the tables of the world's violence and

challenges system of injustice with a nonviolent, contagious love. William
Stringfellow tells us that these politics of biblical spirituality are the politics
of the cross:

> The politics of biblical spirituality involve the renunciation of
> worldly power and the condiments that commonly are associ-
> ated with worldly power: wealth or the control thereof, success,
> fame, applause, ambition, avarice, goals, competitive esprit, and
> the rest of the success syndrome. Biblical spirituality means pow-
> erlessness, living without embellishment or pretense, free to be
> faithful in the gospel, and free from anxiety about effectiveness
> or similar illusions of success. It means living within the ironic
> aspects of holiness, equipped with that realism grounded in the
> biblical insight into the fallenness of the whole of creation. It
> means acting politically in a manner which confesses insistently,
> patiently, fearfully, joyously that Jesus Christ is the Lord and the
> Lord already reigns.[31]

The life of nonviolence means carrying the cross. It also means practicing
the resurrection. We celebrate life even as we resist death. We are always
cognizant of the risen Jesus' presence among us and his gift of peace to us.
We act for peace from the perspective of God's love, God's abiding presence,
from the standpoint of spiritual poverty, simple lifestyle, vulnerability, powerlessness and joy. We accompany the poor, offer solidarity to the oppressed,
resist the forces of darkness with the light of truth and stay in touch with the
beauty of creation itself. In this way God works in us.

Such is a spirituality of nonviolence, the spirit in which the action of nonviolence is lived and enacted, and the understanding, the theology, that lies
behind our commitment to nonviolence. It is the combination of inner transformation and outer transformation, the presence of God acting in our world
to transform us all.

"The soul of peacemaking is the will to give one's life," Daniel Berrigan
writes in his autobiography.[32] Theologian Anne Brotherton defines spirituality simply as "what we are willing to die for."[33] In this same light Henri Nouwen
writes that the Christian of the future is "called to be completely irrelevant
and to stand in this world with nothing to offer but his or her own vulnerable
self . . . [The Christian] will dare to claim his or her irrelevance in the contemporary world as a divine vocation that allows him or her to enter into a
deep solidarity with the anguish underlying all the glitter of success and to
bring the light of Jesus there."[34] This life of nonviolence is a life of powerlessness and humility. Our spiritual journey into nonviolence is a journey into
powerlessness, where we let go daily of every type of domination, control
and violence, so that in the end we become the very presence of God's love
on earth.

Dom Helder Camara, the retired archbishop of Recife, Brazil, and one of
the influential leaders behind liberation theology, has attained this unity of

spirituality and nonviolent action for justice. Living in one of the poorest areas of the globe, Dom Helder maintains a passion for justice and peace, yet he acts with the simplicity, love and joy of a child. He has tried throughout his life to become transparent so that God can act through him. He prays over and over again the prayer of Cardinal Newman: "Jesus, don't extinguish the light of your presence within me. Look through my eyes, listen through my ears, speak through my lips, walk with my feet. Jesus, may my poor human presence be a reminder, however weak, of your divine presence."[35]

Similarly, Thomas Merton stood for justice and peace from the perspective of nonviolence, but he did so rooted in a contemplative love for the God of nonviolence. His last words, spoken to a priest at a conference in Bangkok just before his death, reveal the key to his spirituality of nonviolence: "What we are asked to do at present is not so much to speak of Christ as to let him live in us so that people may find him by feeling how he lives in us."[36]

Merton's words sum up the spirituality of nonviolence: let the nonviolent Christ within radiate through us and lead us to resist systemic violence and proclaim God's nonviolent reign of justice and peace with our lives.

CHAPTER 18

The Sacraments of Nonviolence

Encounters with the God of Nonviolence

We encounter the God of nonviolence in a variety of ways throughout our lives, from dramatic, public actions for justice to the solitude of contemplative prayer. For nearly a thousand years, however, the church has upheld several specific channels of God's love, the sacraments. When examined in the light of nonviolence, in the context of the world's systemic violence, the sacraments are transfigured into nothing less than transforming encounters with the God of nonviolence.

The term *sacrament* finds its roots in the Roman empire's *sacramentum,* "a sacred, public pledge of fidelity, symbolized by a visible sign such as a deposit of money or an oath of allegiance."[1] The imperial soldiers pledged the *sacramentum* as an oath of allegiance to their commander, the emperor and the gods of Rome. Tertullian and early Christian writers co-opted this symbol of imperial allegiance and described Christian baptism as a *sacramentum* that new recruits of the faith ritually professed, not to the emperor and his idols, but to their commander, the Christ. This baptismal *sacramentum* marked a new life of dedicated service to God in discipleship to the nonviolent Jesus. Baptism, like the *sacramentum,* sealed a permanent mark on the soul of the newborn Christian. It declared that this person belonged to Christ, not the emperor, and transformed the person into an instrument of God's love.

Over the centuries the Christian community formalized certain rituals as prayerful encounters with Christ that, in a way, deepen our pledge to Christ. Though Catholic Christian sacramentality has roots in the Jewish and Christian scriptures, seven sacraments were formally legislated and systematized during the Middle Ages—baptism, confirmation, communion, reconciliation, marriage, orders and anointing. Because of clericalization, these seven sacraments were eventually upheld as the primary avenue into the presence of God. Though the sacraments conveyed the mystery of God, they were eventually so absolutized, privatized and ritualized that they often did not invite a greater conversion to the new way of life offered by the gospel. A person could go to confession and receive communion on Sunday and wage war in the name of

Christ the next day. Recent changes in the self-understanding of the church and the human community have led contemporary theologians to rethink our understanding of the seven sacraments. Jesus Christ, they explain, is the sacrament of God, and the church is the sacrament of Christ. In this light the seven sacraments flow from the church; they are "doors to the sacred." The church's age-old definition of a sacrament as "an outward sign instituted by Christ that gives grace" highlights that the sacraments are channels of Christ's love. Today, Catholic Christians are on the verge of seeing the sacraments in a new light, as signs of Christ's presence in our world, as entrees into the reign of God. They are understood anew as paradigms of the human, ordinary symbols transformed by God's initiative, by God's gratuitous grace, in communal, public rituals which uphold what it means to be human. In this new light they help lead us into God's transforming life.

A theology of nonviolence sees the sacraments as channels of Christ's active nonviolence amid the world's brutal violence. The sacraments become occasions of God's grace of nonviolence working in us, transforming us into a people of nonviolence missioned to function as instruments of Christ's nonviolence for the disarmament of the world. The sacraments then emerge as both prophetic and reconciling, as encounters with the God of nonviolence, as moments of personal and communal transformation into God's nonviolent reign. In today's world the sacraments of nonviolence can serve the coming of God's reign of peace.

The Sacraments and Nonviolence

The Second Vatican Council declared that the purpose of the sacraments is "to sanctify men and women, to build up the body of Christ, and finally, to give worship to God."[2] In a church of nonviolence the sacraments open up new channels of God's own transforming nonviolence into our hearts, our communities and our world. They reveal the God of nonviolence and manifest the in-breaking reign of God's nonviolent love. They are channels of the grace of nonviolence and help us fulfill our covenant of nonviolence with God. Since we define nonviolence as the active, ongoing remembrance of our common unity as sisters and brothers, as children of God, and Christ as the way into that transformed, beloved community, the sacraments of nonviolence can help us to remember who we are and who we are called to be. They can be occasions where we encounter the nonviolent Christ, are healed of our violence and missioned to practice Christ's nonviolence publicly in the world. Because the nonviolent, risen Christ is present in the sacraments, the sacraments can be a means for the further liberation of the poor, freedom from the systemic sin of violence and a deeper transformation into Christ's own nonviolent love. The sacraments can be channels for Christ to make peace—in our souls, with God, with one another and with all humanity.

The seven sacraments as occasions for Christ's nonviolent action in today's world can be distinguished from what we might call "sacramental nonvio-

Baptism: somewhat incomplete until "it formalizes our renunciation of all violence" at Confirmation —

lence"—any prayerful, nonviolent action for justice and peace which reveals the nonviolent Christ at work among us (such as prayerful, nonviolent civil disobedience for an end to nuclear weapons research). A review of Christ's nonviolence at work in each of the sacraments will round out our theology of nonviolence and give us a new framework from which to make peace as Christians in today's world.

The sacrament of baptism seals our lifelong, perpetual commitment to Jesus, the way of nonviolence. It formalizes our renunciation of all violence and pledges our journey in the footsteps of Jesus into the God of nonviolence. When the early Christians were baptized, they risked their lives. Becoming a follower of Jesus, a believer in the Christ, meant renouncing belief in the emperor and beginning a life of active, nonviolent resistance to imperial violence. Baptism into the Christian community often led immediately to martyrdom. For Paul, baptism "into Christ's death" leads us to become new creations; it marks the start of new life in the nonviolent Christ. Paul regarded Jesus' death as a moral act and not just some occasion in his life. Through an atoning nonviolence, Jesus died to sin by suffering that consequence of human sin without himself sinning. In Jesus we have forever renounced the violence of this world, Paul suggests, and put on the Christ of nonviolence.

share with Hannah +

Today, through the baptism of infants, the Christian family pledges this lifelong commitment in the name of the child. Later, in the sacrament of confirmation, the young adult recommits himself or herself to follow Jesus by practicing gospel nonviolence. Confirmation celebrates the vocation of nonviolence which we professed or which our families professed for us at our baptisms. By marking the reception of the Spirit's charism, confirmation transforms the people of God into a Spirit-filled people, a transforming people of nonviolence. In this way we build a church of nonviolence.

The sacrament of reconciliation celebrates the forgiving, nonviolent love of God, which continually transforms us anew to live God's nonviolent love. In this sacrament we confess the sins of our violence to a representative of the Christian community and call upon God's forgiving, nonviolent love. We name our inner violence, the violence we have inflicted on others, and our ongoing complicity in systemic violence; we apologize to God, to humanity and to the planet, and we recommit ourselves to Jesus and the gospel of nonviolence. In this graced moment, we encounter the risen Christ of nonviolence, who once again gives us the gift of his peace and sends us forth to be his disciples and instruments of his nonviolent love in the world. The sacrament of reconciliation heals the post-baptismal sins that all do violence, one way or another, to others and the world. It helps us know and grow in deeper awareness of our ongoing need for reconciliation with God and humanity. It invites a renewal of nonviolence within our hearts, in our lives and thus in the world. In this encounter with the nonviolent Christ, our hearts are once again disarmed of violence and we are sent forth as Christ's instruments to disarm the world of its violence.

The sacrament of eucharist recalls through the communal sharing of the word, the bread and the cup, the paschal mystery of Jesus, his incarnation,

+ to explain why baptism in the Catholic church is incomplete until confirmation

teachings, life, death and resurrection. In the eucharist the Christian community gathers in Jesus' spirit of nonviolence to hear the word of God and to share in Jesus' body and blood. After we hear the word and share prayer, we exchange the kiss of peace as a sign of our common unity in Christ's peace and a commitment to gospel peacemaking. Then we enjoy a meal of bread and wine, the presence of Jesus in our midst. This sharing of word and bread and cup help us to remember Jesus and remind us that we are all brothers and sisters, living in peace and love and reconciled with each other. This sacrament heals us of our violence and transforms us into the beloved community of God, a people of nonviolence. It welcomes the poor, the oppressed, the marginalized and the victims of systemic violence, so that Christ can transform and reconcile us all. In the eucharist we encounter the nonviolent Christ. Therefore, we go to the eucharist with disarmed hearts, and we go forth from the eucharist with a disarming love, carrying the good news of gospel nonviolence into the world's war-torn streets.

Early Christian eucharist meant the breaking of the bread and the sharing of the cup as a way to recall the suffering and death—the nonviolence of Jesus on the cross—so as to recall the presence of the risen Christ in the midst of the peacemaking community. Eucharist symbolized the community's acceptance of the risen Christ's gift of peace and his mission for us to go into the world of violence to make peace, seek justice, nonviolently resist evil and love everyone, including our enemies. Today, eucharist can likewise be the most transforming experience of our lives. If we enter into eucharist as a community of nonviolence and fully encounter there the God of nonviolence, we can be forever changed and become better instruments of God's transformation of our world. We can be transformed into saints, apostles, prophets and disciples of the nonviolent Christ, to the point of risking our lives in a nonviolent witness for the coming nonviolent reign of God's justice and peace.

Beginning a lifelong commitment to another person, the sacrament of marriage contextualizes the union of two people within the gospel call to lifelong nonviolence toward each other, God and the world. Marriage proclaims the human vocation of unity, the practice of Christ's nonviolence so that we can live together as God's people of nonviolence. It models human friendship, which is always rooted in vulnerability, disarmament, love and nonviolence. Marriage is not a sacrament because Jesus started marriage but because he redeemed it by rejecting Mosaic divorce practices, by demanding a quality of atoning love from his disciples and by transforming marriage into a ministry. Marriage witnesses to the love between God and humanity. It marks a new journey together on the path of nonviolence with another person in the spirit of ongoing, transforming love. The husband and wife who root their new life in Christ and his way of nonviolence demonstrate to the world the possibility of peace and new life that God offers humanity through the Christ of nonviolence. Marriage, then, is not a private sacrament but a public, lifelong proclamation of the God of nonviolence at work in our lives, uniting us as individuals and ultimately calling us all to be the beloved community of God on earth. In particular, married people are called to nurture nonviolent attitudes in their children and families as a service to the reign of God.

The sacrament of the anointing the sick ritualizes the healing love of the God of nonviolence for us all, beginning for those who suffer and are near death. As Jesus healed not just physical bodies but social ostracism, so too the sacrament of anointing heals the person in body and spirit, and the community and the society through a ripple effect of grace. It models all care for the ill by centering that care in the spiritual presence of Christ's nonviolent love. This anointing missions both the ill person and the community gathered in that person's presence to be instruments of God's healing nonviolence in a broken world of suffering, a world on the verge of destruction. The early Christians "prayed over" and "anointed" those who were ill in a human prayer for healing (see Jas 5:14). They understood this anointing to mark the forgiveness of minor sins. Today this sacrament manifests the nonviolent love that we are called to show to each other, especially those in need, in pain, ill or broken by violence. As we anoint each other with the oil symbolizing Christ's healing love, we are transformed to become the presence of Christ's healing love in our sick world.

Though all Christians participate equally in the priesthood of Christ and all are called to minister to Christ present in suffering humanity, the sacrament of orders ordains people to the lifelong ministry as public spokespersons, facilitators and animators of the church of nonviolence. Priests are called to be peacemakers, prophets of nonviolence, pastors to the nonviolent community and public announcers of God's nonviolent reign of justice and peace on behalf of the Christian community. Priests commit themselves to be at the service of the community and humanity and to speak in the name of the community for Christ's peace and justice. As leaders, they willingly risk their life in service to all human beings for the sake of God's peace, justice and nonviolent love, as Oscar Romero and the Jesuit priest-martyrs of El Salvador demonstrated. Priests model the normal Christian ministry of nonviolence as the normal human life of nonviolence. They help lead the community's active nonviolence in prayer, word and deed for God's transformation of the world.

Today, however, the sin of sexism divides the church, as it has for hundreds of years, by insisting that only men can be ordained priests. There is no adequate reason why women cannot be priests. Biology does not block women from being baptized; it is ludicrous to assert that biology is an impediment to priesthood. A narrow reading of scripture according to the maleness of the disciples fails to understand the radical feminism of Jesus in an age of male domination. The feminist Jesus, who died on the cross in the spirit of nonviolence, called both men and women to be his disciples, yet only his women disciples, as we discussed, were faithful to him through his crucifixion and resurrection. Certainly the great women of the gospels, Mary of Nazareth and Mary of Magdala, model the priesthood of Christ and point to the inclusion of women in all ministries of Christ's church.

The Second Vatican Council's *The Church in the Modern World* declared that sexism is a sin, that the rights and duties of ministers, as long as they are competent, are charismatically grounded and that the hierarchy is not supposed to suppress the Spirit. Following this logic, since sexism is a sin, competent women in the church have the right to be ordained, according to the lead of the Spirit. Certainly the Spirit of God is moving in the Christian community today calling for this conversion and renewal. If the church commits itself to gospel nonviolence, as Jesus desires, then we have to renounce sexism and patriarchy once and for always and open up all ministries within the church community, including priesthood, to women. As the church confronts and renounces its sexism, it then can get on with the prophetic ministry of active nonviolence in today's world. Indeed, when the rule of mandatory celibacy for priests is abolished and women become priests, bishops, cardinals and popes, the church may find it necessary to reorganize itself along a more communal, partnership approach. Then, once it has rooted out the glaring injustice of sexism itself, it can get on with the task of becoming a peace-filled community that actually makes peace in the world.

Once a Catholic bishop asked a first communion class how many sacraments there were. A seven-year-old girl raised her hand and responded, "Seven for men, six for women!" As girls around the world grow in awareness of the unfairness waged against them in the name of Christ, they are beginning to speak out for a real change, for the day when all seven sacraments will be available to them. But this transformation of the church may open deeper questions about power and leadership in the worldwide Christian community. One of the great consequences of patriarchy has been the spirit of domination and control that has taken over the priesthood and disfigured the church. Male domination has created a dysfunctional church. Instead of a community of servants and peacemakers, the church is defined in terms of power institutions, structure, hierarchy and ownership. Such terms were not in Jesus' vocabulary and do not fit within the context of the gospel. Indeed, Jesus incarnated powerlessness, service and nonviolence and he expected his followers (his public ministers) to do the same. Instead, the church modelled itself on the world's empires and its emperors. It turned its back on Christ the Suffering Servant and made its priests into feudal lords, similar to the very authorities who killed the prophets and called for the crucifixion of Jesus. Since the fourth century ordained ministers have been linked to the Levitical priesthood to protect church leadership from imperial encroachment, but as we know, priesthood became the epitome of power and political ambition. Besides abolishing the sexism which excludes women from ordination, the priesthood needs to be renewed in terms of service, prophecy and reconciliation. The world of war and systemic injustice needs women and men as priests to proclaim God's word of nonviolence anew and to lead the church as an instrument of God's nonviolence into the world's violence for the transformation of humanity. The church needs a new kind of priest, a peacemaking priest, a prophetic priest, a priest who addresses the world's violence and offers Christ's nonviolent alternative. The new priest will speak for the church's work for justice and peace and facilitate the church's risky, active nonviolence. In today's world of violence the priest is called to speak God's word of nonviolence. In a world of division the priest will reconcile people in the nonviolence of Christ—whether they are rich or poor, women or men, black or white, gay or straight, friends or enemies. The priest will model the reconciling ministry of every Christian, so that Christ can form all humanity into the beloved community that it was created to be. Priests are not to dominate or lord it over others; they are invited to be powerless servants of the peacemaking people of God. The letter to the Hebrews portrays Jesus as a high priest, not in Levitical terms but in his incarnation, crucifixion and suffering identification with the oppressed. So, too, priests are called to model that same incarnation, crucifixion and suffering identification with the oppressed for the coming of God's reign of justice and peace.

The Sacraments Help Us Become God's People of Nonviolence

When understood in light of gospel nonviolence the sacraments can be transforming experiences leading us more fully into God's reign of nonviolence. They can formalize the next step of our hearts and souls along our journeys with our nonviolent God into that new realm of justice and peace. As channels of God's nonviolent grace they are great gifts to us; they can help us become a people of nonviolence. If we receive the sacraments as encounters with the nonviolent Christ missioning us to the life of active nonviolence, then we will find renewed strength to go forth and be instruments of God's peace and justice.

CHAPTER 19

The Liturgy of Nonviolence

The Peacemaking Community Worships the God of Peace

On Sunday mornings in the basement of St. Aloysius Church, a few blocks north of the Capitol Building in Washington, D.C., people of faith from the surrounding inner-city neighborhood gather to sing, pray, hear the word of God, break bread, share the cup and worship the God of Jesus. The parishioners are mainly low-income African-Americans but include middle-class white people from the surrounding area as well. The sanctuary serves as a shelter for the homeless poor and as a well-used gathering place for demonstrations and anti-war activity. All the people share a desire for justice and nonviolent change and a real faith in the living God. In this common bond they join hands and become the reconciled, beloved community that Martin Luther King, Jr., dreamed about. As people of peace, they worship the God of peace. They model the reconciliation that Jesus offers and go forth to live in that spirit of reconciliation. Worshippers at St. Al's experience joy, heartfelt liberation and spiritual renewal. They are brought together by the God of nonviolence and transformed over and over again into God's own people of peace.

Flannery O'Connor once wrote that belief in Christ is a matter of life and death and that true Christian integrity lies "in not being able to get rid of the ragged figure who moves from tree to tree in the back of the mind."[1] Christian liturgical worship attempts to let that ragged figure take center stage, not only in our minds, but in our hearts, lives and communities. In churches like St. Aloysius around the world, the nonviolent Jesus gathers together peacemakers and practitioners of gospel nonviolence to serve as instruments of his transforming love. As St. Al's demonstrates, peace, justice and reconciliation can and should stand at the center of Christian liturgical worship. Such integral worship brings together our heartfelt longing for God and the reality of systemic violence, which we know is rooted in our own hearts. Together, in

185

"hauntingly beautiful" but no pun intended

liturgical worship, we are real before God; we are present to God as we really are. We listen to God's word and move forward by grace to live as we are meant to live, as God's instruments of peace.

In a world of violence Christians need to gather in prayer, biblical reflection and sacrament to be strengthened for the lifelong journey of discipleship in gospel nonviolence. We congregate as a peacemaking community in a world of war and oppression to worship the God of nonviolence. In a world where violence runs wild, where despair has taken hold, those who follow the nonviolent Jesus assemble regularly, buoyed up in faith, hope and grace to live his struggle of nonviolent resistance to evil.

Ever since that night when Jesus broke bread with his friends, just before he was crucified, Christians have assembled in prayer to praise and worship God, to hear anew God's word of peace, to share the bread and cup of Christ, and to receive the peace that the risen Christ offers. The original meaning of the word *liturgy* refers to "a public work" or "a service to the gods." Over time, Christians redefined the term to mean "public worship and service to God." The Catholic church's official document on liturgy, *The Constitution on the Sacred Liturgy*, begins by quoting Hebrews 13:14 to point out that liturgy "makes the work of our redemption a present actuality."[2] It continues:

> Christ is always present in his church, especially in its liturgical celebrations . . . The liturgy is the summit toward which the activity of the church is directed; at the same time it is the fount from which all the church's power flows. For the aim and object of apostolic works is that all who are made children of God by faith and baptism should come together to praise God in the midst of God's church, to take part in the sacrifice, and to eat the Lord's Supper . . . The church earnestly desires that all the faithful be led to that full, conscious, and active participation in liturgical celebrations called for by the very nature of the liturgy . . . [It] is the primary and indispensable source from which the faithful are to derive the true Christian spirit (nos. 7,10,14).[3]

With these insights, we can define Christian liturgy as a gathering in worship and praise of God within the Christian tradition through humble prayer and petition, scripture readings and reflections, and the sharing of bread and wine as the body and blood of Jesus in a communal experience of God's love and peace. In such liturgy the risen Jesus, present in our midst, sends us out to make peace, practice justice for the poor and transform the violence and injustice of the world into God's reign fully present on earth. A theology of nonviolence understands, then, that worship of the God of nonviolence is what Christian liturgy is all about. Finally, we encounter the peacemaking Jesus, we are transformed by his divine forgiveness and love and missioned to practice gospel nonviolence.

where can we go but to Jesus — the DOOR into the Trinity where all true love originates & diffuses itself

BONUM DIFFUSIVUM SUI

The Crisis of Liturgical Worship

The common practice of most Christian liturgy in North America today, however, falls short of Jesus' vision of gospel nonviolence. More often than not, church assemblies reflect our culture's violence and injustice. Over the last fifteen hundred years, since the time of Constantine, Christians have rarely distinguished themselves in their liturgical worship from the values and goals of the nation, state, empire or feudal reign in which they live. Christian liturgy has often lost its transforming edge. Societal violence and oppression have gone unchallenged by Christians for centuries, even though those Christians attended weekly worship services in droves. This "worship" reached new heights of hypocrisy in Nazi Germany when Catholics went to Mass faithfully on Sundays and returned to work at the concentration camps and other Nazi institutions on Mondays. Similarly today, in the United States, some Catholics go to liturgy in the Pentagon and then walk back to their offices and the work of war. At Colorado's Air Force Academy, Catholics worship in a chapel where stained-glass windows depict a nuclear bomb exploding as a glorious sign of the second coming. In California, 80 percent of the worshipping Catholic population approves the scheduled execution of prisoners on death row. Christians worship in the San Francisco Bay Area on Sundays and ship bombs from the Concord Naval Weapons Station to places around the world or design nuclear weapons at Livermore Laboratories during the rest of the week. The privatization of values and the affluence of our society blind us and block our liturgies from being authentic because we live divided lives. When we separate our worship of God from our participation in cultural violence and pretend that we can have both, we fall into schizophrenic delusion. This grave crisis in worship reveals that we do not understand the nonviolence of God. We still do not know the God of nonviolence. The solution lies in surrendering our lives to the God of peace and becoming God's own people.

True Christian liturgy requires a keen critical awareness of the socio-political context of each particular community. Christian liturgy transcends cultural limitations that blind us to the violence we do to others and to our worship of false gods. It helps us to live more and more attuned to God's universal love, God's nonviolence. When liturgy fails to address the systemic violence and injustice at the heart of a culture, it misses the point of liturgy itself, indeed, the point of the gospel. It loses its spiritual integrity and will not be able to address the world's crisis of domination and death with God's alternative of nonviolent love.

Liturgy and Nonviolence: Worshipping the God of Peace

Liturgy needs to flow from conscious awareness of its context in a culture of violence. Indeed, in Christian liturgy we confess our complicity in the world's violence and accept Jesus' invitation to a life of nonviolence. Liturgy helps us open our eyes to the realities around us, from the bloody wars of the world and the institutionalization of injustice to the active, spiritual presence of God. Because we tend to keep our eyes and hearts closed, to turn away and deny society's systemic violence, liturgies all too easily become a civil religion or what some call the religion of nationalism. In Berkeley, California, where Christian liturgies are held daily at a leading seminary, little mention is made of the bombs shipped from the nearby Concord Naval Weapons Station to third-world military regimes; of the homeless people who wander the neighborhood streets; of the prisoners who sit awaiting execution on nearby San Quentin death row; or of the new forms of laser-beam warfare prepared less than a mile away at the University of California Livermore Laboratories. Unfortunately, these liturgies, presided over by leading experts in the North American church, rarely touch upon the realities of systemic violence in the immediate vicinity—and thus, the world at large.

Because these liturgies seldom confront the surrounding cultural addiction to death, but rather allow this systemic violence to continue without resistance, many people naturally conclude that Christianity is a private, individual affair with little to say to the world's violence. Worse still, they infer that God has nothing to say about our world's violence, or perhaps even that God supports this violence. True Christian liturgy never remains silent in the face of injustice. It always says yes to God, to life, to peace and thus an explicit no to all that is not of God, such as death and war.

Although some liturgists tergiversate and maintain that "liturgy cannot be expected to do everything," by and large first-world Christian liturgy justifies systemic violence through its silent complicity. While some suggest that liturgy is not meant to promote justice, others experience active promotion of injustice in the church's liturgy itself (ask Catholic African-Americans, Native Americans, women, gays, lesbians or other minority and marginalized peoples). Most deadly of all, Christian worship has too often been co-opted by the false spiritual fervor of nationalistic, imperialistic violence, as we saw during the Persian Gulf war. Very quickly churches across the country put up their yellow ribbons, which, in effect, gave their approval to massive violence. Few priests or ministers spoke out against the systematic murder of half a million Iraqi people; few insisted on Jesus' teaching that we love our enemies. (Meanwhile, it should be noted, Christian worship services in Iraq also approved of violence. In this situation of Christian peoples at war with each other, God was presented with prayers for assistance in the killing of God's children in the name of the nonviolent Jesus.)

Long before the Persian Gulf war, however, this co-optation of Christian worship could be seen. Churches with flags in their sanctuaries, for example, send an ambiguous message regarding allegiance to Christ and his way of the cross over against the US government and its wars and systemic injustice. Real Christian worship avoids patriotism. It bespeaks much more than the "feel good" experience of the movies or blind nationalism. If liturgy passes as safe and comfortable, if it endures merely as a passive experience that calls forth no response on our part, if it persists as a participation in civil religion and the evils that derive from nationalism, then the rule of nations will continue unabated and civil obedience, not divine obedience, will be the hallmark of the day. Nothing will be at stake—except perhaps our souls and the lives of millions of people around the world who suffer oppression under "Christian" nations. The liturgical worship that follows the dangerous, costly discipleship of the peacemaking Jesus calls us to something much more dramatic, something that could turn our world upside-down.

Transforming Christian Liturgy

For the early Christians, liturgy was a matter of life or death, a dangerous, risky, all-or-nothing affair. In places in the Third World where Christians are persecuted and killed today for their faith-based nonviolent resistance to evil, liturgy continues in that same spirit. For modern-day peacemakers like Oscar Romero, Dorothy Day, and the martyred Jesuits and churchwomen of El Salvador, everything was at stake in liturgy. Worshipping God and partaking in the eucharist became the high point of their lives, an experience of the peace and justice for which they so longed. Gospel peacemaking charged their liturgies. They challenged the oppression and war around them, and they held out the real hope that peace is God's desire.

Archbishop Romero opened up the transforming potential of Roman Catholic liturgy in the context of brutal El Salvador through his prophetic and reconciling ministry for the poor and for peace. His liturgies were occasionally banned and under constant surveillance by the military because of his outspoken stand for justice and peace. On March 23, 1980, he preached that Salvadoran military soldiers need not obey the laws of the government, that instead they could put down their weapons and obey God's law of peace. Such subversive preaching could have sparked massive disobedience by the soldiers. The next day, while presiding at liturgy, Romero was assassinated. His subsequent funeral liturgy was disrupted by bombings and shootings.

Likewise, Dorothy Day knew the spiritually explosive power of Christian liturgy. "When I'm in church," she said, "I feel like crying, or I flush with anger: to be in church isn't to be calmed down, as some people say they get when they are at Mass. I'm worked up. I'm excited by being so close to Jesus, but the closer I get, the more I worry about what Jesus wants of us, what he would have us do before we die."[4]

I have experienced transforming liturgies in a refugee camp in El Salvador as US bombs fell nearby, and among friends in Washington, D.C., and New York City before acts of nonviolent civil disobedience against US militarism. Such settings put the matter of worship in proper perspective, within the reality of violence and the gospel mandate of nonviolent resistance to evil. The words, symbols and deeds of the ritual prevailed as symbolic and poetic—and actual. Belief became a matter of life and death, as it was for the early Christian community. Such liturgies, centered on the God of peace, are charged with the Spirit. Suddenly, life is transformed, and we take another step forward in risky discipleship to the peacemaking Christ.

Christian liturgy, which includes the liturgy of the word and the liturgy of the eucharist, sets the stage for the graced gift of God's gentle love. This divine love sanctifies us and sends us forth to be God's love to everyone. The public worship of liturgy unites us and transforms us into instruments for God's social, cultural, political, economic and spiritual transformation of the world into a place of nonviolence and justice. Liturgy joyfully celebrates the resurrection of Jesus. Indeed, the risen Christ, present in our midst in the breaking of the bread and the sharing of the cup, breathes the Holy Spirit of peace on us and sends us forth to be signs of peace to all the nations. This spirit brings together the many gifts of the body of Christ, from pastoral and compassionate love to prophetic and critical wisdom, from public responsibility to the mystical and spiritual streams which flow among us all. Such peacemaking liturgy places the poor, the oppressed and the marginalized at the center of our worship of the God of peace so that God's all-inclusive reign of justice and peace encompasses our prayer and praise. This liturgy uses inclusive language and includes everyone. War-making, racism, sexism, classism, consumerism, patriarchy and all forms of violence are renounced. In this way God is not mocked; God's will is done. Such liturgy addresses and renounces the world's violence (our violence) and embraces the God of nonviolence. Such liturgy points to God's reign of nonviolence in our midst. As the US Catholic bishops wrote in their pastoral letter on economics, liturgy "turns our hearts from self-seeking to a spirituality that sees the signs of true discipleship in our sharing of goods and working for justice."[5]

Liturgy incorporates communal prayer, the prayer of the human soul, the disarmed heart and the disarmed community calling out to God in hope and in trust for justice and peace. In this prayer we surrender ourselves to God and allow God to disarm and transform us into the people we already are, God's very own daughters and sons. As we recognize Christ (the nonviolent, disarmed One) in the word, the breaking of the bread and the sharing of the cup, we recognize each other as God's daughters and sons, as sisters and brothers. We are changed again, and we go forth in new awareness, unable to hurt or kill one another or to ignore the suffering of another. We are inspired to love each other unconditionally, as Christ asks us. Liturgy marks the reception of God's gift to us, the gifts of love, peace and reconciliation incarnated in Jesus Christ. It embodies our response, a movement into the praxis of nonviolent love and reconciliation, into God. Liturgy marks the communal following of Jesus along the road of nonviolence.

Liturgy and the Nonviolent Jesus

Christian liturgy centers around the communal experience of the risen Jesus, who is present among us and who once again speaks a word of peace. It gathers the community in a spiritual encounter with Jesus the peacemaker, who incarnated and practiced nonviolence, challenged injustice (even unto death) and breathed a new spirit of peace into humanity. This nonviolent Jesus is the heart of our liturgy. Liturgy uses the scripture and tradition to celebrate the experience of the life, teachings, death and resurrection of Jesus. He then calls us anew to the discipleship of peacemaking and sends us forth at each liturgy to make peace, love unconditionally, resist evil and do justice for the poor. Liturgy invites us to taste God's nonviolent love, God's community of nonviolent love and God's reign of peace coming into our midst.

Christian liturgical worship opens an entrance into the life, death and risen presence of the peacemaking Jesus. It involves a human encounter with God in word, sacrament and community; the ritual, prayerful experience of receiving God's unconditional love and mercy; and a transforming movement into that nonviolent love which sends us forth to be peacemakers in a divided, war-torn world. It is worship of God that promotes God's own nonviolent love, justice and peace. It is therefore more than a holy dance with God, more than a song of divine praise, more than the proclamation of God's presence among us. It includes all this and much more. If our worship of God stays true; if it thanks and praises God for God's presence in Christ among us; if, indeed, it remembers and relives the paschal mystery—the life, death and resurrection, the nonviolence of Jesus—it will transform us in God's peace and nonviolent love and send us forth as a community to make that peace and nonviolent love a reality in the world today. Such liturgy therefore is a celebration, experience, proclamation of and missioning into Jesus' nonviolence.

Centered in gospel nonviolence, Christian liturgy combines both the reconciling and the prophetic work of Christian community. We are transformed by the God who touches our hearts with a peace that revolutionizes our world. It is the gathering of the community of the followers of Jesus to hear Jesus preach the good news once again—the message of God's reign of shalom, the message of the Sermon on the Mount. It recalls the words of Jesus, that before we go to the altar to worship God, we reconcile with anyone from whom we are divided; then, together with our reunited sisters and brothers, we go to the God of peace. "If you bring your gift to the altar, and there recall that your brother has anything against you, leave your gift there at the altar, go first and be reconciled with your brother, and then come and offer your gift" (Mt 5:23). With this command Jesus teaches that reconciliation with our sisters and brothers remains a prerequisite to true worship of the God who reconciles us all.

Set within the context of the Sermon on the Mount and the command to love our enemies, true Christian worship therefore requires that we love our enemies, that we strive toward reconciliation with everyone. Elizabeth McAlister describes nonviolence in this light as "persistent reconciliation."[6] Our worship of a reconciling God is rooted in our reconciliation with one another and the entire human race. Thus, as we break bread and share the cup, we exchange a sign of peace and taste the reign of God in our midst. Liturgy then bears the fruit of reconciliation, love, justice and peace. Paul correctly reflects that we are "ambassadors of reconciliation" (2 Cor 5:18-20). We seek constant reconciliation with one another and with God. Then, reconciled by the word and the table of God, we go forward to proclaim the peacemaking work of Jesus.

Liturgical Nonviolence

Liturgy is revolutionary, Abraham Heschel once observed. In *Seasons of Faith and Conscience* theologian Bill Wylie Kellermann writes that liturgy implies an experience of nonviolence. "Public action offered in the context of worship can express and discipline and nourish a nonviolent spirit."[7] The liturgical nonviolence practiced by Jesus was not limited to his last supper with friends. His entrance into Jerusalem on a donkey staged a classic form of political street theater. This demonstration was rooted in humility and active love and aimed at turning our hearts and allegiance to Jesus and not the emperor and his minions. His nonviolent civil disobedience in the Temple, calling us to worship God in a spirit of prayerful nonviolence, followed upon this nonviolent procession on a donkey. After these public liturgies of active nonviolence, Jesus sat among his friends in an upper room to pray, share his reflections, wash his disciples' feet, break bread and pass a cup. All these actions turn us to the God of peace.

The active nonviolence Jesus practiced can be practiced today in public liturgies of nonviolence, including the public, prayerful, nonviolent protest of civil disobedience aimed at allowing God's transforming nonviolence to transform our world and its structures of violence. Our communal liturgical prayer can take to the streets and go into the marketplace as Jesus demonstrated and as the disciples realized at Pentecost. Gandhi's 1930 march across two hundred miles of India to pick up a handful of salt at the ocean was nothing less than a public, sacramental liturgy of nonviolence in defiance of the British empire. Though it expressed in no uncertain terms a peaceful non-cooperation with systemic violence, for Gandhi it enacted prayer, a long-sustained worship of the God who liberates and offers the gift of true peace. All along the way he and his companions prayed for a revolution of nonviolence. Decades later, in a similar fashion, Dorothy Day and her colleagues sat on public benches in a New York City park, refusing to go underground during public "nuclear weapons air-raid drills." Her prayerful insistence on peace through active, liturgical nonviolence bore fruit as thousands of people joined her. Eventually the drills were canceled. Martin Luther King, Jr.'s ongoing witness for civil rights and peace employed a regular liturgy of nonviolence. After songs, prayer and sermons, he would lead his followers into the streets for boycotts, marches, sit-ins and other demonstrations. On Good Friday, 1963, King and Ralph Abernathy walked through a park in Birmingham, Alabama, knelt down in prayer and were arrested for disturbing the peace in their demand for civil rights. Their march to Selma two years later demonstrated a similar liturgical nonviolence. Such events captured the imagination of the nation and sparked further change for justice.

When Daniel and Philip Berrigan and their friends poured homemade napalm on draft-file records and offered a prayer for peace in Catonsville, Maryland, on May 17, 1968, they took their mission of nonviolence into the public realm. Their public display of nonviolent resistance to the US bombing war in Vietnam ignited the hearts of many and helped change the mind of the nation. Shortly afterward, in an address to the Liturgical Conference, Dorothy Day called their resistance "an act of prayer."[8] Twelve years later, on September 9, 1980, they hammered on nuclear missile nose cones at the General Electric Plant in King of Prussia, Pennsylvania. In this way they took up Isaiah's mandate to "beat swords into plowshares and study war no more," and they offered a public, liturgical act of nonviolence that literally and symbolically called forth God's conversion to peace. "As liturgical direct actions, this ritualized unmaking of a weapons system, this naming and neutralizing of the technology, a literal deconstruction of nuclearism's world, might simply be called a forthright form of confession and praise . . . or an exorcism," Kellermann writes. "These public actions are liturgies insofar as they declare the sovereignty of God. The reign of God is celebrated and enacted in the lives of people and communities. And they are exorcisms insofar as the powers, and the power of death behind them all, are named and exposed and rebuked on behalf of human life."[9]

The public liturgy for peace, organized by the Jesuit Community at the Jesuit School of Theology in Berkeley and held at the San Francisco Federal Building a few days after the massacre of the six Jesuits and Elba and Celina Ramos in El Salvador on November 16, 1989, encompassed the full range of worship: songs of praise, intercessory prayer, biblical reflection, the kiss of peace, a pledge of commitment, political denunciation of injustice and a prophetic call for Christ's peace and nonviolence, beginning with an immediate end to US military aid to El Salvador. As we sang a closing hymn, over one hundred priests, seminarians, sisters and people of faith walked forward and knelt down in the doorways of the main entrance in an act of prayerful civil disobedience as a way to take our prayer for peace to the war-making government officials. Indeed, the civil disobedience embodied an integral part of the worship; it extended the worship—as did our arrests, jailings and trials. All through the afternoon in jail, as we recalled the martyrs, we sang hymns of praise to the God of peace knowing that our prayer had been heard. Our worship was fully integrated in deed and act and, I believe, did honor to the God of the Salvadoran martyrs.

Such liturgical nonviolence, first and foremost, worships the God of nonviolence. As Kellermann suggests, liturgy does not cling to results. "Though it can subvert, resist or even transform a political situation . . . [liturgy] is not firstly instrumental, but always toward God as gift and offering, [and it] permits a tremendous freedom." Kellermann continues:

> Only if liturgical action is firstly a faithful activity of prayer and
> worship may it end by being effective to an extent which ap-

pears very nearly shrewd. The distinction made here is akin to the distinction between nonviolence as a tactic and nonviolence as a way of life deeply rooted in heart and spirit. In the end we are not talking about liturgy as a political tactic, but as life. Our personal life. Our common life before the world. This is not the politicization of sacrament, but the sacramentalization of all life.[10]

If understood correctly, liturgy is political. "Every act of worship, every occasion where the sovereignty of the Word of God is celebrated, every instance where the realm of God is acknowledged," Kellermann concludes, "is always and everywhere expressly 'political.' "[11] Indeed, given our systemic violence, true Christian worship subverts the world; it turns over the tables of this world's suppositions, knocks over its false gods and embraces the God of nonviolence. As Daniel Berrigan wrote while underground during his nonviolent resistance to the US war in Southeast Asia, "I am convinced that contemplation, including the common worship of the believing, is a political act of the highest value, implying the riskiest of consequences to those taking part. Union with God leads us, charged with legal jeopardy, to resistance against false, corrupting, coercive, imperialist policy."[12]

In a world of violence, authentic Christian liturgy is nothing less than subversive nonviolence. In worshipping the God of nonviolence, we cease all worship of the gods of violence, the idols of death, the false gods of war and injustice, who have led us to hurt and kill each other. Christian nonviolence calls for a new style of liturgy: bold, prophetic, reconciling, public and dramatic; a liturgical peacemaking that risks arrest, suffering and death, like Jesus in the Jerusalem Temple, for the sake of God's peace. Today, these questions stand: Will our Christian liturgy be active, outspoken, subversive for Christ's peace and justice? Or will it remain passive, silent, and thus complacent with the violent status quo that is destroying humanity? Will we worship the God of peace as God wants, through active reconciliation with our sisters and brothers and the steadfast practice of gospel nonviolence? Will our worship of God reflect the risky discipleship of our daily lives? Will the God of peace recognize us because of the peace in our hearts, in our communities and in our struggle to transform this world?

CHAPTER 20

The Praxis of Nonviolence

Accompanying the Nonviolent Jesus

The martyred Jesuits of El Salvador understood the theology of nonviolence. They dedicated their lives to promoting the gospel of peace and justice. They followed the peacemaking Jesus all the way to the cross. Ignacio Ellacuría, a liberation theologian and president of the Jesuit-run University of Central America in San Salvador, had invoked the nonviolence of Martin Luther King, Jr., in his theological understanding of Jesus and, like Dr. King, publicly pushed for a dialogue for peace. His peacemaking and bridge-building between the warring sides inevitably led to his death and the massacre of the Jesuits and Elba and Celina Ramos. Though an archbishop, four US church-women and seventy-five thousand people had already died violent deaths, many believe the assassination of the peacemaking Jesuits sparked new international attention on El Salvador, finally forcing both sides to talk peace, lay down their weapons and end the war.

As followers of the nonviolent Jesus, the Jesuits preached and taught peace, and finally gave their lives for the coming of that peace. Ellacuría once told me that his work sought to promote the reign of God in El Salvador, which, he explained, meant the end of the killing and the promotion of justice for the poor. With the massacre of the Jesuits, El Salvador turned a new corner and took a significant step on the road to disarmament and justice. The martyrdom of the Jesuits paved the way for the peace treaty of February 1, 1992. One year after that, soldiers from government death squads and the F.M.L.N. revolutionary forces sat down together for the first time and discussed their lives, their sufferings, the war and their common hope for a peaceful future.

To paraphrase the early Christians, the blood of the martyrs makes peace. With the final gift of their lives in a nonviolent struggle for justice and peace, the Salvadoran martyrs demonstrated that fidelity to the peacemaking Jesus bears fruit. These martyrs, like all martyrs for Christ's peace and justice, teach us a theology of nonviolence. They point us back to the nonviolent Jesus and the coming of God's reign of justice and peace.

195

The potential of nonviolence is breaking out around the world as never before in history—from the "People Power" revolutions of the Philippines, Haiti and the Soviet Union to the nonviolent revolutions of Poland, East Germany, Hungary, Czechoslovakia, Bulgaria, Brazil, Chile, Latvia, Lithuania and Estonia, not to mention the nations that have been touched by major movements of nonviolence, as in South Africa, Burma and South Korea.

Though violence and death pervade our world, there is hope! Violence does not have the last word! Gospel nonviolence insists that God is transforming us all and will transform the violence and injustice in every human heart and every unjust structure into God's reign of love and peace. Indeed, Christ proclaims that the God of nonviolence has already won the victory, that violence has not only been overcome, it has already been transformed. This already-won victory of God through nonviolence gives us the hope and the faith to go forward in the lifelong struggle of transforming nonviolence.

After all is said and done, a theology of nonviolence roots itself in Jesus of Nazareth, the way of nonviolence. The nonviolence of Jesus offers an alternative to the world's crises of violence. The world can still grasp this divine nonviolence as the way to live humanly. More than anyone in human history, Jesus points the way to peace, to the disarmament of hearts and nations. The world stands on the possibility of being transformed. A theology of nonviolence upholds this exciting new possibility and places it at the center of our contemporary understanding of God, church and humanity. Finally, we are turning the corner to realize the God of nonviolence loves every human being unconditionally and nonviolently and invites us to do likewise. We are beginning to see this invitation not as impossible, but quite possible and, indeed, as the only option left if we are not to destroy ourselves in a final outburst of violence.

The theology of nonviolence we are beginning to trace understands every area of theology through the peaceful eyes of the nonviolent Christ. With the nonviolent perspective of Mohandas Gandhi, Dorothy Day and Martin Luther King, Jr., we can look upon each realm of theology and find new light for our life mission of witnessing to Christ and making peace in Christ's name. This book contributes a mustard seed to the growing, worldwide consciousness of gospel nonviolence. It invites us to reflect on our experience of God within the realities of our violence and self-destructive potential. It charges us to explore further what nonviolence has to contribute to each area of theology-scripture, God imagery, the Trinity, Christology, sin, grace, theodicy, soteriology, eschatology, anthropology, ecclesiology, social teaching, "just war" theorizing, feminism, liberation theology, a consistent ethic of life, spirituality, sacraments and liturgy. If we are to survive the kairos moment of violence that threatens humanity in these times, the theology of the future will have to proclaim a theology of nonviolence. The gospel pushes us to get on with the task of nonviolence.

Living centered in Jesus demands the practice of nonviolence. A theology of nonviolence speaks the language of praxis. It does not make empty speeches; it advances prayerfully, committed to action for peace and justice, as Jesus demonstrated. The Jesus of the gospels upholds a vision of nonviolence that offers the only alternative to a world of violence, injustice and death. Though the world clings to the ways of violence, a new age is dawning as we embrace Jesus' nonviolence. As we do, we shall put away the age-old reliance on war and killing and begin to live together as brothers and sisters of one another, children of a gentle, all-loving God. This life of active nonviolence will require that we enter struggles for justice, peace and disarmament with heartfelt love. It will mean giving over our lives in companionship to Jesus, turning to Jesus our peacemaker in our prayer, joining hands with him and following his lead into God's nonviolent reign. Undoubtedly, his way will take us to the cross. We will have to die to ourselves and surrender our hearts and lives to the God of peace to enter God's reign of peace. As we take up the cross of nonviolence, we can trust Jesus that we will follow him in resurrection and rise with him into that new life of peace with God.

Jesus' message is simple: "Put away your sword. Stop the killing. Disarm your weapons. Love one another. Love your enemies. Love God. Be compassionate like God. Turn and embrace the God of peace. Let the God of nonviolence transform you into God's people of nonviolence. Go forth and teach nonviolence. Practice nonviolence. Live in God's reign of nonviolence. Let your faith life be rooted in the deep peace that God offers you as God's children. For behold, God is giving you the gift of peace. God's peace is at hand. You are blessed, you are God's children, you are peacemakers."

Gospel nonviolence envisions a new world order of nonviolence, the coming of God's reign of justice and peace. It foresees the day when nations will transcend borders and all human beings will join hands across the barriers that divide us in a global circle of prayer and praise to the God of peace. Gospel nonviolence not only proclaims that coming day, it enacts it here and now through Jesus' way of loving enemies. It summons us to break the laws that legalize systemic violence and nuclear holocaust. It invites us to risk arrest, imprisonment and execution for our insistence on disarmament, justice and peace. As Gandhi said, nonviolent social change does not come from governments, courts or schoolrooms, but from within prisons and sometimes on the gallows.[1] The praxis of nonviolence requires civil disobedience to preparations for war and nuclear destruction and divine obedience to the God of peace. Though we may be jailed or killed for proclaiming the truth of nonviolence, we will be found faithful. We will be blessed.

We are getting to know Jesus as the unarmed and disarming Christ of peace. We are learning from Jesus to plumb the spiritual depths of nonviolence in our hearts so that our lives may be a nonviolent explosion of God's peace in the world. We are becoming a people of nonviolence. We look into the eyes of the nonviolent Christ and find ourselves at last at peace with God, with all humanity, with ourselves.

We are finally beginning to recognize our God as the God of peace.

Notes

1. From Violence to Nonviolence

1. Thomas Gumbleton, "Peacemaking as a Way of Life," in *One Hundred Years of Catholic Social Thought*, ed. John Coleman (Maryknoll, N.Y.: Orbis Books, 1991), 310.

2. *Gaudium et Spes* (1965), no. 80.

3. "Vatican Statement on Disarmament" (1975).

4. Ruth Leger Sivard, *World Military and Social Expenditures: 1991* (Washington, D.C.: World Priorities, 1991), 5.

5. The 1991 figure of daily deaths worldwide due to starvation is from Oxfam Relief Agency. The annual figure is from Jack Nelson-Pallmeyer, *War Against the Poor* (Maryknoll, N.Y.: Orbis Books, 1989), 10.

6. Sivard, *World Military and Social Expenditures: 1991*, 9; see *The State of the World's Children—1993*, UNICEF Report (Oxford, U.K.: Oxford University Press, 1993), 50.

7. Tom Cordaro. *A Shoot Shall Rise Up: Building an Alternative to the New World Order* (Erie, Penn.: Pax Christi USA, 1992), 7.

8. Ibid. 11.

9. Ibid. 20.

10. Ibid. 7.

11. Ibid. 11.

12. Ibid. 16.

13. See Michael Wines, "Aspin Orders Pentagon Overhaul of Strategy on Nuclear Weapons," *New York Times*, October 30, 1993, A8.

14. *The Defense Monitor*, vol. 22, no. 1 (1993). Published by the Center for Defense Information, 1500 Mass. Ave., N.W., Washington, D.C., 20005.

15. Walter Wink, *Engaging the Powers* (Minneapolis: Fortress Press, 1992), 26, 13.

16. James Washington, *A Testament of Hope: The Essential Writings of Martin Luther King, Jr.* (San Francisco: Harper & Row, 1986), 280.

17. See Elizabeth McAlister's foreword in John Dear, *Our God Is Nonviolent* (New York: Pilgrim Press, 1990), xiv.

18. For further reading on the question of violence, see John Dear, *Disarming the Heart* (Mahwah, N.J.: Paulist Press, 1987), 13-29; idem, *Our God Is Nonviolent*, 1-25.

19. From a talk by Wally Nelson at the Catholic Worker, New York City, Spring 1986.

20. Thomas Merton, ed., *Gandhi on Nonviolence* (New York: New Directions, 1965), 32.

21. Ibid. 44.

22. Richard Attenborough, ed., *The Words of Gandhi* (New York: Newmarket Press, 1982), 55.

23. Ibid. 47.

24. Merton, *Gandhi on Nonviolence*, 25.

25. Arthur Laffin and Anne Montgomery, eds., *Swords Into Plowshares* (San Francisco: Harper & Row, 1985), 20.

26. William Miller, "Dorothy Day, 1897-1980: 'All Was Grace,' "*America* (December 13, 1980), 385.

27. Jim Forest, *Love Is the Measure* (Maryknoll, N.Y.: Orbis Books, 1994), 99.

28. Martin Luther King, Jr., *Stride Toward Freedom* (New York: Harper & Row, 1958), 78-79.

29. Ibid. 83.

30. Washington, *A Testament of Hope*, 224-25.

31. King, *Stride Toward Freedom*, 83-88.

32. Ibid. 84.

33. Ibid. 85.

34. Ibid. 88.

35. Wink, *Engaging the Powers*, 217.

2. The Nonviolence of Jesus

1. Thomas Merton, *Gandhi on Nonviolence* (New York: New Directions, 1965), 26.

2. For further reading on the six antitheses, especially this command of nonviolent resistance, see Walter Wink, *Violence and Nonviolence in South Africa: Jesus' Third Way* (Philadelphia: New Society Publishers, 1987); idem, *Engaging the Powers* (Minneapolis: Fortress Press, 1992), 175-93; also, John Dear, *Our God Is Nonviolent* (New York: Pilgrim Press, 1990), 26-51.

3. Merton, *Gandhi on Nonviolence*, 40.

4. Ibid. 34.

5. For the clearest study of Jesus' campaign of nonviolent resistance to evil, see Ched Myers, *Binding the Strong Man: A Political Reading of Mark's Story of Jesus* (Maryknoll, N.Y.: Orbis Books, 1988).

3. God Is Nonviolent

1. See Robert McAfee Brown, *Unexpected News* (Philadelphia: Westminster Press, 1984), 33-48.

2. Richard McBrien, *Catholicism* (San Francisco: Harper & Row, 1981), 337.

3. Thomas Merton, *The Sign of Jonas* (New York: Image Books, 1956), 351.

4. Francis Schüssler Fiorenza and John P. Galvin, eds., *Systematic Theology*, vol. 1 (Minneapolis: Fortress Press, 1991), 92.

5. Ibid. 93; See also, Austin Flannery, ed., *Vatican Council II*, "Dogmatic Constitution on Divine Revelation," no. 2.

6. Schüssler Fiorenza and Galvin, *Systematic Theology*, 133.

7. Ibid. 136-38.

8. Ibid. 138.

9. Roger Haight, *Dynamics of Theology* (Mahwah, N.J.: Paulist Press, 1990), 58.

10. Ibid.

11. Schüssler Fiorenza and Galvin, *Systematic Theology*, 145-46.

12. Walter Wink, *Engaging the Powers* (Minneapolis: Fortress Press, 1992), 146-47, 149.

13. *The Challenge of Peace: God's Promise and Our Response* (Washington, D.C.: National Conference of Catholic Bishops, 1983), nos. 30-36.

14. Ibid. nos. 40-43.

15. Ibid. nos. 47-50.

16. Ibid. nos. 52-55.

17. Ibid. no. 111.

18. Ibid. no. 112.

19. Ibid. no. 113.

20. Ibid. no. 114.

21. Ibid. nos. 115-16.

22. Mohandas Gandhi, *All Men Are Brothers* (New York: Continuum, 1982), 83.

23. Ibid. 52-53.

24. Coretta Scott King, ed., *The Words of Martin Luther King, Jr.* (New York: Newmarket Press, 1983), 71.

25. Martin Luther King, *Strength to Love* (Philadelphia: Fortress Press, 1963), 53, 55.

26. Helder Camara, *Questions for Living* (Maryknoll, N.Y.: Orbis Books, 1987), 17.

27. Wink, *Engaging the Powers*, 116.

28. Ibid. 141-42.

29. *The Challenge of Peace: God's Promise and Our Response*, no. 333.

30. William Shannon, *Seeking the Face of God* (New York: Crossroad, 1988), 168-69.

31. Wink, *Engaging the Powers*, 217

4. The Peacemaking Trinity

1. Dorothy Day, *The Long Loneliness* (San Francisco: Harper & Row, 1981), 286.

2. Leonardo Boff, *Trinity and Society* (Maryknoll, N.Y.: Orbis Books, 1988), 32.

3. For further reading, see "Peacemaking in the Early Church: From Paul to Constantine," in Ron Musto, *The Catholic Peace Tradition* (Maryknoll, N.Y.: Orbis Books, 1986), 31-45.

4. Boff, *Trinity and Society*, 49.

5. Ibid. 57.

6. *The Classics of Western Spirituality: Richard of St. Victor*, "Book III: The Trinity," trans. and intro. Grover Zinn (Mahwah, N.J.: Paulist Press, 1979), 373-97.

7. Ibid.

8. Boff, *Trinity and Society*, 84

9. Ibid.

10. Ibid. 13.

11. Ibid. 16.

12. Ibid. 20.

13. Ibid. 22.

14. Ibid.

15. Ibid. 4-5.

16. Ibid. 6-7.

17. Ibid. 22-23.

18. Ibid. 108.

19. Ibid. 120.

20. Ibid. 152.

21. Ibid. 154.

22. Ibid. 158.

23. Ibid. 163.

24. Martin Luther King, Jr., *The Words of Martin Luther King, Jr.* (New York: Newmarket Press, 1983), 21.

5. The Christ of Peace

1. Richard McBrien, *Catholicism* (San Francisco: Harper & Row, 1981), 430.

2. Ibid. 431.

3. Jon Sobrino, *Christology at the Crossroads* (Maryknoll, N.Y.: Orbis Books, 1978), 291.

4. Ibid. xiii.

5. Rosemary Radford Ruether, *Sexism and God-Talk* (Boston: Beacon Press, 1983), 135.

6. James A. Will, *A Christology of Peace* (Louisville, Ky.: Westminster/John Knox Press, 1989), 9-10.

7. Sobrino, *Christology at the Crossroads*, xiii.

8. Ibid. xxi.

9. Ibid. 3.

10. Ibid. 305.

11. Ibid. xxv.

12. Ibid. 139.

13. Ibid. 135.

14. Ibid. 340.

6. The Sin of Violence

1. William Stringfellow, *The Politics of Spirituality* (Philadelphia: Westminster Press, 1984), 38.

2. Jim Wallis, *Agenda for Biblical People* (San Francisco: Harper & Row, 1984), 41.

3. Gerald O'Collins and Edward Farrugia, *A Concise Dictionary of Theology* (Mahwah, N.J.: Paulist Press, 1991), 222.

4. Richard McBrien, *Catholicism* (San Francisco: Harper & Row, 1981), 1256.

5. O'Collins and Farrugia, *A Concise Dictionary of Theology*, 222.

6. Walter Wink, *Engaging the Powers* (Minneapolis: Fortress Press, 1992), 151-52.

7. Paul Achtemeier, ed., *Harper's Bible Dictionary* (HarperSan Francisco, 1985), 190-91.

8. O'Collins and Farrugia, *A Concise Dictionary of Theology*, 85-86.

7. Human Suffering and the God of Peace

1. Tim Golden, "Salvador Massacre Site Unearthed: Skeletons of Victims, Mostly Children, Support Story of 1981 Killings," *San Francisco Chronicle*, October 2, 1992, A17; see also, Mark Danner, "The Truth of El Mozote," *The New Yorker*, December 6, 1993, 50.

2. Richard McBrien, *Catholicism* (San Francisco: Harper & Row, 1981, 238. See also, Wendy Farley, *Tragic Vision and Divine Compassion* (Louisville, Ky.: Westminster Press, 1990); John Douglas Hall, *God and Human Suffering* (Minneapolis: Augsburg Publishers, 1986).

3. Walter Wink, *Engaging the Powers* (Minneapolis: Fortress Press, 1992), 69.

4. Ibid. 314-17.

5. Coretta Scott King, ed., *The Words of Martin Luther King, Jr.* (New York: Newmarket Press, 1983), 72.

6. Gandhi, quoted in James Douglass, "Through the Cross of Jesus, We Are Saved," in *Gospel Peacemaking* (Winter 1992-93), published by Bay Area Pax Christi, 1 (Bay Area Pax Christi, 2808 Lakeshore Ave., Oakland, CA 94610). See also, James Douglass, *The Nonviolent Coming of God* (Maryknoll, N.Y.: Orbis Books, 1991), 7-28.

7. Ibid.

8. James Douglass, *The Nonviolent Cross* (New York: Macmillan, 1968), 71.

9. Ibid.

9. An Eschatology of Nonviolence

1. Karl Rahner, quoted in Gerald O'Collins and Edward Farrugia, eds., *A Concise Dictionary of Theology* (Mahwah, N.J.: Paulist Press, 1991), 172.

2. Richard McBrien, *Catholicism* (San Francisco: Harper & Row, 1981), 1157.

3. Walter Wink, *Engaging the Powers* (Minneapolis: Fortress Press, 1992), 70.

4. Martin Luther King, Jr., quoted in James M. Washington, ed., *A Testament of Hope: The Essential Writings of Martin Luther King, Jr.* (San Francisco: Harper & Row, 1986), 280.

5. James W. Douglass, *The Nonviolent Coming of God* (Maryknoll, N.Y.: Orbis Books, 1991), xii.

6. Ibid. 34.

7. "Pastoral Constitution on the Church in the Modern World," in *Vatican Council II*, ed. Austin Flannery (New York: Costello Publishing Company, 1975), nos. 39, 938.

8. Douglass, *The Nonviolent Coming of God*, xii.

9. Rosemary Radford Ruether, *Sexism and God-Talk* (Boston: Beacon Press, 1983), 254-58.

10. Douglass, *The Nonviolent Coming of God*, 141.

11. Myers, *Binding the Strong Man* (Maryknoll, N.Y.: Orbis Books, 1988), 399, 401.

12. Douglass, *The Nonviolent Coming of God*, 141.

13. Daniel Berrigan, *Portraits of Those I Love* (New York: Crossroad, 1982), 158.

14. Daniel Berrigan, in *Words of Peace: Selections from the Writings of Daniel Berrigan*, ed. John Dear (Erie, Penn.: Pax Christi USA, 1990), 22.

15. Daniel Berrigan, *The Discipline of the Mountain* (New York: Seabury Press, 1979), 119-20.

16. Douglass, *The Nonviolent Coming of God*, 33.

17. Monika Hellwig, "Eschatology," in *Systematic Theology*, vol. 2, ed. Francis Schüssler Fiorenza and John P. Galvin (Minneapolis: Fortress Press, 1991), 371.

10. An Anthropology of Nonviolence

1. See Gordan Zahn, *In Solitary Witness: The Life and Death of Franz Jägerstätter* (Collegeville, Minn.: Liturgical Press, 1964), especially pp. 212-38.

2. Walter Wink, *Engaging the Powers* (Minneapolis: Fortress Press, 1992), 151-52.

3. William Stringfellow, *A Second Birthday* (New York: Doubleday and Co., 1970), 67-68.

11. An Ecclesiology of Nonviolence

1. See Marcus Borg, *Jesus: A New Vision* (San Francisco: Harper & Row, 1987), 139; Walter Wink, *Engaging the Powers* (Minneapolis: Fortress Press, 1992), 209-20; Richard McSorley, *New Testament Basis for Peacemaking* (Scottdale, Penn.: Herald Press, 1985), 68-80; Ron Musto, *The Catholic Peace Tradition* (Maryknoll, N.Y.: Orbis Books, 1986), 31-47.

2. Musto, *The Catholic Peace Tradition*, 41, 45.

3. Ignatius Jesudasan, *A Gandhian Theology of Liberation* (Maryknoll, N.Y.: Orbis Books, 1984), 114-15.

4. Wink, *Engaging the Powers*, 216.

5. Ibid. 216-17.

6. Ibid. 212; Musto, *The Catholic Peace Tradition*, 45.

7. Leonardo Boff, *Church: Charism and Power* (New York: Crossroad, 1988), 50-51.

8. Ibid. 53.

9. Ibid. 54-55.

10. Ibid. 60.

11. Avery Dulles, *Models of the Church* (New York: Image Books, 1978).

12. Boff, *Church: Charism and Power*, 51.

13. Ibid. 27.

14. Ibid. 115.

15. US Catholic Bishops' Conference, *The Challenge of Peace: God's Gift and Our Response* (Washington, D.C.: 1983), no. 333.

16. James Washington, *A Testament of Hope: The Essential Writings of Martin Luther King, Jr.* (San Francisco: Harper & Row, 1986), 297.

17. Ibid. 298-300.

18. Ibid. 300.

19. Oscar Romero, in *The Violence of Love*, ed. James Brockman (San Francisco: Harper & Row, 1988), 43.

20. Ibid. 227.

21. Ibid. 174.

22. Ibid. 211.

23. Ibid. 35.

24. Ibid. 156.

25. Ibid. 40.

26. Ibid. 184.

27. Ibid. 200.

28. Wink, *Engaging the Powers*, 217.

29. Ibid.

12. Catholic Social Teaching and the Gospel of Peace

1. *Pacem in Terris*, no. 109.

2. "Gaudium et Spes," *Vatican Council II*, ed. Austin Flannery (New York: Costello Publishing Company, 1975), "Gaudium et Spes," no. 77.

3. James Douglass, *The Nonviolent Cross* (New York: Macmillan, 1969), 109.

4. Ibid.

5. Ibid. 126.

6. US Bishops' Conference, *The Challenge of Peace* (Washington, D.C., 1983), 36.

7. US Bishops' Conference, *The Harvest of Justice Is Sown in Peace* (Washington, D.C., 1993), 10-11.

8. Pope John Paul II, "Near Northern Ireland: A Plea for Peace," *Origins*, vol. 9, no. 17 (October 11, 1979), 273-74.

9. Pope John Paul II, "War Is Death," *Origins*, vol. 10, no. 39 (March 12, 1981), 620.

10. Pope John Paul II, "War, a Decline for Humanity," *Origins*, vol. 20, no. 33 (January 24, 1991), 525.

13. From Just War to Nonviolence

1. Walter Wink, *Engaging the Powers* (Minneapolis: Fortress Press, 1992), 214-215. See also, US Bishops' Conference, *The Challenge of Peace* (Washington, D.C., 1983), nos. 80-110; John Howard Yoder, *When War Is Unjust* (Minneapolis: Augsburg Publishers, 1984).

2. Wink, *Engaging the Powers*, 215, 385.

3. US Bishops' Conference, *The Challenge of Peace* (Washington, D.C., 1983).

4. "Christian Conscience and Modern Warfare," *La Civilta Cattolica* (Rome, Italy) July 6, 1991.

5. Ibid.

6. Ibid.

7. Ibid.

8. Ibid.

9. Ibid.

10. Ibid.

11. Ibid.

12. Ibid.

13. For further information, see Gene Sharp, *The Politics of Nonviolent Action* (Boston: Porter Sargent, 1973); Richard Taylor and Ronald Sider, *Nuclear Holocaust and Christian Hope* (Downers Grove, Ill.: Intervarsity Press, 1982); and Walter Wink, *Engaging the Powers*, 243-57.

14. Yoder, *When War Is Unjust*, 81-82.

15. John Dear, ed., *It's a Sin to Build a Nuclear Weapon: The Collected Writings on War and Peace of Richard McSorley* (Baltimore: Fortkamp Pub. Co., 1991), 66-67.

16. Ibid. 68.

14. Feminism and Nonviolence

1. Ntozake Shange, "We All Have Immediate Cause," in *Nappy Edges* (New York: St. Martin's Press, 1978), excerpted in the *National Catholic Reporter*, April 20, 1990, 2.

2. Joan Chittister, "Questioning the Limited Status of Women's Lives," *Origins* (1989), 35.

3. Sandra Schneiders, *Women and the Word* (Mahwah, N.J.: Paulist Press, 1986), 13-14.

4. Ibid. 3.

5. Ibid.

6. Ibid.

7. Ibid.

8. Ibid. 5-7.

9. Ibid. 20-27.

10. Ibid. 36-37.

11. Chittister, "Questioning the Limited Status of Women's Lives," 35.

12. Schneiders, *Women and the Word*, 37.

13. Virginia Mollenkott, quoted in Schneiders, *Women and the Word*, 40.

14. Schneiders, *Women and the Word*, 41.

15. Ibid. 44.

16. Ibid. 46.

17. Ibid. 55.

18. Ibid. 55-56.

19. Ibid. 58.

20. Ibid. 58-62.

21. Ibid. 62-63.

22. Ched Myers, *Binding the Strong Man: A Political Reading of Mark's Story of Jesus* (Maryknoll, N.Y.: Orbis Books, 1988), 396.

23. Ibid. 396-97.

24. Rosemary Radford Ruether, *Sexism and God-Talk* (Boston: Beacon Press, 1983).

25. Ibid. 138.

26. Schneiders, *Women and the Word*, 71

15. Liberating Nonviolence and Institutionalized Violence

1. Mev Puleo, "How Do You Tell the Poor God Loves You? An Interview with Gustavo Gutiérrez," in *St. Anthony Messenger* (February 1989), 10.

2. Ibid. 11.

3. Gustavo Gutiérrez, *A Theology of Liberation* (Maryknoll, N.Y.: Orbis Books, 1973), 15.

4. Francis Schüssler Fiorenza, "Systematic Theology," in *Systematic Theology*, vol. 1, ed. Francis Schüssler Fiorenza and John P. Galvin (Minneapolis: Fortress Press, 1991), 65.

5. Gustavo Gutiérrez, quoted in Puleo, *St. Anthony Messenger*, 13.

6. Oscar Romero, quoted in Jon Sobrino, *Archbishop Romero* (Maryknoll, N.Y.: Orbis Books, 1990), 16.

7. Robert McAfee Brown, *Theology in a New Key* (Philadelphia: Westminster Press, 1978), 72-73.

8. Walbert Bühlmann, *With Eyes to See* (Maryknoll, N.Y.: Orbis Books, 1990), 68-69.

9. Brown, *Theology in a New Key*, 91; also, Gutiérrez, *A Theology of Liberation*, 194-95.

10. Gutiérrez, *A Theology of Liberation*, 298-99.

11. Ibid. 275.

12. Ibid. 275-76.

13. John Dear, *Seeds of Nonviolence* (Baltimore: Fortkamp Publishing Co., 1992), 261-63.

14. Gutiérrez, *A Theology of Liberation*, 300-301.

15. John Dear, *Oscar Romero and the Nonviolent Struggle for Justice* (Erie, Penn.: Pax Christi USA, 1991), 20.

16. John Dear, "In Every Heart, There Is Love: An Interview with Dom Helder Camara," *Pax Christi* (Fall 1991), 20-21.

17. Adolfo Perez Esquivel, *Christ in a Poncho* (Maryknoll, N.Y.: Orbis Books, 1983), 136-37.

18. Ibid.

19. John Dear, "The Liberating Force of the Gospel: An Interview with Adolfo Perez Esquivel," *Pax Christi* (June 1986), 16-17.

16. The Seamless Garment of Nonviolence

1. James Douglass, "Patriarchy and the Pentagon Make Abortion Inevitable," *Sojourners* (November 1980).

2. Gandhi, quoted in Thomas Merton, *Gandhi on Nonviolence* (New York: New Directions, 1965), 24, 26.

3. Martin Luther King, Jr., quoted in David Garrow, *Bearing the Cross: Martin Luther King, Jr., and the Southern Christian Leadership Conference* (New York: William Morrow, 1986), 572-73.

4. Garrow, *Bearing the Cross*, 573.

5. Elizabeth McAlister, "The Concern Is for Human Life," *Sojourners* (November 1980).

6. Thomas Merton, quoted in James Forest, *Thomas Merton's Struggle with Peacemaking* (Erie, Penn.: Pax Christi USA, 1985), 27.

7. Ibid. 21-22.

17. Spirituality and Nonviolence

1. Richard Attenborough, ed., *The Words of Gandhi* (New York: Newmarket Press, 1982), 71.

2. Mohandas Gandhi, *All Men Are Brothers* (New York: Continuum, 1980), 54.

3. Roger Haight, "Sin and Grace," in Francis Schüssler Fiorenza and John Galvin, eds., *Systematic Theology*, Vol. 2 (Minneapolis: Fortress Press, 1991), 135.

4. Richard McBrien, *Catholicism* (San Francisco: Harper & Row, 1981), 1057, 1093.

5. William Stringfellow, *The Politics of Spirituality* (Philadelphia: Westminster Press, 1984), 21.

6. Ibid. 25-26.

7. Thomas Merton, *The Nonviolent Alternative* (New York: Farrar, Straus, Giroux, 1980), 216.

8. Gandhi, quoted in Eknath Easwaran, *Gandhi the Man* (Berkeley, Cal.: Nilgiri Press, 1978), 116.

9. Thomas Merton, *The Asian Journal* (New York: New Directions, 1975), 308.

10. Ibid. 318-19.

11. Ibid. 296.

12. Thomas Merton, quoted in James Douglass, *Lightning East to West* (New York: Crossroad, 1984), 7.

13. Thomas Merton, *Gandhi on Nonviolence* (New York: New Directions, 1965), 6.

14. Gandhi, quoted in Douglass, *Lightning East to West*, 43.

15. Attenborough, *The Words of Gandhi*, 23.

16. Gandhi, quoted in Merton, *Gandhi on Nonviolence*, 44.

17. Attenborough, *The Words of Gandhi*, 44.

18. Merton, *The Nonviolent Alternative*, 183-84.

19. Gandhi, quoted in Merton, *The Nonviolent Alternative*, 184.

20. Attenborough, *The Words of Gandhi*, 52.

21. Gandhi, quoted in Merton, *Gandhi on Nonviolence*, 65.

22. Attenborough, *The Words of Gandhi*, 94.

23. Merton, *Gandhi on Nonviolence*, 45.

24. Gandhi, *All Men Are Brothers*, 89.

25. Prayer of St. Francis, in *Peacemaking Day by Day* (Erie, Penn.: Pax Christi USA, 1985), 5.

26. William Sharmon, ed., *The Hidden Ground of Love: The Letters of Thomas Merton*, vol. 1 (New York: Farrar, Straus, Giroux, 1985), 294-96.

27. William Shannon, *Silence on Fire* (New York: Crossroad, 1991), 155.

28. James Douglass, *Resistance and Contemplation* (New York: Doubleday and Co.,1972), 179-80.

29. Ibid. 180-81.

30. Douglass, *Lightning East to West*, 18.

31. Stringfellow, *The Politics of Spirituality*, 44-45.

32. Daniel Berrigan, *To Dwell In Peace* (San Francisco: Harper & Row, 1987), 163-64.

33. Anne Brotherton, "A Spirituality of Nonviolence," talk presented to Pax Christi Berkeley, September 3,1991, at the Jesuit School of Theology in Berkeley, California.

34. Henri Nouwen, *In the Name of Jesus* (New York: Crossroad, 1988), 17.

35. Jim Wallis and Joyce Hollyday, *Clouds of Witnesses* (Maryknoll, New York: Orbis Books, 1991), 217.

36. Thomas Merton, quoted in James Forest, *Living With Wisdom: A Life of Thomas Merton* (Maryknoll, New York: Orbis Books, 1991), 216.

18. The Sacraments of Nonviolence

1. Joseph Martos, *Doors to the Sacred* (New York: Image Books, 1982), 11.

2. "The Constitution on the Sacred Liturgy," *Vatican Council II*, ed. Austin Flannery (New York: Costello Publishing Company, 1975), no. 59.

19. The Liturgy of Nonviolence

1. Flannery O'Connor, *Wise Blood* (New York: Farrar, Straus and Giroux, 1962), 1.

2. Mary Ann Simcoe, ed., "The Constitution on Sacred Liturgy," in *The Liturgy Documents* (Chicago: Liturgy Training Pub., 1985), no. 2.

3. For details, see Gordan Zahn, *German Catholics and Hitler's War* (New York: Sheed and Ward, 1962).

4. Dorothy Day, quoted in *Modern Liturgy* vol. 18, no. 8 (1991), 10.

5. U.S. Catholic Bishops, *Pastoral Letter on Economics*, no. 331, in Robert McAfee Brown, *Spirituality and Liberation* (Louisville, Ky.: Westminster Press, 1988), 86.

6. Elizabeth McAlister, foreword, in John Dear, *Our God Is Nonviolent* (New York: Pilgrim Press, 1990), xiv.

7. Bill Wylie Kellermann, *Seasons of Faith and Conscience* (Maryknoll, N.Y.: Orbis Books, 1991), 126.

8. Ibid. 104.

9. Ibid. 104-5.

10. Ibid. 128-29.

11. Ibid. xxvi.

12. Daniel Berrigan, *America Is Hard to Find* (New York: Doubleday, 1972), 78.

20. The Praxis of Nonviolence

1. Louis Fischer, *The Life of Mahatma Gandhi* (New York: Harper & Row, 1950), 204.

Index